The Hidden Hall

PORTRAIT OF A CAMBRIDGE COLLEGE

The Hidden Hall

PORTRAIT OF A CAMBRIDGE COLLEGE

EDITED BY
PETER PAGNAMENTA

WITH AN INTRODUCTION BY PROFESSOR PETER CLARKE

THIRD MILLENNIUM
PUBLISHING, LONDON

First published in 2004 by Third Millennium Publishing Limited, a
subsidiary of Third Millennium Information Limited

Farringdon House
105–107 Farringdon Road
London
United Kingdom
EC1R 3BU
www.tmiltd.com

ISBN: 1 903942 31 4

Consultant Editor: Peter Pagnamenta

Editor: Catharine Walston of Honeychurch Associates, Cambridge, UK

Design: Matthew Wilson

Produced by Third Millennium Publishing,
a subsidiary of Third Millennium Information Limited

Printed and bound by Mladinska, Slovenia

Editor's foreword

PETER PAGNAMENTA (1960)

Though the longer articles for this anthology were requested by the editors, most of the other elements spring from an invitation to alumni to contribute material, promulgated through *Front Court* in 2003. In the months that followed the College was inundated with letters and emails full of personal recollections, and brown envelopes arrived bulging with photographs, receipts for Proctors' fines, and edicts from long-gone Bursars on the maximum wattage of electric light bulbs to be used in undergraduate rooms. One or two staggered in with heavy albums assembled by fathers or grandfathers. We need to thank everyone who responded to this trawl.

What proved hard, apart from the normal editorial constraints of space and time, was balancing the first-hand testimony from the different eras, so that sections dealing with the last twenty years would come across with the same texture as earlier periods. One problem was that men and women who studied at the Hall in the 1980s and 90s are busy getting on with their lives and careers and may see this sort of exercise as a little regressive. A greater difficulty was the shortage of pictures and printed ephemera for the later years. It is a paradox that though we are better at recording images than ever before, we are less good at keeping them in a way that future generations will be able to refer to easily. There is no substitute for those old photo albums.

What proved easy was securing the co-operation and enthusiasm of a whole range of College members and staff, who were caught by the idea and wanted the book to work. We are grateful to all the Fellows, present and Emeritus, who agreed to write pieces and found the time to do so. We owe a particular debt of thanks to some of the longest serving of them who, as well as writing, were able to provide the folk memory and continuity. Jonathan Steinberg, Sandra Raban, Graham Howes and David Thomas were particularly helpful with background comments and suggestions. David Thomas not only wrote about law teaching but also took many of the photographs. We thank John Pollard, the Archivist, who helped find material, and warned us on those days when the archives were flooded. Drew Milne and the College librarians, Alison Hunt and Andrew Lacey, gave valuable help. Tristan Rees Roberts drew the sketch plans that accompany his own contribution. Bridget Wheeler did extensive research before she started to write about Hall Olympians and sport, and Julian Ebsworth put on a heroic spurt to deliver the Boat Club at a late stage.

We owe special thanks to Victoria Fangen, who sorted the Halliana which poured onto her desk with efficiency and calm, and fielded the College contributions. At the publisher, Third Millennium, we are grateful to Matt Wilson who designed the book, Bonnie Murray who handled the production, and Louise Wilson who co-ordinated the project, not forgetting Julian Platt, the supremo of TMI, who persuaded Trinity Hall that this would all be a good idea in the first place. Within the College Jocelyn Poulton has been the book's keenest advocate, and gave us great assistance and encouragement. Finally, I need to thank Catharine Walston, who provided an intelligent and invaluable sense of perspective as co-editor. With an enterprise like this, with so many elements coming in from so many sources, it is hard to know quite what the total impact will be, until it is too late to do anything about it. But we hope the result is a revealing and not reverential, affectionate though not sentimental, account of a living institution with a long future ahead of it.

Picture and copyright acknowledgements

The editors wish to thank the British Library for permission to reproduce the frontispiece to Robert Herrick's *Hesperides*; the Cambridgeshire Collection in Cambridge Central Library for wartime photographs from the *Cambridge Daily News*; Charlie Colmer; Chris Copp of Staffordshire Arts and Museum Service; Thomas Firbank and Gerald Duckworth & Co. for the use of the photograph of Ronald Firbank's room; Dona Haycraft; Melvin Jefferson of Corpus Christi College; JET Photography; Jayne Lownsbrough of Yorkshire Post Newspapers Archive for cuttings on Philip Mickman; Lucy Martin of the Scott Polar Research Institute for the photograph of Launcelot Fleming in Antarctica; the Middleton Foundation, Charleston, South Carolina for permission to reproduce the painting of the Middleton family; Paul Norris; the Pepys Library, Magdalene College, Cambridge for the portrait of Samuel Pepys; Peters Fraser and Dunlop and the estate of J.B. Priestley for permission to use an extract from *Instead of the Trees*; *Playboy* Magazine; the Syndics of the University Library, Cambridge for permission to reproduce David Loggans' plan of the College; THBC; Third Light Photography; the Trustees of the Fitzwilliam Museum for the photographs of the Louis Clarke bust by Jacob Epstein and *Smuggling in – An Old Varsity Trick* by Thomas Rowlandson.

We would also like to thank the following for the use of their personal photographs and ephemera: Roger Aldridge; William Ballantyne; Rosie Beaufoy; Tom Breeze; Kenneth Brown; Andrew Burr; Jonathan Burton; Sarah Chew; Rosamunde Codling; Bill Coldrey; Frank Conley; Piers Crocker; Richard Devitt; Mario

Doucet; Nick Eastwell; Julian Ebsworth; Frederick Eirich; Peter Freeman; Robert Hunt-Grubbe; Vicki Iovine; Andrew Ives; Alan King-Hamilton; Neil Laverty; Donald Legget; Carsten Lund; Caroline Lynas; John McCaig; Simon Moore; Tony Nixon; Michael Page; David Ranc; Wyn Richards; Kenneth Rimmer; James Runcie; John Russell; Bevis Sanford; Andrew Senior; the Sims-Williams family; David Swann; David Thomas; Derek Thomas; Peter Trier; Iain Tuddenham; J. Michael Woolley; and all those who sent in photographs and mementoes which we were not able to include.

Contents

Introduction

PROFESSOR PETER CLARKE
(MASTER 2000–2004)

Peter Clarke at a sitting with artist Joe Plaskett who was commissioned by the College to paint his portrait.

At a formal dinner in Trinity Hall – and there's none better in Cambridge – the menu tells you the set order of courses, proceeding with its own logic and with a parallel progression in the accompanying wines. Legendary College battles have been fought over whether the pudding should come before or after the cheese but nobody suggests that the pudding should come before the fish or the meat course. The palate is prepared stage by stage for what follows – it makes sense to begin at the beginning and continue to the end. And much the same is true of Charles Crawley's *Trinity Hall: the history of a Cambridge College*, a book read with much profitable enjoyment since its original publication in 1976 (and its revision by Graham Storey in 1992). It remains indispensable; anyone who reads it from cover to cover will benefit from its systematic account of our varied and rich-textured history.

The Hidden Hall is different. Here is a tempting buffet of dishes (call them hors d'oeuvres, tapas or smorgasbord as you like) to be sampled, scoffed or savoured, just as you fancy. It has been compiled by many hands, with contributions from dozens of dons and unnumbered undergraduates – from a myriad of members who have made this an album or anthology of the Hall as they know it.

There is much good lively writing here. Some of it is the fruit of research in the College archives, retrieving an understanding of past events which has often been lost or obscured by later legends. Some of it draws on memories of the Hall, not all of which are airbrushed by sentimental nostalgia, thus juxtaposing accounts of happy sunlit days in a lost golden age with wry comments on the inequities and privations experienced by others at exactly the same time. And there are pictorial as well as literary evocations of the past, with ancient menu cards of impossibly grand dinners, old photographs of undergraduates looking improbably elderly, not to mention some stunning views of Trinity Hall as we see it today.

What, then, is hidden? Some secrets are self-consciously spilled by alumni who seize their chance to blow the gaff, with a now-it-can-be-told bravado licensed by the passage of time. There are some glimpses behind the scenes which reveal aspects of the College that were once carefully concealed. But what is hidden depends partly on who you are, just as what is revealed depends partly on what you know already. The undergraduates of past generations (who never thought of themselves as 'students'), just like the College servants (who were likewise not yet known as 'staff'), had perspectives on the Hall that will seem arcane to those of us at the Hall today. 'The past is a foreign country: they do things differently there,' as L.P. Hartley put it. But, conversely, for many of our alumni the doings of our current students can seem pretty foreign too. Perhaps this book can act as our own go-between.

Here is a handsome volume, not too heavy, but replete with evocative text and pictures, which we hope will encourage you to discover your own Hidden Hall.

Crossing Front Court

HOW ARCHITECTURE CAN DEFINE CHARACTER

JONATHAN STEINBERG

Nobody who has gone in and out of Cambridge colleges can miss the differences in atmosphere. King's opens its broad vistas and its huge monuments as if to remind the visitor to be humble in the presence of such regal grandeur. Fellows of King's shuffle across the vast lawn while hordes of Japanese tourists photograph them. It must be hard not to succumb to delusions of grandeur. Corpus presents its romantic façades, a mock Middle Ages, built by enthusiasts who had done the grand tour. John's looks oddly unbalanced with Giles Gilbert Scott's cathedral creating an open space to the right while ahead a Tudor range sits uneasily at right angles to E and F staircase, which gained modern façades in the eighteenth century. And Great Court at Trinity, still the most spectacular collegiate space in the University and one of the most beautiful, produces awe and wonder.

Do college buildings shape the communities that live in them? Is social life in King's made more distant by the broad lawns that separate the buildings? And what about Trinity Hall? Are we what we are because of the configuration of our buildings? Do the walls convey a spirit which changes us and makes us behave in certain ways?

To look for an answer, we have to begin in Front Court with its pleasing regularities, 'comfortable and phlegmatic,' Pevsner calls it. Front or Principal Court has marked the space called Trinity Hall since the mid-eighteenth century. When any of us thinks of Trinity Hall, we think of that even, regular, unpretentious, comfortable space. Its length and width and squares of green define our space, the casual comings and goings, the experience of life at Trinity Hall.

Above: *Sir Nathanael Lloyd, Master from 1710–35. This portrait hangs in the Dining Hall and is probably by Sir James Thornhill.*

Right: *Front Court.*

Left: *A blocked-up Gothic window on C staircase uncovered during the renovations of 1928–29.*

Below: *Garret Hostel bridge, 1880s.*

The façades of 1728–29 also represent a substantial benefaction from Sir Nathanael Lloyd, who lived from 1669 to 1741 and presided over the College from 1710 to 1735. Lloyd, whose immense portrait looks benignly over the heads of his successors dining in hall, came to Cambridge from Oxford and arrived with a reputation for being difficult, haughty and overbearing. And he was all those things. A rich man and a successful civil lawyer, he practised all the arts of blackmail which the wealthy employ to bend institutions to their wills. Lloyd was a Fellow of All Souls and, as Charles Crawley put it, 'after bombarding the Warden with letters, he was allowed to retain his fellowship at All Souls on becoming Master here,' an outrageous abuse. Lloyd took a robust view of giving. He had been an undergraduate at Lincoln College, Oxford, and in 1735 gave them the sum of £500 [in present money about £46,000]. In his will he wrote 'it not being laid out as I directed – so no more from me.' He bequeathed £1,000 to All Souls 'to finish the North Pile or, if finished, towards completing the Library'. All three of his colleges took pains to have his portrait painted and to be nice to him in other ways. Lloyd was not fooled. On his large marble monument in Trinity Hall chapel he had inscribed in Latin: 'epitaphs should be truthful; telling lies is wicked. This place is holy; go and tell lies outside.'

Like many benefactors before and since, he was careful with his money and knew exactly what he wanted. In 1728–29 he concocted a deal worthy of the best modern campaign director. He gave £1,000 pounds to the College in return for an annuity of £50 so that they could start to replace the Gothic frontage in Front Court with the latest sash windows and ashlar facings. When he died, he left a further £3,000 to remodel the dining hall completely and to extend the College to the Cam, knocking down the Old Library and flattening the gardens along the way. The plans had been drawn by Messrs James Burrough and James Essex, fashionable architects of the time, to whom we owe Clare chapel, the only chapel in the University where, I am assured, it is impossible to pray to a personal God.

The great inflation of the eighteenth century, not the aesthetic reservations of the Fellowship, saved the Old Library and the

'A little Handel sonata in stone…'

Fellows' Garden. Lloyd's £3,000 pounds proved insufficient for the scheme and other benefactions, such as that of John Andrew, came with strings. What was done was considered by contemporaries to be an improvement. William Warren, who was a Fellow from 1712 to 1745, tells us that the former dining hall was 'one of the most ancient buildings at present remaining in the University… roofed with old oak beams, very black and dismal from the Charcoal which is burnt in the middle of the Hall and over it an old awkward kind of Cupolo to let out the smoak.'

Lloyd's legacy allowed the College to build an eighteenth-century dining chamber, light and airy, its fireplace modern and equipped with a good draught. The ceiling must have been white and curled with those vines, tendrils and sheaves of grain so beloved of the eighteenth century. It was an expression of the Age of Reason. Its length was twice its width, and even today one can recapture its proportions by walking ten paces from High Table so that the fireplace sits in the middle of the wall, where it was intended. By the 1890s, undergraduate numbers had grown beyond the capacity of Lloyd's space, so the College engaged Messrs Grayson and Ould to enlarge the hall. They moved Lloyd's eighteenth-century reredos with its coupled Corinthian columns further to the east, and, as Pevsner puts it, 'unfortunately and incomprehensibly – a Tudor roof was substituted for the eighteenth century ceiling.'

Lloyd's world was corrupt, full of abuse and privilege. Lloyd was a shameless pluralist and gathered up office and stipends with that unembarrassed greed which made Dr Johnson, a near contemporary, observe, that 'a man is never so innocently employed as when he is making money'. Yet Lloyd clearly loved this College and wanted it to be beautiful. He succeeded. It is beautiful in its cosy way. He made a space in which the young people who study there chat and bump into each other. Most of them know nothing of him. Many have never even noticed his huge portrait behind the High Table. Yet they are his heirs and live with his benefaction as we all have, all of us, who have lived in his enlightened eighteenth-century space over the past two and a half centuries.

This abiding, timeless continuity makes Oxford and Cambridge colleges what they are, alike and yet incredibly different. It was pure chance that for once in its six and a half centuries Trinity Hall elected a seriously rich Master in 1710 and that he imposed on the following ages the taste of his time, but it was a happy chance. He bequeathed us a part of his world, its values and symbols, its sense of itself. The Front Court is a little Handel sonata in stone and it makes us glad to be in it.

Jonathan Steinberg read economics at Harvard University, graduating in 1955. He came to Trinity Hall as a Fellow in 1966 and served as Director of Studies in History, Tutor, and was Vice-Master from 1990–94. He is currently Walter H. Annenberg Professor of Modern European History at the University of Pennsylvania.

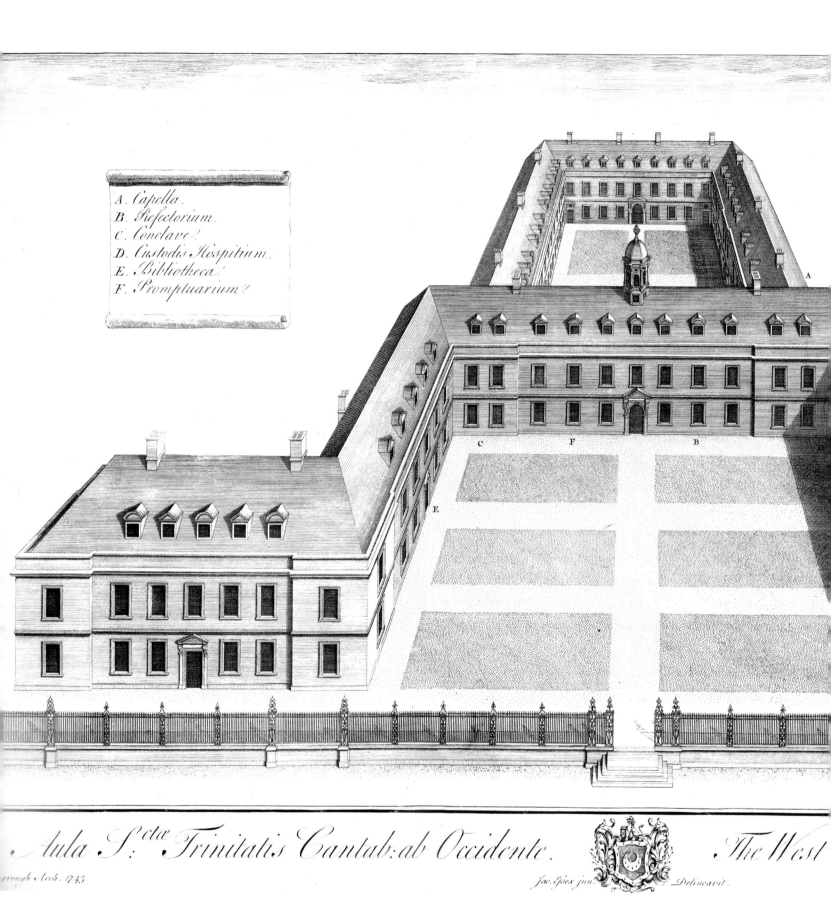

A. Capella.
B. Refectorium.
C. Conclave.
D. Custodis Hospitium.
E. Bibliotheca.
F. Promptuarium.

Aula S:tæ Trinitatis Cantab: ab Occidente.   The West

...rough Arch. 1743.   Jac. Essex jun.   Delineavit.

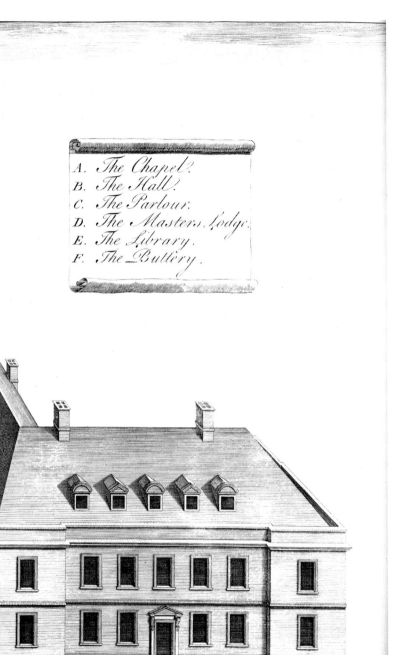

A. The Chapel?
B. The Hall?
C. The Parlour.
D. The Masters Lodge.
E. The Library.
F. The Buttery.

S.t Trinity Hall in Cambridge.

W.H.Toms Sculp

The Hall that never was 02

ABANDONED BUILDING SCHEMES

JOHN POLLARD

Trinity Hall might have had a very different feel to it if some of the building projects proposed during its history had been implemented. The first of these was the Burrough–Essex proposal of 1743. This would have resulted in a drastic rebuilding of the College frontage towards the river. Consisting of two classical wings, in more or less the same Palladian style as the then façade, with further wings at right angles, the rebuilding and extension would have replaced both the Old Library and the Master's Lodge. In one sense, the project was simply an extension of the process of ashlaring the walls of Front Court, inserting sash windows and giving the whole the classical appearance then fashionable in Cambridge, a process funded by the Master, Sir Nathanael Lloyd. But there was a dispute between the College and the executors of the estate of Dr John Andrew, and the money he left for the project went to St John's College, Oxford, instead. The proposal by Sir James Burrough and his pupil James Essex was only one of many circulating in the mid-eighteenth century for the reconstruction or extension of college and University buildings yet, curiously, there is no mention of the rebuilding project with the others in F.A. Reeve's book, *The Cambridge That Never Was* (1971).

The proposed remodelling of the river frontage by James Burrough and James Essex dated 1743, which would have changed drastically the College's character.

Plans submitted in 1971 by Cambridge architects Barry Gasson and John Meunier for new buildings that would have created an entirely new block between the Fellows' Garden and the Latham Lawn.

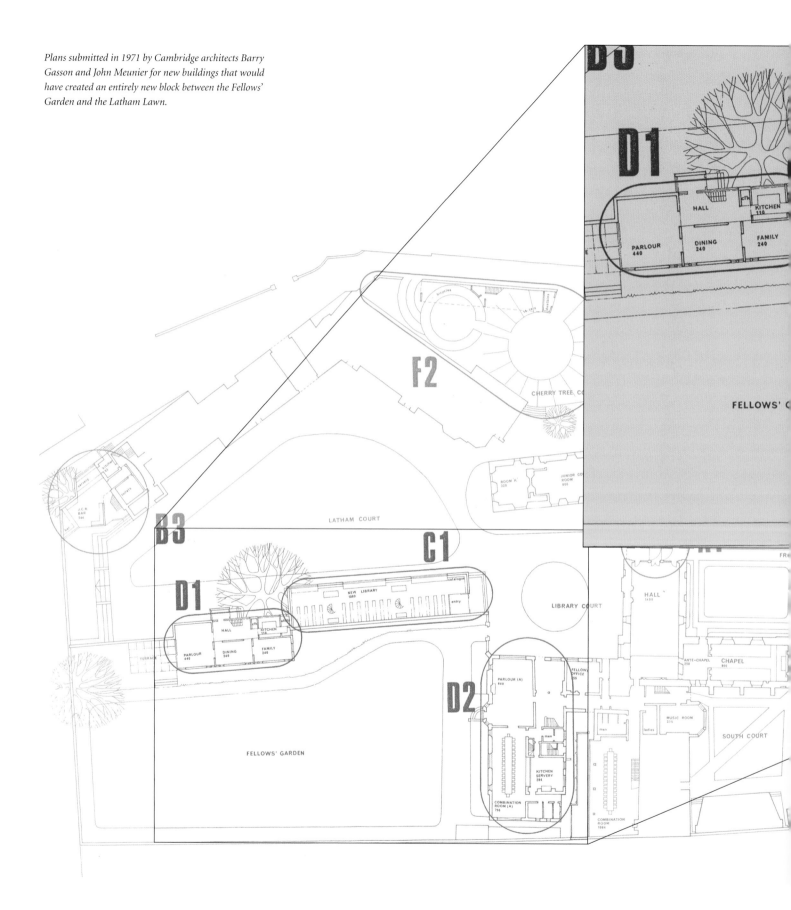

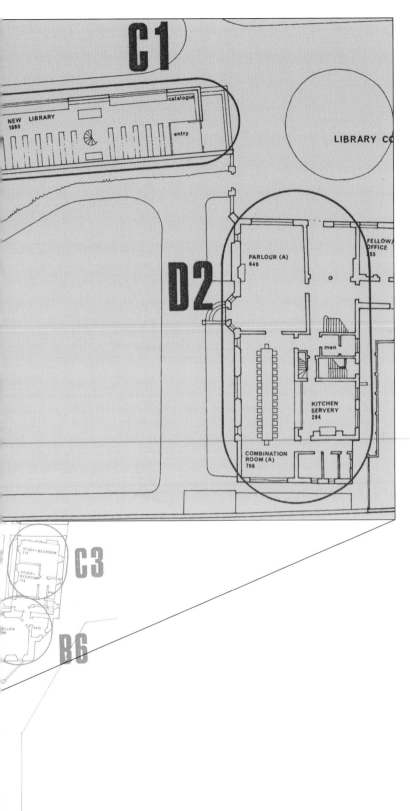

Another scheme which would have substantially changed the appearance of the College surfaced in 1971, over two hundred years after the Burrough–Essex proposal. A *Report on the Development of the Central Site, Trinity Hall, Cambridge* by architects Gasson and Meunier proposed a variety of options, including redeveloping the Master's Lodge as Fellows' and students' sets and as a new library, with an almost complete closure of the view towards the river by means of an extension(which itself could possibly have been part of the new library) towards the Old Library, thus forming a 'Library Court'. An even more radical option was the proposed building of a 'Master's house' along the wall with the Latham Lawn in the Fellows' Garden and a new library on the other side of the wall. In what once was Cherry Tree Court, now the site of the JCR, music and lecture room complex, there was to be a circular, semi-underground car park with workshops. None of these designs was, of course, executed and a rather more comprehensive redevelopment of Cherry Tree Court was carried out instead later in the 1970s.

Finally and more recently, the archive reveals that there was a more modest proposal dating from 1983, for a pleasant conservatory to be built on the terrace outside the Fellows' parlour. It looks rather splendid, but I have serious doubts about the very much more ambitious plans of both Burrough–Essex and Gasson and Meunier. In my humble opinion, both projects would have destroyed the very fine balance between architecture and landscape which gives the Hall its special character and the peculiar picturesqueness of the front towards the garden would have been lost had either of the projects been implemented.

John Pollard read history at Trinity Hall, graduating in 1966. He was Professor of Modern European History at Anglia Polytechnic University, 1990–2003. He is an historian of modern Italy and the papacy. He was elected into a Fellowship at the Hall from October 2003 and is the College Archivist.

Confident assumptions

03

HALL LIFE 1700 TO 1939

AN EIGHTEENTH-CENTURY STUDENT DIARY
GRAHAM HOWES

In May 2001 the College acquired at auction a battered, vellum-covered notebook, its frontispiece elegantly inscribed 'Spencer Penrice May Ye 29 1736'. Born 4 August 1719, the only son and heir of Sir Henry Penrice, a former Fellow of the College and a Judge of the High Court of Admiralty, Spencer was admitted – no doubt on his father's initiative – a Fellow Commoner on 29 June 1736. In the eighteenth century, Fellow Commoners were usually from well-born or wealthy families, were charged higher University and College fees than undergraduates, and not required to proceed to a degree. Lord Chesterfield (Trinity Hall 1712–14) is our best-known

Fellow Commoner of the period, but as Charles Crawley remarks in his exemplary history of the College, 'many... were on the books for a very short time... and little is known about many of them.'

Spencer Penrice's diary should help to redress this. Its 365 closely written, double-sided pages, covering the academic year 1736–37 provide a vivid and exceptionally detailed picture of his daily life at the Hall and during his vacations at the family home, Offley Place, Hertfordshire. Although it is essentially a factual rather than literary account – perhaps aimed at his father, who bought him the diary in the first place, and at his younger, bluestocking sister Anna Maria – and its tone more one of dutiful record than self-conscious introspection, a glance at virtually any page (see opposite) reveals, in a clear, unfussy hand, an almost obsessively precise chronology of student life here in the early eighteenth century.

For today's reader, four impressions predominate. One is that his College life-style was a relatively privileged one. Indeed he arrived here in some style. 'Oct 18th... we got here about 2. I then went immediately for Dr Dickins [Fellow and Regius Professor of Civil Law] and brought him to my father at the Rose Inn. Dr Warren [Clerical Fellow and compiler of *Warren's Book*] came after dinner. They drank tea and Dr Warren supped with us'. Next day 'my father and I and Dr Monson [Fellow and later Regius Professor of Civil Law] breakfasted with Dr Dickins and saw my Chamber. My father gave directions about it... we dined in Commons and he gave a treat for me. I had my gown made by noon.' Once installed in his 'chamber' (with new bookshelves erected for him), Penrice

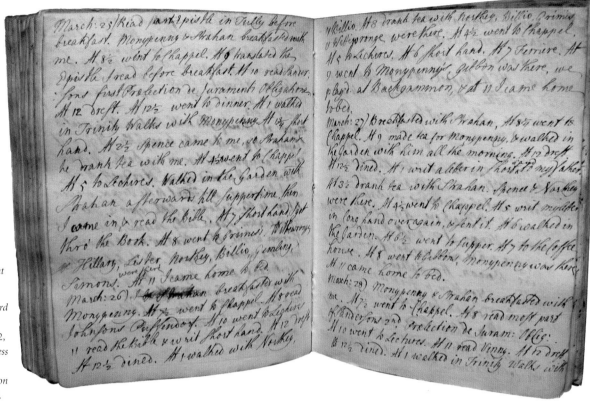

Right: *The diary of Spencer Penrice, a Fellow Commoner at the Hall from 1736.*

Far left: *Oil painting by Richard Bankes Harraden, entitled Trinity Hall, Cambridge, 1822, with a game of bowls in progress in the Fellows' Garden. It was bought by the College at auction in 2001 and hangs in the SCR.*

usually breakfasted with one or two other close friends, and, although occasionally opting for 'bread, cheese, and small beer in the buttery', he invariably dressed for 'dinner' (i.e. lunch) at 12.30 with the Fellows, whom he also joined for a less formal supper. He rarely provides details of the cuisine, although on one occasion (a farewell supper for twelve 'treated' by a retiring Fellow named Brand), 'we had… Scotch scallops, syllabub sammon [sic] and mackerel, ham and beans, chicken, partridge and quails.' Afterwards 'we went into the parlour… and staid there till 12…. There were some set Healths [i.e. Toasts]. The Master drank Church and King, Queen and all the Royal Family, the University, Queen's Colledge [sic], the Chancellor of the University. He said he had lost one by the High Steward being dead.' On another occasion, after the Eden Oration, 'we had a feast. It was the first time that the Master came into the Hall. We went into the Parlour afterwards. There were two tables of cards, one of quadrille and the other whist'. Both games were a regular feature of Penrice's daily life here, and the diary also abounds with references to piquet, bragg, backgammon, chess and billiards, as well as to bowls, swimming in the 'sophs' pool' and tennis (presumably the real variety). His other recorded College activities included much tea-drinking with others, attending debates in Hall [tantalisingly unspecified, alas], weekly attendance at 'the Musick Club… where I was Steward,' re-

arranging and cataloguing his personal library, and sorting out his dirty linen and crockery for his bedmaker. The latter, although never named here in person, clearly performed a variety of functions, from cooking breakfast to running errands (e.g. 'May 12 writ a letter to my father. At 5.30 finding no bedmaker I carried my letter myself to the Postmaster.') College discipline rarely intruded, especially on Fellow Commoners, save when, as he dutifully notes 'Apr 6. Mem. Enacted by the Fellows in College that we must pay 6 pence for missing gates or having company of another college in our rooms after 10.' However, the diary does contain one interesting example of tutorial care. On March 23, 'I received a very angry letter from my father which disturbed me all the afternoon… then I went up to Dr Dickins who gave me some good advice and comforted me. At 5.30 came down and thought of something to say to my father.' Beyond the College gates, Penrice, if not exactly a young man about town, nonetheless purchased new gloves, new clothes and a new wig (for the latter some friends 'cut off my hair quite bare'), was a regular *habitué* of a well-known coffee house, and, less frequently, of the Tuns public house 'where I drank a bottle of French wine.' He cruised the bookshops, attended auctions at 'the Wrestlers', visited a puppet show and 'Puff Fair' ('people of all sorts there') and saw bull-baiting on Parker's Piece. On 9th and 10th March he made two attempts to attend a criminal

trial at Cambridge, 'but could not get in.' At 3pm on the 12th, he 'walked to the Castle to see the prisoners… there's three to be hanged and two transported.' Finally, on the 15th, 'at 11 to the Castle Hill to see the prisoners hanged, but was too late.'

Such an intensely varied pattern of activity both inside and outside College was, however, contained and structured by two major commitments: One was to Christian practice and belief. To the conventional piety of his family background (morning and evening prayers were held daily at Offley, and lengthy mental preparation made before taking the Sacrament), Penrice added, while at the Hall, reading the Bible at least once a day, attending College chapel (which he invariably spells 'Chapell') twice daily – at 7.30am and 6.30pm, and 'Church' on Sunday mornings – presumably St Edward's, the College's own 'peculiar', although sometimes Great St Mary's, the University church, where on November 21st 'there was a Turk… with two attendants.' Occasionally we also find him visiting King's (where he makes no comment on the chapel architecture) or Trinity ('to hear their anthem. There were six fiddles there') or Christ's, whose chapel 'is a very neat one, wainscoted with oak and has got an organ.' Such regular religious practice was supplemented by reading well-known devotional texts such as Beveridge's *Private Thoughts*, Tillotson on the Sacraments and, more surprisingly, the ex-ploughman poet and priest, Stephen Duck.

If Penrice's religious obligations were relatively demanding, his academic ones were almost as rigorous and daunting as any today. He seems to have committed himself to the equivalent of what we would now call a joint honours course – in Penrice's case a combination of law, mathematics, classics and astronomy. Even as a self-evidently hard-working and intelligent young man, he seems to have been fully stretched, not only in attending lectures and writing them up fully afterwards, but in solving prescribed (and sometimes self-administered) mathematical exercises as well as helping some of his less able – or perhaps more idle – fellow students with such tasks. Nonetheless, for Penrice, mathematics

was not all plain sailing. He has trouble when 'I try to extract the Square Root', needs help with algebra from a clever contemporary ('Kidlington showed me how to do one of my algebraick problems') and at one point he seeks out Sanderson (the famous blind mathematician) and asks him to 'scratch my name from his course', and then thinks better of it. Classics, especially for an ex-St Paul's pupil, presented no such problems. He reads Horace, Homer, Juvenal and others fluently, turns passages of Greek into Latin and then into English, and sometimes comments on how much of the work set is 'already familiar from my schooling'. Astronomy, taught by Roger Long (who went on giving virtually the same lecture course until well into his eighties) was merely boring ('at 5 read Dr Long's lecture over again out of a book he gave us' speaks volumes.) But law, given his father's professional eminence, and evident expectations of his son, together with the Hall's contemporary reputation as a 'law' college, inevitably loomed largest in Penrice's academic timetable. He attends lectures punctiliously, and appears to read Vinny's *Legal Commentaries* every day. Not far behind is the German jurist Puffendorf: '25 January, I walked to the booksellers to get Johnson's Puffendorf and got it at last.' Many pages of the diary reflect his variegated, tightly packed and sometimes physically punishing schedule. Listen to him on November 11th: ' I went to chapel, breakfasted with Colebrooke. I studied Vinny from 9 to 11, then went to lectures till 12 and afterwards compared Wood's *Institutes* with Parry's. Dressed for dinner. Afterwards I took a little walk and came in to read Corvinus till Cust and Hall came. They stayed till 4. Then I went to Logick and from thence to Puffendorf,

and then to Chapell and supper and thence to the coffee house.
I came home about 8, read Vinny till 9 when I could hardly keep
my eyes open. So I studied Mathematics till ten and then went to
bed.' Unsurprising therefore that on several occasions he records
'slept till 8 for shame' or 'I overslept myself' and on one occasion
bursts into doggerel: ' Let travellers their early vigils keep/The
morning rose, but I lay fast asleep.' Unsurprising, too, perhaps that
his non-academic and non-devotional reading does not appear to
have extended much beyond the *Tatler* and the *London Magazine*
and occasional play-readings with friends. Vanbrugh's *The Relapse*
was a favourite. His political awareness remained, on this evidence,
muted and rudimentary throughout.

Yet, overall, the accumulated material in this diary is rich,
fascinating and does much to document Penrice's day-to-day
activities in precise and vivid detail. It was, of course, never
intended for other than personal or family scrutiny. This volume
stops abruptly in mid-sentence on 14 August 1737,and hence
almost certainly it extends beyond this date, and another volume
may still be extant somewhere. Meanwhile we hope to publish –
if sufficient financial support is forthcoming – an edited and
annotated version of the full text on which this glimpse of the
'hidden Hall' of the early eighteenth century is based. As for
Spencer Penrice himself, we do not know whether he completed his
time at the Hall or not, for he died at home, tragically, of smallpox
on 6 January 1739. He was twenty years old. His grieving father
incorporated a reference to his only son on the imposing family
memorial in Great Offley Church. It describes him as 'a youth of
great virtues. And expectations.' This is more than simply
eighteenth-century panegyric. It is also palpably true, as the
evidence of this diary attests.

*Graham Howes came up to Trinity Hall in 1959, and read history. He
was elected a Staff Fellow in Social and Political Sciences in 1968, and
has, in his time, been Tutor, Deputy Librarian, Fellow Archivist and
Picture Steward.*

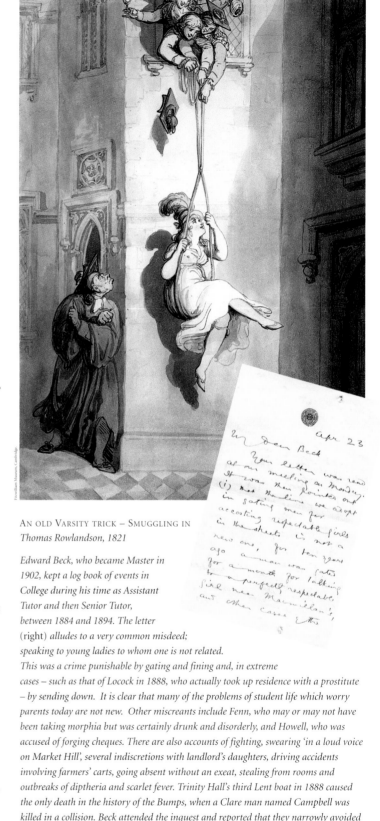

Fitzwilliam Museum, Cambridge

An old Varsity trick – Smuggling in
Thomas Rowlandson, 1821

*Edward Beck, who became Master in
1902, kept a log book of events in
College during his time as Assistant
Tutor and then Senior Tutor,
between 1884 and 1894. The letter
(right) alludes to a very common misdeed;
speaking to young ladies to whom one is not related.
This was a crime punishable by gating and fining and, in extreme
cases – such as that of Locock in 1888, who actually took up residence with a prostitute
– by sending down. It is clear that many of the problems of student life which worry
parents today are not new. Other miscreants include Fenn, who may or may not have
been taking morphia but was certainly drunk and disorderly, and Howell, who was
accused of forging cheques. There are also accounts of fighting, swearing 'in a loud voice
on Market Hill', several indiscretions with landlord's daughters, driving accidents
involving farmers' carts, going absent without an exeat, stealing from rooms and
outbreaks of diptheria and scarlet fever. Trinity Hall's third Lent boat in 1888 caused
the only death in the history of the Bumps, when a Clare man named Campbell was
killed in a collision. Beck attended the inquest and reported that they narrowly avoided
a charge of manslaughter.*

Left: *May Ball photograph, Market Square, 1888.*

Below: *Proctor and Bulldogs, 1902. The Proctor is George Shirres, who was Vice-Master from 1902 until his death in 1919. The bulldog on his left is Mr Halls, gyp for B and C staircases.*

LESLIE STEPHEN ON THE COLLEGE IN THE 1860S

… It is enough to say that our college has all that is essential to the ideal of a college. There is the ancient corner of building, half merged in more modern structures, which our founder acquired or did not acquire, together with an adjacent field, from certain monks. There is the less venerable court, which affords a perfect example of Elizabethan architecture. There is the atrocious pile of obtrusive ugliness which some sixty years ago repaired the ravages of a fire. We have of course a hall, which has been restored to show the old oak roof, and a chapel, which causes me to live in daily fear of another restoration and another liberal subscription. Of course, too, we are 'bosomed deep in tufted trees', though, in spite of University commissioners, no beauty lies as yet beneath our towers and battlements. We have a lawn of velvet turf, hitherto devoted to the orthodox game of bowls, but threatened by an invasion of croquet, for female influence is slowly but surely invading our cloisters. Whether, like the ivy that gathers upon our ancient walls, it may ultimately be fatal to their stability, remains yet to be seen….

When the intelligent foreigner of fiction expresses his surprise at our English devotion to classics and mathematics, this is the answer which is invariably thrown at his head. Your students, he says, are kept hard at work till twenty-one upon matters which nine-tenths of them have utterly forgotten at thirty. They have been filling their minds pertinaciously with a lumber which is only to be consigned to vaults and cellars. Ought they not rather to be supplied with some useful stock-in-trade for future life? What can be the use of keeping them grinding at this mental treadmill, which is actually recommended by the inutility of its products? Ah, we reply, see how it strengthens the prisoners' thews and sinews. When we once let them out, there is no nut which they won't be able to crack, and no work which they won't find easy by comparison. We teach classics and mathematics because they are the best of all mental gymnastics. They strengthen the intellectual faculties, as lifting weights and jumping bars strengthen the muscles. If asked why they are the best, we appeal to 'all experience' – an appeal to experience being a well-known method of at once refusing to argue, and looking preternaturally wise.

From an article in The Pall Mall Gazette, *1865, when Stephen was about to resign his fellowship to become a writer, republished in* Sketches from Cambridge *(OUP, 1932). Leslie Stephen was a Clerical Fellow at the Hall from 1854 to 1868, when he became an agnostic and resigned his Fellowship. A noted athlete and mountaineer, he was an enthusiastic rowing coach for THBC. He is celebrated as a writer on literature and philosophy and was elected an Honorary Fellow in 1891. (see also article by Jan-Melissa Schramm, chapter 7)*

THOMAS THORNELY ON DRINKING IN THE 1870S

… In the case of wine-parties alone were the rigours of etiquette relaxed. Restraint there was thrown to the winds, and all that was insisted on was that there should be no stinting of measure. The results were frequently so unedifying that there was a general though unacknowledged relief when, under the combined pressure of authority from without and discomfort from within, wine-parties fell gradually into disuse, or were confined to those occasions of

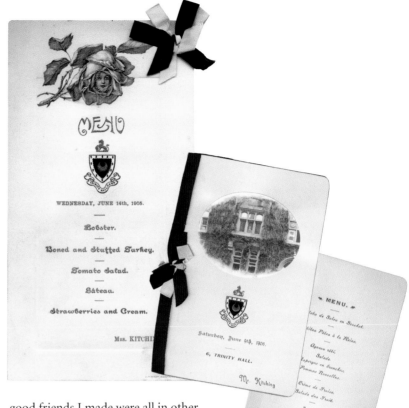

Right: *Private dinner party menu cards.*

Bottom: *Undergraduate rooms of F. Sims-Williams, 1877.*

general rejoicing when strict sobriety would be obviously out of place. In addition to conventions common to the University, I was given to understand that there were many things permissible in some Colleges which were not open to members of the Hall, which set itself a high standard in social matters, and was indeed thought by jealous outsiders to have more than an adequate opinion of itself. That such feeling existed, and that the 'swelling port' we may sometimes have exhibited was resented, was brought vividly home to me when my first landlady – a formidable dragon – met a mild remonstrance at some gross piece of carelessness by a long tirade, which ended with these never to be forgotten words – 'I did think as how I wouldn't have no more Trinity Hall gents, they his so huppish.'

From Cambridge Memories *(Hamish Hamilton, 1936), in which the writer recalls his time as an undergraduate in the 1870s. Thomas Thornely was the first College lecturer in history. He became a Fellow in 1886 and served under three different Masters. He died in 1949 at the age of 93.*

J.B. PRIESTLEY RETURNS FROM THE TRENCHES

… Cambridge treated me very decently when I was up there. Strictly speaking, I didn't deserve to be there at all, having no claims to scholarship, with my school-days long gone, working in an office before spending four-and-a-half years in the army, and an outsider, an uncouth Northerner if there ever was one. Yes, going there was a stroke of luck, even if I was a trifle unlucky in the college I was assigned to, for Trinity Hall was devoted to the Law, rowing and an expensive kitchen if you could afford to patronize it. I couldn't; I wanted (then and since) to have nothing to do with the Law; and I was in no shape to start rowing. The

good friends I made were all in other colleges; I had only one at the Hall, who had the very literary name of Byron-Scott but was actually a musician; and he and I used to play duets, chiefly arrangements of Haydn symphonies, in which I was never given a shot at the treble. However, I had these good friends. Writing for the *Cambridge Review* and occasionally for some London periodicals and publishing a little book, *Brief Diversions*, that had longer and more admiring London reviews than it deserved to have, I became some sort of character in the place….

The truth was I never felt really happy there, never even felt cosily at home. The University itself wasn't to be blamed; it had done its best for me, even though it has given me only sour or blank looks ever since I left it. The trouble was that I had gone up there at the wrong age, in my middle twenties. It was all very well for these shining-faced freshmen, newly released and promoted from school, all happy and busy buying college ties and blazers and tobacco jars with the college arms on them. It was all very well for the mature men, the dons, returning to their lecture rooms or labs. I belonged to neither group, not fowl, not

23

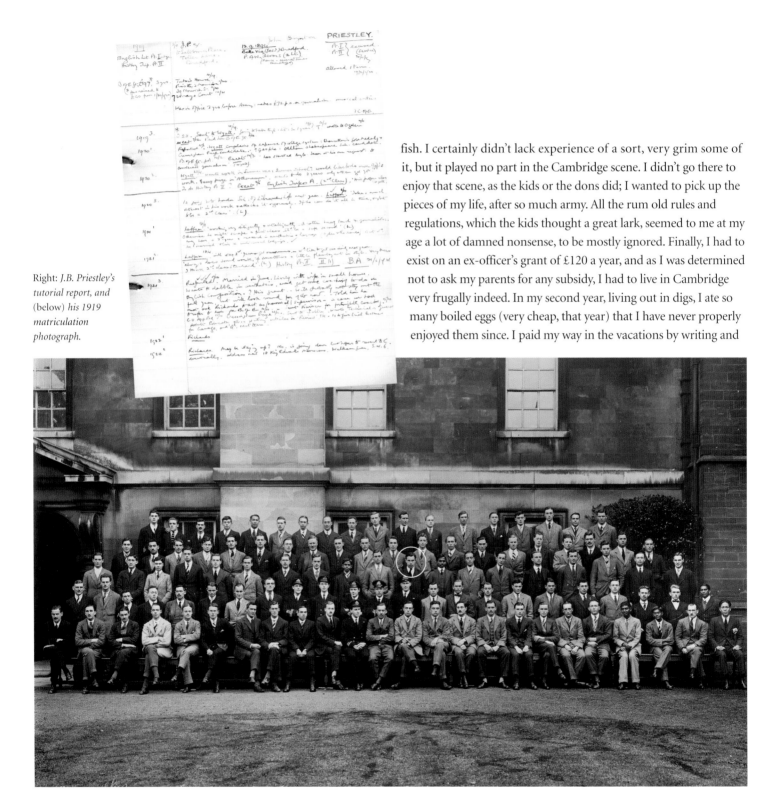

Right: *J.B. Priestley's tutorial report, and (below) his 1919 matriculation photograph.*

fish. I certainly didn't lack experience of a sort, very grim some of it, but it played no part in the Cambridge scene. I didn't go there to enjoy that scene, as the kids or the dons did; I wanted to pick up the pieces of my life, after so much army. All the rum old rules and regulations, which the kids thought a great lark, seemed to me at my age a lot of damned nonsense, to be mostly ignored. Finally, I had to exist on an ex-officer's grant of £120 a year, and as I was determined not to ask my parents for any subsidy, I had to live in Cambridge very frugally indeed. In my second year, living out in digs, I ate so many boiled eggs (very cheap, that year) that I have never properly enjoyed them since. I paid my way in the vacations by writing and

giving lectures to schools. But I had to go very carefully during term time. In those days – and I don't know what happens now – it was the Cambridge fashion to provide monster teas, crammed with muffins and crumpets and fairy cakes, and I remember how it irritated me to see men I knew, round about four o'clock, carrying fat bags of confectionery. I never provided anyone with those Cambridge breakfasts of buttered eggs from the kitchen. I lived a spare, inhospitable existence, totally unsuited to my temperament.

Moreover, neither the weather nor the environment brought any pleasure. I have been both colder and hotter in Cambridge than in any other English town. I arrived in October 1919 during a coal strike, and I well remember sitting in my overcoat, in a room like a refrigerator, trying to read books that shook in my chilled grasp. Yet I took my first tripos exam in what seemed to me a May heatwave, when my dripping hands stuck to the paper and my writing, never a good feature, looked more illegible than ever. Again, brought up in hill country, I couldn't enjoy the Fens and those enormous depressing fields they offered me. I took walks, just for exercise, and exercise is all I got from them....

From Instead of the Trees *(Heineman, 1975). Jack Priestley came up in 1919 after active service in the First World War, during which he was twice wounded. He read history and political science at Trinity Hall before pursuing his career as a journalist, novelist, playwright and broadcaster. He was made an Honorary Fellow in 1978 and died in 1984.*

Alan King Hamilton (1923)

I went up to the Hall in 1923, but had spent two nights there in the previous year to sit entrance examinations for both the College and University. Dinner in the Dining Hall that first night was made memorable because for dessert there were strawberries and cream, a luxury never enjoyed at school.

On that earlier visit, in 1922, I was given a large room at the top of R staircase (the one nearest to the river). As one emerged from the staircase entrance, there was a tall hedge on the right which concealed a single-storey building containing six or seven lavatories backing onto the river, from which it was obvious what the building was. None of those lavatories had a door! They had all been ripped off to feed the large bonfire on the adjacent lawn to celebrate the Hall having gone Head of the River in the May races two or three months earlier. When I went up in 1923 I was pleased to note that the missing doors had been replaced.

In my first year in residence, as was the custom on those days, I had rooms in College on the second floor of G staircase. And the rooms had not been adapted to house two undergraduates. On that staircase we were looked after by a gyp and a bedder. The gyp was lazy, always surly, and never known to smile. On reflection, having to wake up a number of undergraduates on bitterly cold mornings with a can of supposedly hot water could not have been a cheerful occupation. But he was just the same in the summer. Maybe we didn't tip him sufficiently. The bedder used to arrive on a tricycle which she parked in the Court and was never pleased when we tried to ride it, not easy because the small lawn was triangular in shape!

The Master was a fine man, Dr Henry Bond, one of the two greatest authorities in Roman law. Those of us reading Roman law were invited, four at a time, for supervision into the drawing room of the Master's Lodge. It had a most comfortable couch which seated four. Sometimes it was difficult to prevent oneself nodding off and I recall once being awakened with a sharp rebuke.

I had, of course, joined the College and University Law Societies over both of which I eventually presided, and also the Union Society of which, eventually, it was a great honour be elected President, although it did interfere with work. To have held that position was especially pleasing because, on a visit to Cambridge with my father before going into residence, we went to see the Debating Chamber and he said to me, 'Before you go down, you must occupy that chair!'

Two Hall Presidents of the Union: Alan King Hamilton (centre) *and Lionel Elvin* (right) *with Hugh Foot, 1927.*

In May or June 1926, just as we were about to take on Finals, there was the General Strike and everything in the country came to a standstill and there was a national appeal for volunteers. The vast majority of undergraduates leapt at the opportunity to undertake a variety of occupations. I had no difficulty in refusing a suggestion that I should go to the Midlands and harangue the coalminers and persuade them to return to work! Instead, I joined a party of Hall men who went to Scotland Yard and were sworn in as police officers. Our job was to escort petrol bowsers being driven from Thameshaven to Hyde Park, which had become a huge food distribution area. Between each bowser was a car with three of us in the back and beside the driver sat a sailor with a tin-hat and a rifle with a fixed bayonet. Happily, we were never called upon to exert our authority.

The strike was called off after about ten days. Those of us who had missed their exams were offered a fourth year at University which most of us accepted, including myself, thanks to the generosity of my father.

Actually receiving one's degree involved returning to Cambridge to appear before the Vice-Chancellor a month or so later. To obtain the MA one had to do so again, about a year later. I missed the train at Liverpool Street and immediately telephoned to the never-fussed, imperturbable Stanley Brown, Chief Clerk of the Union Society and explained my problem.

'That's alright, Sir, leave it to me!'

And thus, by proxy, I obtained by MA.

Alan King Hamilton read law at Trinity Hall, graduating in 1927. He was President of the Union Society in his final year. He was called to the Bar in 1929 by the Middle Temple. After service in the RAF during the Second World War, he took silk in 1954 and became a judge in 1964. He retired in 1980.

LIONEL ELVIN (1924)

Although the forces of change were slowly at work, the Trinity Hall to which I came up in 1924 still had more of the old than of the new about it. It was true that the old scandal of men staying up even though they had not passed the 'Little Go', the modest examination that gave them entrance to the University, had ended. But a good number were still taking the ordinary, not the honours degree. Some of these no doubt could have got their third-class honours, but what time would that have left for living the life of the place? On the whole, though, anyone who had gone away in 1914, had he survived the war, would have recognised his old college.

I saw all this from a particular, and a minority, point of view. I came from public elementary schools and a municipal high school, not one of those affluent private institutions that are oddly called Public Schools. People like myself would never have been at Cambridge except for the scholarships we had won and the grants from local authorities that brought them up to the bare minimum we needed to live on. I felt it to be almost a miracle that I was at Cambridge at all. I remember an impulse to put out my hand to touch the walls to reassure myself that it was real.

Anyway, here I was in October 1924, ready to enter eagerly into everything that Cambridge had to offer and to meet everybody in a friendly way who was similarly ready to meet me. And so I did, and

Below left: *The* Silver Crescent *magazine suggests a radio broadcasting schedule in the style of the newly created BBC, 1926.*

Below: *The Quinquagenta band, which included the Hall's Kenneth Thomas on banjo, played at many May Balls in the 1920s.*

TO-DAY'S BROADCASTING

Trinity Hall. Wave length (by Marcel), 2 inches 1 ell and a metre (gas).
7.30 a.m. Chorus of bedders and gyps, "Arise, ye blighters."
7.35 a.m. Morning Carol, "I'm a bit o' the ruins that Cromwell knocked abaht a bit." By Auntie Unwon.
7.45 a.m. Obligato on Chapel bell in F.
Hymn: "As pants the hart for cooling streams
When heated by the Chase."
8.30 a.m. Organ recital by the Dean.
8.59 a.m. Time signal. Weather forecast: Deep depression; foggy, light at intervals.
9.30 a.m. Negro Spirituous by the Porters, "My Lord, what a Morning."
Bass solo by Albert of Albert Hall.
9.59 a.m. Rev. C. F. Angus's alarm clock broadcast.
10.0 a.m. Rev. C. F. Angus on "How to Get Up Plato."
10.30 a.m. Mr. A. Pamplin arrives.
10.59 a.m. Mr. A. Pamplin will give a few hints to beginners on "How to sign off Hall."
11.15 a.m. Mr. K. D. Harris on "Self-compression; or, how to make a camel go through the door of an Austin."
11.30 a.m. Rowing notice broadcast. (Announcer, C. A. Potter.)
11.45 a.m. Rowing notice corrected.
11.55 a.m. Rowing notice re-corrected.
12 noon. Weather report. No rowing.
12.15 p.m. Solo by Mr. Campbell, "You must be Bursanary, Mary."
(Relayed from the Oratory House.) Recitation, "Wingkle, Wingkle, little bur."
12.45 p.m. The T.H.P.C.'s will sing "Crawling through the Hops," followed by "The Dales of England." Mr. Strangman will repeat the last verse *ad lib.*
1.0 p.m. Mr. Archibald and Mr. Jameson will give their celebrated imitation of "Feeding Time at the Zoo."
2.0 p.m. Woman's hour.
1. Pollarditics for Women; or, The Gregory Powder in the Jam.
2. The Best Pottery for the Ideal Home.
3. Mr. Pollard will speak on the Sex Femmae.
2.45 p.m. Mr. Richards on "The Use of the English Language." (Relayed from the tow-path.)
3.0 p.m. (Relayed from Hall Soccer Ground.) Conversations between players and Ref.

6

3.30 p.m. Mr. Baggs will sing, "When I was a Girl."
3.45 p.m. Gramophone music, by kind permission of the Senior Tutor. (Winder, R. Hayes.)
4.0 p.m. Mr. Nairn will plead for funds for Oriental Students.
4.15 p.m. (Relayed from the Baths.) Selection from "What is this Pinney for?"
4.10 p.m. (Switch over to Jesus.) The Master of Christ's on "Shipleys that Pass in the Night."
5.30 p.m. Mr. R. Paton on "My Scheme for the Construction of a Channel Tunnel."
6.0 p.m. Mr. Harvey (junr.) and Mr. Pamplin will sing a duet, "Drink to me only with thine eyes."
6.15 p.m. Mr. Harvey on "Spoon-Feeding."
6.30 p.m. Song, "I am a Most Superior Pearson."
6.45 p.m. L. Tetley will make an appeal for the blind.
7.0 p.m. Bad-time Stories, by Auntie M.A.B.
7.30 p.m. Mr. Grant on "Bottles I have Administered."
7.45 p.m. (Switch over to the Vic.)
8.0 p.m. (Switchback again.)
8.15 p.m. Humorous recitation, "Instal Pups and Bulldogs." By Mr. Chandler.
8.30-10 p.m. Medley, accompanied by Leighton (of Leighton and Johnson—no connection with the Lord.)
Mr. Rubinstein will sing, "I wonder where my baby is to-night."
Mr. Aston, "Song without words."
Mr. Currie will sing, "I didn't want to do it."
Mr. Salamon will sing "The Messiah," accompanied by Mr. Macdonald on the bagpipes. (S.R. to the Zionist Society.)
By request for R. G. Wilson, "Will he no come back again?"
10.0 p.m. Bar closes.
10.1 p.m. Gate closes.
10.5 p.m. News items. (R. F. Henniker, announcer.)
10.35 p.m. Topical talk on the Report of the Special Commission on the Coales Situation.
11.0 p.m. Mr. Jack getting up before breakfast will be broadcast.
11.30 p.m. Evening Prayers. By Mr. Oliver. Close down.
3.0 a.m. Mr. H. G. G. Herklots from KDKA, relayed, on "I've got my pants on upside down."

7

enjoyed my time immensely. Yet I found – and this must be said – that I had entered a very class-conscious society. J. B. Priestley, who went down a year or two before I came up, had found the same, I was told, and resented it. I think it was easier for me because I enjoyed my games and the track at Fenner's and that is a considerable social solvent.

I want to put this matter fairly, though it is not easy to get the balance right. There were people from the privileged schools who took you as you were, or gave you the benefit of the doubt; particularly, I noticed, northerners or the occasional American or Australian or New Zealander. But there was a perceptible 'distancing'. None of my intimate friends in the College – those whose rooms you could drop into to talk about all the things undergraduates do talk about, from the state of the College food to the meaning of life, was from an independent school. We were a separate group, supposed to be brighter than the rest and expected to get Firsts, but these other people, with their hands in their jingling pockets, seemed to be the lords of the place.

Only a few of them were positively ill-mannered. By these, even if you had been playing football or cricket with them that same afternoon, you could expect to be cut dead in the College or on the street. The reason was that they had been badly brought up. As one man said to me many years later, when we had become good friends and golfing partners: 'We just assumed that anyone who hadn't been to a Public School must be a **** ,' and he used a word that does get into print now but that then was a pretty forceful unprintable.

The class structure of College society was reflected in the relations between the dons and undergraduates on the one hand and those who were employed by the College on the other. These were then always referred to as the College servants. Now, a little ambiguously, but more decently, they are called the staff. It embarrassed me that they called me 'sir' while I was expected not even to put a Mr in front of their names. But, as Marx pointed out, in a stable feudal society in which both classes accept their stations personal relations can often be quite good, and in College society, which in a minor way was a feudal survival, I think on the whole they were. In some cases the more affluent or even aristocratic a young man was the more glory rubbed off on to his gyp, so long as he behaved like a gentleman. I was very amused

Silver Crescent *magazine, 1930.*

when my first gyp after I became a Fellow, that impeccable gentleman's gentleman Chandler, told me that in the war he had been a batman to four officers, all of them old Etonians, he said. My word, I thought to myself, I must be a let-down for you! But, he assured me, he always voted Labour. In fact, we got on excellently and he looked after me so well, even wanting to pack my bag if I was to be away for a weekend, that I was almost spoiled. In the end I had to make a rule or two. I said that however cold it was I would not have a hot-water bottle. 'But why, sir, if it's really cold?' he asked. 'Just to save my self-respect,' I replied, leaving him, I think, a little mystified.

The Head Porter when I came up was one Albert Pamplin. I am afraid he represented the less acceptable face of College feudalism. On a summer evening after hall he would hang about in Front Court being mildly – and I thought ill-manneredly – ragged by some of the Boat Club types, and laughing as if he enjoyed it. No doubt he did well enough out of their tips at the end of term; when he died it was said that he owned several houses. But the other porters and staff were different, and Grant, Boggis and the rest I liked. Chase [Senior Tutor] had told me that at the end of term I should leave such a tip as I could afford at the Porters' Lodge, and if it had to be smaller than the tips some other people left, this would not in the least affect their readiness to be helpful; and this was true. Services were more personal, less mechanised, than now. Boggis brought the post round to your rooms every morning, always with a cheerful greeting, just as 'Bicycle Bill' mended your punctures for you. Similarly Ludman, that mighty carver, carved the joints in hall, with no cutting up in the kitchens first; however he got through so fast and with such skill I never knew.

From a memoir deposited in the College archive. Lionel Elvin read English at Trinity Hall and was elected President of the Union Society in 1928. He was a Fellow from 1930 to 1944. He was Professor of Education and then Director at the Institute of Education, London. He retired in 1974 and was elected an Honorary Fellow in 1980.

DENIS RICHARDS (1928)

Trinity Hall, to which I went up in October 1928,… was at that time socially a cut above some of the other colleges but not particularly distinguished intellectually. As an exhibitioner, I was entitled to rooms within the College throughout my three years – the ordinary undergraduate had two years out and only one year in. However, as part of the building was under reconstruction I had for my first year to put up with lodgings in town. They had only one good feature, a fair-sized sitting-room with a strong table and a couple of comfortable armchairs. Everything else was dismal. My bedroom had no gas or electricity, and was so small that I could put my candle on the dressing-table at one side of the room and blow it out from my bed at the other. The house had no water upstairs, and if there was a bath downstairs we were not allowed to use it. Toilet facilities in the bedroom consisted of a jug, a basin, and a jerry-pot. During the exceptionally cold weather of early 1929, when the Cam was rock-hard for weeks on end and some enthusiasts skated right up to Ely, the contents of these utensils repeatedly froze over in the course of the night.

The occupant of the other set of rooms in the house, a freshman like myself, was to become my closest companion in the three years that lay ahead. He was a lively and good-looking boy whose brilliant blue eyes went well with his dark hair and fresh complexion. He had had a fairly strict Methodist upbringing in Cornwall, and had won a scholarship to the Hall in natural sciences. I was soon to observe that in the struggle between the calls of his spirited disposition and those of his Methodist upbringing, the former won hands down every time. While I was out on the first day after our arrival some members of the THBC called at our lodgings on a recruiting campaign. They invited him out for a drink, took him to a pub and stood him his first pint of beer. I saw him at lunchtime and he told me that he would never touch another drop of it as long as he lived. That evening he fell in with these oarsmen again. This time the beer went down better. They brought him back after closing time much the worse for wear and he needed a friendly hand to reach the safe haven of his bed.

In the Borough of Cambridge.

To *John Michael Page*

of M.S. Trinity Hall

in the Borough of Cambridge.

Information has been laid this day by ROBERT JOHN PEARSON, Ch'

charging you with the following offence :—

STATEMENT OF OFFENCE.

Extinguishing light of a street lamp

contrary to **section 28 of the Town Police Clauses Act 1847.**

PARTICULARS OF OFFENCE.

On the   **22nd**   day of   **February**   193 6 ,

at and   in the said Borough

you did **in a certain street there called St. John's Street to the annoyance of passengers then in the said street wilfully extinguish the light of a certain lamp there.**

You are therefore hereby summoned to appear before the Court of Summary Jurisdiction, sitting at the Guildhall, in the said Borough, on **Monday** the   **2nd**   day of   **March**   1936 , at the hour of Eleven in the forenoon, to answer to the said information.

Dated the   **27th**   day of   **February**   1936 .

Justice of the Peace for the Borough aforesaid.

Take Notice. If you are unable to attend either personally or by a Solicitor in answer to this summons, and do not wish for an adjournment of the hearing to enable you to appear, a communication acknowledging receipt of the summons should be sent.

Any communication with respect to this summons should be addressed to THE CLERK OF THE JUSTICES, 21, ST. ANDREW'S STREET, CAMBRIDGE, *and accompanied by a stamped addressed envelope for reply.*

BOROUGH OF CAMBRIDGE POLICE COURT. A2024

2nd March, 1936.

Received of *J. M. Page*

the sum of *One* Pounds

Shillings

Pence, Penalty and Costs

imposed on *2/3/36*

£ 1 : —

pp. JASPER LYON,
Clerk to the Justices.

Extinguishing a street lamp in 1936 led to a proctor's notice, a police summons and a short article in the newspapers for Michael Page.

own bat, gloves, pads, cricket bag, etc. The pair of buckskin boots I bought at Joshua Taylor's in 1929 cost £7.10s – equivalent to over £200 in 2000 – but at least they lasted well.

The debating I never got in the Union [due to the tedium of the debates and the large number of other, more persistent contributors] I made up for in a much more enjoyable way – in my College Debating Society, of which I became Secretary. It was a very light-hearted body indeed, known as the XYZ and, being light-hearted, it perished during the increasingly solemn 1930s. We debated on Sunday evenings after hall, about twenty of us, and took it in turns to meet in one another's rooms. The host of the evening had one obligation – to supply port and chocolate biscuits. The motion was invariably frivolous and several of the members were extremely skilled in exploring the more inane aspects. Denis Blundell, the cricket blue, was my predecessor in office; and another lively speaker was Mervyn Griffith-Jones, later famous for prosecuting at Nuremberg and for asking the jurors at the Lady Chatterley trial whether they would be happy for their servants to read the book. Typical of our deliberations was a motion 'that the higher up the mountain, the greener grows the grass'. This was very heavily defeated after Baron de Rutzen had demonstrated conclusively that the characteristic fauna of the mountain was the mountain goat; that the excreta of the mountain goat were globular in shape; that being globular, they would roll to the bottom of the mountain and it was therefore the lower slopes that would be better fertilized and hence greener.

Extracted from his autobiography, Recalling the Flavour *(Smithson Albright, 1998). Denis Richards read history and left Trinity Hall to take up a career as a school master in 1931. He served in the RAF during the Second World War, becoming one of its official historians. His post-war career spanned adult education, voluntary work and historical writing.*

With my total work for the week, including lectures, amounting to about sixteen or seventeen hours there was ample time to enjoy other aspects of a university education. Fortunately, I had money enough to do so; and with £250 from all sources, and my parents also providing a home and pocket-money in the vacations, I was quite as well off as the average undergraduate of that time and a great deal better off than most undergraduates nowadays. [To equal what £250 p.a. would buy in 1928, a student in 2000 would need about £8,000 p.a.]

I played cricket many times for the College, but drew some odium on myself by withdrawing from the teams a fortnight before the examinations – the long hours in the fresh air and the beer afterwards made work impossible in the evenings. It was, of course, a more expensive game than soccer since one had to provide one's

TRINITY HALL,
CAMBRIDGE.

ELECTRIC LIGHT.

The standard equipment of electric light in College rooms is three lamps of 20 watts each at a charge of £1 5s. per term. This charge covers repairs arising out of fair wear and tear (but not the replacement of bulbs) and also a contribution towards the public lighting of the College.

Lamps of higher power may be used but if so an extra charge is made each term on the following scale:

Up to 20 watts extra	...	...	10/-
Between 20 watts and 40 watts extra			15/-
„ 40 „ 60 „			£1

For higher power than 60 watts the charge is in proportion.

TRINITY HALL,
CAMBRIDGE.

FIRE.

A patent fire extinguisher will be found in every bedroom in College. This is for use in emergencies only and the occupant of each set of rooms will be held responsible for the safe keeping and proper use of the instrument in his rooms.

If the extinguisher be tampered with or used improperly, the occupant of the rooms will be fined a minimum of £1 1s. by the Bursar, plus the cost of replacement, without reference to any other action taken by the Tutor.

Domestic aspects of Hall life in the early 1930s.

ESTIMATE OF THINGS NECESSARY

FOR MEN COMING INTO COLLEGE ROOMS OR LODGINGS

(not including furniture).

SHEETS 3 pair	†TEAPOT
*BLANKETS	†COFFEE-POT
TOWELS 6 ordinary and 3 bath	KETTLE
PILLOWCASES 3 or 4	TRAYS
TOILETCOVERS 3	
	†SPOONS
	Not fewer than 6 each of table, dessert, tea, egg; and 2 salt.
*TABLECLOTH, coloured	†KNIVES AND FOLKS
TABLECLOTHS 3 small and 2 large	Not fewer than 6 each both of large
NAPKINS 12 or fewer	and small; with small carving-knife and
GLASSCLOTHS 6	fork.
DUSTERS 6	
	CRUETS
	TEA AND BREAKFAST SERVICE
*TOILET-SERVICE, including splasher	TUMBLERS
	WATER JUG
	WINE-GLASSES(?)
All linen should be plainly marked with the owner's name and initials.	DECANTERS(?)
* These are supplied in Lodgings.	† Electroplate is preferable to silver.
	In hanging pictures, wall hooks should be used.

Rooms in College are unfurnished, but usually the furniture of the outgoing tenant can be taken over on valuation; in Lodgings furniture is supplied.

Extra plate, linen, knives and forks, glasses, &c., can when necessary be obtained on hire from the Kitchens at moderate rates.

TRINITY HALL.

SAPPERS AT THE HALL BETWEEN THE WARS
BILL ADAMS (1936)

From the early 1920s up to the outbreak of the Second World War, all Royal Engineer Officers commissioned from the RMA Woolwich (known as the Shop) automatically came to Cambridge to read mechanical sciences and were joined by perhaps two a year from the RMC Kingston (Canada) and occasionally one or two from the Royal Signals. Academic standards especially in applied mathematics at the Shop were high and we were therefore excused the first year of the course. Obtaining an honours degree was the standard required to draw Engineer pay, a small increment to one's salary abolished after 1945. The number of officers involved probably varied between 30 and 35 a year.

I can remember what a warm welcome we received in October 1936 from the tutors (Owen Wansbrough-Jones and Charles Crawley) both of whom had family connections with the Sappers. Wansborough-Jones was later to become scientific adviser to the Army Council. Three of us joined, two from the previous year were already there and finished in July 1937 and three more took their places in October 1937. I can remember well how easy it was to make friends and be accepted in spite of our perhaps rather narrow Army background. It was like a breath of fresh air to us to sample and savour all the activities offered. The Union, amateur dramatics, Christian societies, eating asparagus, breakfast with the Master, societies of every description, apart from all the opportunities for every kind of sport. At the Engineering Laboratories we went straight into the second year. To start with we found this baffling but gradually got on top of it. Two hours of lectures first; these

Trinity Hall work camp for unemployed miners at Eastnor Castle in the Malvern Hills, August 1937. Seated centre are Launcelot Fleming and Robert Martineau. The camp was attended by about 70 unemployed Welsh miners and 20 undergraduates.

College chaplain. For my first year this was Victor Johnson, who was acting as a locum. Launcelot Fleming returned from the Antarctic for my second year and he remained a friend for all my life, which he certainly influenced in many ways.

I think all of us Sappers took part in a lot of sport. Hunter Gordon was Captain of the College Rugger Club whilst I became Treasurer of the University Vandals and toured Scotland with them in 1938. I also learned to play hockey which, though I never reached a high standard, I was still playing on the parade ground of my unit in Libya some twenty years later. Peter Oliver who was Captain of the University Hockey side kindly invited me to go to the Rhineland with the University Muddlers in 1938 as trainer and we had an overwhelmingly successful tour. Frederickson got a half blue for fencing.

Long vacations were spent continuing our military training at Chatham but, in 1938, I was given leave to join the Cambridge Spitzbergen Expedition as surveyor which made a glorious finale to my time at Cambridge.

Bill Adams came to Trinity Hall as a Second Lieutenant in the Royal Engineers in 1936. He saw active service in Burma and served in India until partition. He was Deputy Commandant at the School of Military Engineering at Chatham from 1961 to 1963 when he retired to pursue a career as a civil engineer.

FREDERICK EIRICH (1939)

When I was called up to the Army in 1938, Austria had already been annexed by Germany and I was finding difficulties with academic life there. I had, however, no intention of fighting for Hitler so used the excuse of a Faraday Society meeting in Cambridge to ask for and obtain an exit permit. I sent my family abroad to my wife's sister and used my remaining time in Vienna to put in order my household, belongings and academic position. By September, after Chamberlain's visit to Berchtesgaden, I knew war was imminent. After a short stay in London, I went to a

were slightly unusual as the lecturer wrote his lecture word for word on the blackboard which we copied down, but this approach was perhaps necessary as they had a high mathematical content. Supervision for Sappers was on a centralised basis and we didn't use College facilities, although the Hall Engineering Fellow, Robin Hayes, nevertheless became a good friend.

Because of getting a First in the Mays I was to spend my whole two years in College and had a room at the top of E staircase, alas no longer in single occupancy. The gyp was Langley who became a very good friend. He had seen Army service in the Rifle Brigade and I think was slightly disappointed with me as my life style was so different from that of an officer in the Greenjackets. There was a big plus living on E staircase as my rooms were directly above the

Frederick Eirich with Sir Eric Rideal who helped him find a refuge at the College.

prearranged position with Sir Eric Rideal in the Department of Colloid Science in Cambridge and joined his college, Trinity Hall. I cannot emphasise enough how welcoming and reassuring the English population were after the hectic time in Austria. In particular, College life had a great appeal for me and Sir Eric's efforts to secure me honorary MA status helped a great deal. In Sir Eric's lab, I busied myself setting up an air-driven ultra centrifuge, and at the same time was engaged in teaching at the neighbouring institute of Dr Norrish [Physical Chemistry].

Life in England and especially academic life in Cambridge was so congenial that, if I'm ever homesick, it is for our life in Cambridge rather than for our birthplace of Vienna.

Frederick Eirich moved to New York after the war where he became a professor at the Polytechnic University of Brooklyn and Dean of Research in 1962. He is now retired and lives in New Jersey.

Beautiful hypotheses and ugly facts

04

SCIENCE AT TRINITY HALL

NICK BAMPOS

Trinity Hall is not known as a science college. We are, after all, an institution founded to teach canon and civil law, and one significantly founded by a bishop. Instinctively, the teaching of science would not have figured prominently in the minds of the early Fellowship. For the first 300 years since foundation, science as we understand it today was an unknown discipline. The celestial bodies were thought to rotate around the earth until the late sixteenth century, and any attempt to understand or tamper with the state of nature was considered heretical. Simply extracting a medicinal agent from a plant by boiling it in water, in the way that we prepare countless infusions today, was tantamount to witchcraft, especially if the substance had the desired effect. While many individuals had done great work, mostly in secret, it is only with hindsight that we can begin to appreciate their role in subsequent discoveries. My own discipline, chemistry, can be considered to have been derived from alchemy, in which gold could supposedly be transmuted from base metals, or elixirs formulated for prolonging life. While scientific progress, in any form, thrives in environments which embrace change, change was the last thing the Middle Ages were prepared to deal with. If science was to flourish, it needed patronage both financially and politically. Ironically, the necessary knowledge was there all along and only needed great minds to disentangle it from the superstitions which encrusted it. But all this lasted well into the late seventeenth and early eighteenth century. Let us not forget that it was not until 1687 that Isaac Newton offered the world his landmark *Philosophiae naturalis principia mathematica,* or 1859 when Charles Darwin revolutionised our perception of our role in the world around us. Many of these significant events were taking place within walking distance of the Hall, and ultimately shaped how science was to be taught.

Teaching science in Cambridge during the eighteenth and nineteenth centuries, was a very personal affair, with the vogue for a particular subject being dominated by the interests (not necessarily strengths) of the individual Fellows. Outside the established chairs in subjects such as divinity and law, only mathematics was seen as a credible discipline from which many of the modern areas of science have derived. Newton originally came to Cambridge to study law, and only by turning to philosophy, under which much of mathematics was taught, did he begin to formulate the ideas which led to the great achievements for which he is known today. The Natural Science Tripos was only introduced in 1848 as a postgraduate course for those having previously sat one of the other Triposes. By Newton's time, physics and mathematics were gaining academic credibility in Cambridge and were destined for great things. Chemistry, however, was not honoured with a chair in the University until 1702, when Giovanni Vigani, an apothecary and enthusiast in investigating chemical reactions, was elected as the first Professor in Chemistry. It is significant that the University Senate finally recognised chemistry as a 'safe' science, rather than a practice sullied by supernatural connections as late as the early eighteenth century. At that time, colleges were exercising significant power and influence in areas of research and teaching. Some of the colleges built and maintained their own observatories and laboratories, and

Nick Bampos, Senior Tutor, 2003–.

independently appointed science Fellows who ultimately directed what was being taught and how it was going to be taught. What soon became clear to the colleges was that the business of research and teaching science was an expensive enterprise, which offered few financial benefits. The only solution was to pool resources and allow the University some control over the newly established disciplines. University laboratories began to dot the Cambridge streetscape in the late eighteenth century, and since then the decision to consolidate centralised science departments has been richly rewarded with groundbreaking discoveries and an unequalled bounty of Nobel Prizes in Physics, Chemistry, and Biology and Medicine. The establishment of various cognate sciences blossomed in the nineteenth and twentieth centuries, today placing this University at the forefront of scientific research. However, good research scientists were once students, and it is in this area that Trinity Hall has played its role.

Early science Fellows at Trinity Hall in the nineteenth century would not have been too taxed by work, as there would not have been more than a couple of students admitted to read 'science'. It is unlikely that the first science Fellow would have carried out research, or have had more than a secondary interest in the subjects he was expected to teach. For example, Edward Lovett Henn was one of the few science Fellows I could identify, but he fulfilled this role as a Fellow in Mathematics (1875–89) and at the same time practised as a barrister. Teaching science in those days might have involved informal discussions based around information gained from the Cambridge grapevine, or extracted from the published proceedings of the Royal Society. Over the next one hundred years, things did not change significantly, with the College growing very slowly both in terms of undergraduate numbers and the size of the Fellowship.

Catastrophic events such as epidemics and wars dramatically affected academic life at Trinity Hall as elsewhere, but because of our size and lack of wealth, these events hit Trinity Hall harder than most, at times paralysing our capacity to teach core subjects. For example, in 1919, there were only six resident Fellows struggling to cope with a flood of ex-service undergraduates and the huge task of reconstruction. One can only imagine the magnitude of the task from an administrative perspective, let alone an educational one. The period after the First World War offered much hope in terms of provision for science at Trinity Hall, with a string of eminent academics. Robin Hayes (1919–46) acted as Director of Studies for the engineers throughout his tenure at Trinity Hall, and was a committed teacher. Sir Eric Rideal (1920–46) was one of two science Fellows elected under the Mastership of Henry Bond (1919–29). His brilliant career as a physical chemist led to his appointment as the first Professor of Colloid Science, Fellow of the Royal Society and President of the Royal Institution. The other scientist elected in 1928 was Sir Clive Cooper (1928–38) who was Director of the Museum of Zoology, acted as College Bursar, and went on to become Director of the Natural History Museum in London; unfortunately his commitments meant he did no College teaching. In the tradition of excellence in colloid science at Trinity Hall, Sir Owen Wansbrough-Jones (1930–46) was elected under the next Master of the College, Henry Dean (Fellow 1922–29, Master 1929–54), who was an eminent pathologist and the first scientist to be elected Master in the history of the College. By this time, the importance of science in the Fellowship was reflecting the demands of the increasing proportion of science students in the undergraduate body. Dean was followed by two further scientists elected to the Mastership; William Deer (1966–75) who was Professor of Mineralogy and Petrology, and Sir Morris Sugden (1976–84) whose career as a physical chemist spanned academia and industry. A significant number of committed teachers and science Fellows followed, too many to list here, many moving on to chairs at other universities. Three 'scientists' acted as Vice-Masters, all having taught in their respective subjects; Howell ('Bill') Grundy (Pharmacology, 1962–87) from 1974–78, Denis Haydon (Biophysics, 1965–88) from 1978–82 and John Denton (Turbomachinery, 1977–) at present. The Senior Tutorship has been held only three times by scientists; firstly by Ernest Frankl, an engineer who served the role with commitment between 1968–85, then Kareen Thorne, a biochemist who was the first woman to serve as Senior Tutor (1985–93) and one of the first female Fellows at Trinity Hall, and finally by myself, a chemist appointed to the Senior Tutorship in 2003. The uncommon union of Church and science was successfully fused by two Deans, Launcelot Fleming (Divinity and Geology, 1933–49), and John Polkinghorne (Mathematical Physics, 1986–90).

The period between the wars saw great advances in every area of science, and with each stride forward the establishment of new and exciting disciplines. Teaching during this time would have been handled exclusively by the Fellows, as it was still possible for one individual to be aware of almost all that was known about their discipline – and I assume rather romantically that there were fewer administrative distractions and forms to complete. Oh, and no email! The Second World War brought great change, both to the University, Trinity Hall and science in general. It can be argued that this war was driven by science, and one that certainly ended with what should have been one of the greatest scientific advances. Unfortunately two flashes of light, in Hiroshima and Nagasaki in 1945, are the events which stamp the atomic age into the pages of history. Many of the key individuals, not only on the atomic programme, but in many of the science-related programmes in the war effort were Cambridge educated or academics in Cambridge.

Sitting next to Shaun Wylie at a dinner recently, and listening to stories about his years at Bletchley Park, will rate as one of the highlights of my time at Trinity Hall. The Second World War also saw the birth of the computing age, a development embraced early by Trinity Hall. We were the first college to appoint a Fellow in Computer Science, William Clocksin, in 1986 and our Fellowship provided Cambridge with its first Professor of Information Engineering, Frank Fallside, in 1983.

Just after the war, a science student might have commanded the attention of a Fellow on a one-to-one basis for the duration of their degree, although the success of such relationships depended on the personalities of the two parties. Teaching would involve attending lectures and practical classes, as well as tuition within the College. The advantage of centralised lectures is based on the student being lectured by the person best suited to present the course, rather than the Fellow who happens to be attached to the College. The fact that the Fellow will have carried out research in the University laboratories will have led to a productive exchange of ideas which result in better teaching across the University. This system of teaching pretty much reflects how we teach scientists today.

In 2003–04 the College admitted 110 undergraduates, of which just under half were scientists, mathematicians, medics and engineers. Throughout our history, science Fellows have made up a small component of the overall Fellowship, although the students reading natural science make up about one fifth of the undergraduate body. Currently, due to the disparate nature of the course, the convention is to divide scientists into those with an interest in biological subjects or physical subjects. For this very reason, providing suitable teaching is quite a challenge. At present, a typical week for an undergraduate reading science at Trinity Hall is rather busy. Most mornings, often including Saturdays, an undergraduate attends three to four hours of lectures in large groups (about 500 in their first year, but shrinking to about 10–50 by their final year depending on subject). The lectures aim to distil the important aspects of a particular specialised course and are accompanied by comprehensive notes produced by the lecturer. If lucky, one manages a spot of lunch before embarking on a practical session lasting three to four hours; depending on how well the experiment goes. Of course, there are still revision sessions to be organised and the results from the practical classes to be analysed and incorporated into a report that will be marked. Thankfully, not every afternoon is committed to practical classes, as problem sheets related to the lectures need to be attempted before attending regular supervisions based on the problems. Supervisors are often demanding individuals who are convinced that it was all so much harder during their undergraduate days, and insist on setting a few extra questions, just to better illustrate the subtleties of the course. After life's necessary functions there is barely time in the day to stop to talk to a friend on Latham Lawn! For those bold enough to take on rowing as well, the day starts before the sun rises. In short, and contrary to popular myth, our undergraduate scientists work very hard.

At the end of every term, our supervisors submit reports for each of our undergraduates, commenting on their progress, any potential problems and predicting how they would perform if sitting an exam on the course. The more one gets to know the students individually, the easier it becomes to comment on their progress. I have always found supervision reports a fascinating documentation of the developing relationship between the undergraduate and their subject (and supervisor). Of course, much praise is heaped on those students who take their work seriously. But the intimate nature of supervisions achieves a great deal more than a training session for glittering examination results. College teaching forges friendships. A supervisor can detect in the written work if a student is struggling with the work, or if some other problem is looming in the background. Exhaustion, frustration, depression and homesickness can be detected within minutes of embarking on an hour-long session dealing with quantum mechanics, partial differential equations, genetics or chemical synthesis. More often than not, students feel comfortable enough to seek advice on non-academic matters. This makes the supervisor part teacher and part counsellor, and ultimately a good friend. Supervisions are, however, a very expensive way of teaching. As the number of students increases, and the diversity of courses flourish, our capacity to offer supervisions (as we now know them) will become increasingly difficult. At Trinity Hall, especially in the sciences, the majority of teaching is done by a talented pool of graduate students and post-doctoral researchers, with only a handful of courses in the final year supervised by Fellows at other colleges who are ideally suited to teach highly specialised courses. This offers an effective balance of enthusiasm from the graduates and post-docs, and experience from permanent members of staff. In my opinion, this is as close to a perfect system of teaching as is possible, but in the future we may need to turn to College-based revision classes or seminars to allow Trinity Hall Fellows (of whom there are far too few for the number of students) the option of interacting with complete year groups, and offer students the opportunity to gauge the depth of their understanding against their colleagues. In this respect, teaching science is different to arts subjects, where the need to dissect an essay or develop an idea may be best served in smaller groups. There is, however, another difference between science and arts-based subjects that may affect the relationship students develop with the College. Arts supervisions are typically conducted in College rooms, leading to a greater appreciation of the College environment. Science supervisions are most often conducted in the departments, where supervisors spend most of their time carrying out research in purpose-built laboratories. By the final and subsequent years, most scientists shift their base from College to their respective departments, leading to a very different relationship with the College.

The composition of the science undergraduates is remarkably different to that of a generation ago. In any year, there are a number of overseas students who bring a fresh approach to the subjects they take. Of the natural science intake, about half

Stephen Hawking, Lucasian Professor of Mathematics, was a research student at the Hall from 1962–65 and is an Honorary Fellow.

and present results at major conferences, but they also contribute to the teaching, as mentioned earlier. They also bring a maturity and enthusiasm to the College that enriches the collegiate experience for all. Stephen Hawking is our best-known graduate student of recent times and is an Honorary Fellow, but I have no doubt that many others will follow in his wake. Unfortunately, funding is the determining factor in graduate admissions, and any change in funding policy will influence the composition of the graduate community and the nature of their interaction with the College. Many science graduates go into industry, with some staying on in academia, one or two to take up Fellowships at Trinity Hall.

As a teaching university, Cambridge has a proud tradition, one that we would like to think is unrivalled. I am happy to state this as an outsider, having completed all my degrees in my native Australia. Those who choose to teach in Cambridge appreciate the privileged community we work in, and are galvanised by our common sense of purpose. We work hard, but our efforts are rewarded by the effort our students invest in their degrees. Despite our humble foundation, the Hall is today a dynamic, progressive and committed academic institution which is well prepared to deal with the various challenges ahead.

Nick Bampos completed his BSc and PhD at the University of Sydney, before coming to Cambridge in 1993. He became a Fellow of Trinity Hall in 1999 and Senior Tutor in October 2003, and still conducts research and teaches organic and inorganic chemistry.

(predominantly male) intend to specialise in physical subjects, while half (predominantly female) express a preference for biological subjects. All, however, respond to the challenges of their courses, with just under half our finalists applying to graduate courses either in Cambridge or other research-active universities.

Graduates are often the forgotten communities within the Cambridge college setting. Thankfully, at Trinity Hall our graduates are a valued and respected group of individuals. Not only do they undertake world-class research, publish in international journals

ERNEST FRANKL (1936–1992): AN APPRECIATION
MICHAEL KELLY

Ernest Frankl was born in Vienna and came up to Trinity Hall in 1936 to read engineering. He was interned for two years during the Second World War, in spite of having volunteered. From 1941 on he taught for the University and several colleges, while researching aspects of stress analysis in structures. He became a Fellow of Trinity Hall in 1956 and Senior Tutor in 1968, a role in which he

Right: *Sir Morris Sugden, Master from 1975–84.*

Bottom: *Ernest Frankl (second from right) as an undergraduate, with Hugh Forbes, Kenneth Brown and another, 1937.*

served the Hall for many years and with great distinction. He retired from the University in 1982 and from the Hall in 1985.

In both Department and College things got done quietly and effectively when he was in the team, and more so when he was in the chair. Reforms in engineering education and the tripos examinations were his legacy. In the Hall he developed an efficient tutorial system, and was involved in all the important Hall decisions over nearly twenty years. His great outside interest was photography, which in the latter part of his life became a professional activity. His photographs of Oxbridge colleges showed a keen insight into their whole fabric. His quiet, sceptical style, his wry humour, contained manner and gentle wisdom was made available to all in College, and I was one of many who benefited from Ernest's advice at several stages.

SIR MORRIS SUGDEN (1975–1984): AN APPRECIATION
MICHAEL KELLY

When Dr Sugden was elected Master of Trinity Hall in 1975, he was returning to Cambridge after an absence of twelve years. At the time he was Chief Executive of Shell Research Limited, with over 800 scientists at their Thornton Research Centre, where he had

established a major research group on the chemistry of combustion. Between 1938 and 1963 he had been variously a student at Jesus College, a lecturer then reader in the Department of Chemistry and Fellow of Queens' College. His research interests throughout where the study of flames in a wide variety of chemical settings and with a wide range of analytical techniques, for which he was elected FRS in 1963.

On his return, Dr Sugden, (Sir Morris from 1983) served the College well as Master, as a particularly effective chairman. He paid a personal attention to the interests of the Fellows, the students and the staff. He was a talented pianist and was widely read and travelled. He and Marian were great entertainers in the lodge, not least for students at Saturday morning breakfasts! He soon acquired several other important roles, not least the Physical Sciences Secretary of the Royal Society, Chairman of the Faculty Board of the Engineering Faculty and Chairman of the Syndics of the University Press. He died in January 1984 after a short illness.

Michael Kelly was a Fellow between 1974 and 1981 in theoretical physics, and 1989 and 1992 in semiconductor science. He has been a Professorial Fellow since 2002. He is now the inaugural Prince Philip Professor of Technology, and Executive Director of the Cambridge-MIT Institute.

GWR locomotive 5916 Trinity Hall. *Built in 1931, she was withdrawn from service in 1962. She was one of a series of 'Hall Class' locomotives, which GWR named after 'famous Halls'.*

RESEARCH DEMANDS AND COLLEGE LIFE
MICHAEL HOBSON

I have been asked many times by colleagues in the Physics Department 'Why do you bother being a member of a College?' It is, after all, not uncommon for scientists in the University to concentrate solely on their research and departmental responsibilities. The life of an academic in the sciences is very different to that of one in the arts or humanities. Modern science is a collaborative pursuit. Most projects involve a large number of researchers around the world and rely on expensive pieces of equipment. As a result, much of one's research life is spent in the Department, working with colleagues and students, coordinating research, and visiting other institutions in the UK and overseas. This can leave precious little time for College life, and hence many scientists choose not to become Fellows. In my opinion, this is a great loss to both constituencies. I would like to take this opportunity to answer my colleagues' question, and to set down the reasons why I have found the past ten years at Trinity Hall a profoundly rewarding experience.

I must begin by admitting that, in my own case, the decision to join a college in the first instance was extremely straightforward. In 1994, I was fortunate enough to be awarded a Research Fellowship at Trinity Hall. Such a position gives a young academic a unique opportunity to spend three years pursuing their research, and affords complete intellectual freedom, without the usual responsibilities of a standard postdoctoral position. It thus provides an ideal start to one's academic career. It was, however, far more than financial support that the College provided. I soon found that Trinity Hall also afforded an extremely supportive environment for academic study and research. I was very warmly welcomed into the Fellowship and immediately given the opportunity take part in many aspects of College life and have a say in the decision-making process. Beyond that, I was delighted to find that the other Fellows, irrespective of their own areas of expertise, showed an honest and real interest in my research and in

" Hall " Class

No. 5916, " Trinity Hall "

each other's. In my opinion this is the true strength of the College system in general, and something at which Trinity Hall in particular excels.

It is the fact that one is part of a broader academic community that makes being a Fellow at Trinity Hall such a worthwhile experience. This is a benefit easily underestimated by those without a college affiliation. The chance to discuss one's work outside of the immediate departmental environment can provide not only a welcome opportunity to vent one's frustrations at the inevitable setbacks one encounters, but also allows one to place one's research in a wider context. I am fortunate that my own area of research, namely astrophysics and cosmology, holds a general interest for many people, and I have found it both extremely challenging and rewarding to explain how and why I undertake my research to my friends in the Fellowship who work in the arts and humanities. By the same token, it is a pleasure to be educated in the numerous fascinating areas of research pursued by the other members of the Fellowship. It is often said that one only really understands a subject when one has to explain it to someone who is not expert in the field. It is a great benefit to any academic to have the chance to do so.

The new bridge on Garret Hostel Lane under construction, June 1960.

Beyond the opportunity to discuss one's work with people outside the discipline, the Fellowship also provides invaluable support and advice on academic and research matters. The relatively small Fellowship at Trinity Hall means that there are only one or two Fellows in any given subject. Nevertheless, I have benefited on numerous occasions from the advice of these colleagues, and those in related areas. Amongst the Fellows in the physical sciences, engineering, mathematics and computer science, I have found that there is almost always someone who can answer whatever technical question has been troubling me. This is a profoundly important resource. It is very common in scientific research to come across a problem that lies beyond one's immediate area of expertise. I have been fortunate indeed to have colleagues within the Fellowship of such ability that I have often been able to discover the solution to such problems simply by coming into lunch and asking the appropriate expert, or by dropping a note in their pigeon-hole. Needless to say, I have also benefited from expert advice in other areas unrelated to science. If one requires legal advice, for example, there is usually no shortage of people willing to help. Indeed, on a number of occasions, I have enjoyed amazing some unwitting solicitor in my employ by pointing out a legal subtlety that had escaped his attention, but had

been spotted by one of our eagle-eyed law Fellows. Of course, I always take full credit for the insights I provide!

Despite the great advantages of being a member of the Fellowship, this group forms only one part of the College. The main reason for the College's existence is its students, the undergraduates and graduates, and a major benefit of being a member of Trinity Hall is the opportunity to interact with young people of such intelligence and enthusiasm. From early in my Research Fellowship, I supervised Trinity Hall undergraduates for various courses in physics and mathematics within the natural sciences. I found the experience extremely rewarding. In due course, my Research Fellowship came to an end and I was given the opportunity in 1997 to remain at Trinity Hall as a Staff Fellow and Director of Studies in Physical Sciences. I continue to perform this role today, and have thoroughly enjoyed the opportunity to teach and advise what is fast becoming a significant number of students. It has indeed been deeply satisfying and a great priviledge to have been involved in the education of so many bright young people.

Without the friends I have made at Trinity Hall, and the opportunities and challenges that define being a science Fellow, my academic life would not have been nearly so interesting and enjoyable. I have no doubt that I am better equipped to fulfil my departmental responsibilities and pursue my research having had the chance as a Fellow of Trinity Hall to engage in educational activities beyond the narrow world of astrophysics and cosmology, and interact with people from a wide variety of academic disciplines. I consider my role as a Staff Fellow and Director of Studies to be time well spent, and have found the experience to be entirely rewarding. Oh, by the way, the food is pretty good too!

Michael Hobson is Reader in Astrophysics and Cosmology in the Astrophysics Group of the Cavendish Laboratory. He is also a Staff Fellow and Director of Studies in Physical Sciences at Trinity Hall and enjoys an active role in the teaching of undergraduate physics and mathematics.

A uniselector switch of the type used by Tony Nixon
and Hall engineers for their covert exchange.

ERIC RIDEAL (1907–1946)

Eric Rideal came up to the Hall in 1907 to
study natural sciences. He studied for his PhD
on the electrochemistry of uranium at Bonn and
was awarded a gold medal for his work. He then
worked in the London laboratory of his father,
a public analyst, who sent him, aged 23, to
Ecuador to see to the water supplies and
sanitation in Quito and the port city of
Guyaquil. The Rideal-Walker Test remained
for a long time the standard method for
testing the efficacy of disinfectants. His
name graced the lavatories of millions of
English homes for many years where bottles
of disinfectants carried an indication of their
potency in terms of the Rideal-Walker Test. He
returned to England in 1914 to enlist in the Artist's Rifles,
but was wounded on the Somme and assigned to military research.
He became a lecturer in physical chemistry at Cambridge and a
Fellow of the Hall in 1920. Ten years later, he became Professor of
Colloid Science and Director of the Colloid Science Laboratory,
which was deeply involved in research into explosives, fuels and
polymers during the Second World War. He left Cambridge in 1946
for chairs at the Royal Institution and then King's College, London.

MICHAEL CARLILE (1951)

As a microbiologist I knew many pathologists, and I heard tales
about Daddy Dean that were circulating in that community. Once,
when a conscientious young visiting examiner was worrying about
the principles to be used in assessing the candidate's examination
performance, Dean said, 'Simple – if they know less than I do, we
fail them, if they know the same amount, we pass them, and if they
know more, we give them honours.'

Sir Eric Rideal told me that Cambridge was one of the first
universities to have pension arrangements for academic staff. Then,
when a national scheme was introduced,
Cambridge joined and discontinued its own
scheme. All prudent members of staff,
including Rideal, took the option of
transferring their accumulated pension
funds to the national scheme, and duly
ended up as poor as church mice. Two
reckless individuals, Dean and a chemist,
exercised the other option of withdrawing their
pension fund. Dean spent the money on Georgian
silver, then little esteemed and cheap, resulting in a
collection that at the end of his life was very
valuable.

TONY NIXON (1973)

In 1973 a simple clandestine telephone system had been
installed in King's. A group of us engineers decided that
the Hall needed such a system. So we set about building one. We
had nine extensions and no privacy, as all calls could be heard by
anyone picking up their phone. Those in the system had to be
involved in its installation. I was not keen on climbing round the
rooftops at dead of night laying cables, but I did have a room at the
top of D staircase where it was possible to put the exchange (in a
'Rover' biscuit tin) just outside the window. An outside location for
the exchange was essential, because of the noise that it made. Not
all those connected were engineers we had at least one lawyer, a
theologian and one or two mathematicians.

The building of the 'new' JCR allowed us to link the first
exchange with a second one in Latham Court. At dead of night in
January 1974 we used the scaffolding alongside the Old Library to
install cables in the guttering. The cables went down inside a
drainpipe, were buried in the gravel to L Staircase and then up
inside another drainpipe to emerge and become tucked in amongst
the extremely untidy 'official' telephone wiring. The wires,
camouflaged with black paint (a sticky job) ran all along the front

Tom Körner, Director of Studies in Mathematics for over thirty years.

of the Thornton and Latham Buildings to the exchange. This second exchange had the most ambitious part of the scheme, a submarine cable, which often needed nocturnal repairs, connecting our system to the one at King's. This would not have been possible had some of us not had shares in our own punt, H103.

We handed the system on in 1976 and it continued for at least another year. The cables proved much more durable. In 1998 there were still wires along the front of L staircase.

MATHEMATICS: THE MORNING IS STILL PERMISSIBLE
TOM KÖRNER

The philosopher and mathematician Whitehead wrote that omitting mathematics from the history of thought would not be equivalent to omitting Hamlet from the play… 'But it is certainly analogous to cutting out Ophelia. The simile is singularly exact. For Ophelia is quite essential to the play, she is very charming – and a little mad.' A similar claim can be made for the place of mathematics in the history of the University but, so far as Trinity Hall is concerned, mathematics finds herself cast among the attendant lords and ladies.

From the nineteenth century we have Leslie Stephen's loving portrait of the mathematical coach who asked by one of his students whether he could take Christmas day off, replied that, 'The morning was permissible'. We also have a splendid Victorian picture of *Degree Day* which hangs outside the SCR (see p.81) and shows the only time that a Trinity Hall student became Senior Wrangler (came top of the Tripos) during the period – over a hundred years – in which the exam positions were published. (We have had rather more *in petto* since.) We may also take vicarious pride from the fact that it was the daughter of one of our Fellows, Miss Philippa Fawcett, who in 1890 was placed above the Senior Wrangler. (In other words, beat all the men; an event which, according to the *DNB*, 'materially advanced the cause of higher education for women and naturally gave her mother the greatest satisfaction'.)

During the twentieth century the number of undergraduates studying mathematics rose slowly. It seems there was a grand total of three in 1923! By 1974 numbers had grown to near the present total of about twenty. Trinity Hall's contribution to the world of mathematics rose in parallel. Shaun Wylie both symbolised and assisted in this rise. He joined the College as a Fellow just before the Second World War and was recruited by Bletchley Park. He was in charge of the shift when the decisive break was made in the German U-boat code. After the war, he and a fellow code-breaker wrote the first textbook in the new subject of algebraic topology. More importantly, he supervised the PhDs of Adams and Zeeman who became leaders in the field. (Adams, one of the great British mathematicians in the second half of the century, was a Fellow here for three years.)

Shaun and his contemporaries completed the process of professionalisation of Cambridge mathematics. During their time, the opening of educational opportunities drove the standard of the student body up to what it is today. They took advantage of the rise in standards to remodel the mathematics course along lines which have stood the test of time.

I came up to take the Cambridge entrance exam during the bitterly cold winter of 1963. (I can still recall the unpleasant gas fire in my room and the sheer panic induced by the mathematics papers.) Has anything changed since then? The admission of women caused hardly a ripple in the smooth waters of the College. The move of the Mathematics Faculty from a few offices to temporary quarters in a very lightly converted factory and warehouse and thence, after a mere thirty years, to palatial accommodation on Clarkson Road was one of outer circumstance only.

If asked for changes which go beyond mere appearances, I would suggest the growth of graduate and postgraduate numbers and the internationalisation of the University. When I started Part III (essentially our mathematics MSc), I was, I think, the only Trinity Hall candidate. Nowadays we regularly have six or more Part III candidates, most of whom come from abroad. There were several exotic accents among my teachers, but this was a 'one off' consequence of the wave of refugees in the 1930s. Today, Cambridge students take up posts all over the world and people from all over the world take up posts in Cambridge. These changes have produced great strains within the University and its constituent colleges, but, unless we welcome these changes and adjust to them, Cambridge mathematics will lose its leading position. I hope that Trinity Hall will rise to the challenge.

In the meantime, let me reassure my past and present students: 'The morning is still permissible.'

Tom Körner arrived at Trinity Hall in October 1964 to study mathematics. He has been successively undergraduate, Part III student, PhD student, Research Fellow and teaching Fellow at the College. He has been Director of Studies in Mathematics for over thirty years.

STUDYING MEDICINE
ROY CALNE

The undergraduate years for medical students are predominantly scientific and the high quality of the science in the academic departments responsible for their teaching may seem to be excessive for their needs as medical practitioners. Some, however, will be enthused by the studies and decide to pursue a research career in the biological sciences. Others will wish to combine research with clinical practice. Medicine has a wide variety of possibilities between

general practice, requiring day-to-day compassionate contact with patients, and laboratory science where patients are not part of the scene. Hospital medicine is in between. At Trinity Hall, the tutorial system permits undergraduates to have a glimpse of a number of options which may eventually be their career choice.

My own contact with students has been in the hospital, teaching those preparing for qualification and graduates training specifically in surgery and especially in transplantation. I found the College atmosphere refreshing after previously working only in hospital and medical school environments. If there is not an expert in any subject one wishes to pursue in Trinity Hall, there is certainly somebody there who will know where to point you for the specialist knowledge you need, usually without having to leave Cambridge. There is also the possibility to widen interests beyond science and medicine. In return, I have been a source at table of specialist surgical opinion and often medical opinion far distant from my own field of interest. There was a time when I seemed to be working my way through the Fellowship in terms of operations that they needed. I am sure our system is not perfect but it seems to provide a good grounding and the medical curriculum is now tending increasingly to introduce patients to students during their undergraduate studies. This gives them a chance to realise that the application of science to someone who is in pain or frightened and an explanation to their loved ones can be a very difficult and stressful task, but central to those who intend to practise medicine.

Roy Calne, FRCS, FRS has been a Professorial Fellow at Trinity Hall since 1965. He has a world-wide reputation as a transplant surgeon and has made important discoveries in the study of immunology. He was knighted in 1986 and is an accomplished and prolific painter.

WILLIAM HORSFALL (1938)

I went up in October 1938 to read medicine having already completed the 1st MB exam while at school. I was studying for the Tripos which led to the degree of BA in Natural Science. The

Professor Sir Henry Roy 'Daddy' Dean, Master from 1929–54.

subjects I was taking were anatomy, physiology including pharmacology and two half subjects of organic chemistry and pathology. Passing these subjects exempted me from the 2nd MB.

I loved the study though much time had to be spent rote-learning anatomy. I would have preferred to devote that time to physiology. I found that I knew much of the organic chemistry and devoted little time to it only to find that it was of a higher standard than the 1st MB. I ended up wishing I had worked harder at it. But my favourite subject was physiology.

Besides the lectures and practicals we had to attend, the College organised tutorials in all subjects. There were eight of us at Hall doing medicine in my year. Davis took us in anatomy while Solandt, a visiting Fellow from Canada, took us in physiology and Wansbrough-Jones in organic chemistry. He was my main tutor. He kept an eye on my overall performance and my behaviour in College.

To pass in medicine one did have to work. It was at this time that I discovered I was an 'early bird' and that any study after 10pm was just a waste of time. My tutorial class with Wansbrough-Jones was early in the morning, possibly 7am. I had no problem getting up at this hour but others did. The number of contact hours with lecturers was much less in other disciplines though to get high-class honours one did need to do long hours of study. Many students, however, were only interested in passing and they spent many hours at other activities. There was a bridge club in College and they sometimes played all night till the sun came up.

PETER TRIER (1938)

When he was getting on for 80, there was pressure to get the Master, Henry Dean, to hand over to a younger person, but he simply refused to listen. At a College reunion dinner in 1960, feeling quite merry, he made a speech, which ended: 'As you all know, the tenure of my chair has for a considerable time been an anomaly. By now, it is nothing less than a crying scandal. And I have every intention to live to the day when it has become a bloody disgrace!'

EDWARD CHASE (1971)

According to our family lore, when elected Master in 1929, Henry Dean was not entirely happy. He explained to the Senior Tutor (our relative), Revd George Chase, that his family were very anxious about their bulldog as dogs were banned from College. The Senior Tutor organised a meeting of the Fellows at which, after a solemn vote, the dog was officially appointed an honorary cat. As there was no ban on cats in College, the newly appointed 'cat' was allowed to take up residence in the Master's Lodge.

Poets, decadents, and irritants

05

WRITERS AND BOOKS

WILD CIVILITY: TRINITY HALL'S LITERARY HISTORY
DREW MILNE

In his introduction to *The Complete Ronald Firbank*, Anthony Powell suggests that Trinity Hall, 'the house *par excellence* of hunting, racing and rowing men, was another of those unaccountable choices for his son on the part of Sir Thomas Firbank. However, Ronald seems on the whole to have enjoyed the university, where he liked to read poetry aloud to himself….' There were some who listened, some who evidently took solace in Firbank's aestheticism, as an antidote perhaps to the prevailing culture, if culture be the word. Crawley's history of the College also notes that Firbank was a 'seemingly incongruous figure in pre-1914 Trinity Hall,' but one whose 'later novels earned him a rather special niche in literary history.' This judgement errs on the side of understatement, suggesting a diplomatic reluctance to sing the praises of such an engagingly decadent writer.

Occasional decadents aside, the historical record suggests that the College has rarely been a congenial place for literary types. While the last century or so has seen a number of distinguished scholars and writers emerge from Trinity Hall, the College's pre-modern contributions to literary history are rather modest and underwhelming by comparison with many Cambridge colleges. Crawley, for example, tactfully resists calling Thomas Tusser (*c.*1524–80) a *poet*, describing his writing as 'artless verses…. They are the source of many farming proverbs and still provide a mine of information to economic historians'. A few lines from his versified autobiography will suffice:

When gaines was gone, and yeres grew on,
And death did cry, from London flie,
In Cambridge then, I found agen
   a resting plot:
In Colledge best of all the rest
With thanks to thee, O Trinitee,
Through thee and thine, from me and mine,
   some stay I got.

(Thomas Tusser, *The Authors life*, from *Fiue hundred pointes of good Husbandrie* [1580], stanza 31)

There's a touch of pleasing bathos in the final lines, but this is poetry perhaps best left hidden.

Crawley is also quietly unimpressed by the way in which Edmund Spenser learnt from Gabriel Harvey (*c.*1545–1630) and Harvey's 'ingenious but graceless experiments in writing English verse in classical metres'. Harvey's claim to literary fame is as an irritant and provocateur who goaded other writers on. Even less can be said of Robert Aylett (1583– *c.*1655), LLD of Trinity Hall in 1614 and someone who found 'relaxation in publishing religious poems.' Aylett is hardly a household name and with good reason. He was too minor even for inclusion in the two thousand pages of George Saintsbury's *Minor Poets of the Caroline Period* (Oxford, 1905–1921). Why? Perhaps there is something unpromising about the idea of relaxing religious verse:

RUSSELL DAVIES

Previous page: *Trinity Hall Old Library, showing the door which originally gave onto a walkway running along the top of a wall linking the library to the Master's Lodge.*

Left: *This caricature of Ronald Firbank hangs in the MCR.*

Of that *dread love* by which the *Trinity*
Ineffably doth in it self delight,
Of *Persons three* making one *Unity*
I dare not undertake so high to write.

(Robert Aylett, *The First Book,* Meditat. I. *Of Heavenly Love,* st. 5. *The Brides Ornaments,* from *Divine and Moral Speculations* [1654])

There seems to be a long tradition that those passing through Trinity Hall prefer to ignore the theological challenges posed by the speculative truths of the Hall's grand titular claims. If only Aylett had kept his word, for this turns out to be a touch of false modesty. Much of the rest of this long poem dares to write at heights much too high for its own resources:

As *Body, Spirit, Faith, Lord, Baptism's* one,
So but one true and living *Hope* we finde:
But as her *Objects* infinite become,
We may distinguish her in different kinde.
    If heav'nly Objects be to her assign'd,
She like the Object, is Celestiall,
If she on worldly Object, set her minde,
As doth the Object she doth rise or fall,
Lo then, the Object of our *Hope* is all in all.

(Aylett, *The First Book,* Meditat. V. *Hope,* st. 12).

This perhaps hints at the *all or nothing* logic of Pascal's wager, but not with a quality of poetry that is likely to divert or persuade even the most mathematically challenged theologian. Recent debates have ascribed to Aylett the authorship of the book-length volume *David's Troubles Remembered* (1638), a book which has been put forward by Barbara Kiefer Lewalski as a source for Dryden's *Absalom and Achitophel*. But perhaps even Aylett would not own up to the lameness afflicting lines such as:

But he indeed is Master of his Art,
That keeps th'infection from the *head* and *heart,*
The *King* and *Army,* for by these, lo all
Monarchs and *Kingdomes* flourish, rise and fall;
And sure we seldome see a remedy
Of such infection, but *Phlebotomy.*

(from *The Third Booke. Bathsheba bathing,* from *David's Troubles Remembered* [1638], lines 37–42)

Rather than engaging in such literary blood-letting, it might be better to follow Southey's example, who said of another Trinity Hall poet, his friend William Hayley (1745–1820), that 'everything about that man is good except his poetry'. This said, Hayley's ballads were illustrated by his friend Blake. Southey's critique of one of Trinity Hall's literary giants is at least gentler than Dr Johnson, who said of Philip Stanhope, 4th Earl of Chesterfield, that his *Letters* 'teach the morals of a whore and the manners of a dancing-master'. If only all blurbs were so enticing.

Amid the history of Trinity Hall's decadents, irritants and literary footnotes, there are some notable figures who deserve to be kept out of hiding and whose names are still deservedly commemorated. Thomas Preston (1537–98), Master of Trinity Hall, 1584–89, was the author of *A Lamentable Tragedy mixed full of Mirth conteyning the Life of Cambises, King of Percia* (1569). The College's dramatic society, founded around 1950, is named after Preston. His play *Cambises,* as well as having claims to be considered the first Elizabethan tragedy, is notable for its Senecan sensationalism and violent knockabout comedy. Critics have even found it unlikely that someone of Preston's academic distinction could write a play with such populist intentions. Sample the following lines from the vice character, Ambidexter, who speaks through his weeping, beginning with 'A' sounds that could be modernised as a loosely phonetic series of 'ah's, a precedent for King Lear's O, O, O, O.

Ambidexter: A, A, A, A, I cannot chuse but weep for the Queene:
    Nothing but mourning now at the Court there is seen.
    Oh, oh, my hart, my hart, Oh my bum wil break:
    Very greef so torments me that scarce I can speake.
    Who could but weep for the losse of such a Lady?
    That can not I doo, I sweare by mine honesty.

(Cambises, 1127–32)

Cambises became notorious for the ridiculous quality of its bombast. Shakespeare made Falstaff declaim 'in King Cambises' vein', and briefly parodied *Cambises* in *A Midsummer Night's Dream.* Through *Cambises,* then, the Hall can be said to have had a slight and surprisingly vulgar influence on Shakespeare. Two notable literary scholars, Leslie Stephen (1832–1904) and Graham Storey, have College rooms named after them. Stephen wrote important essays in literary criticism and intellectual history, edited the *Dictionary of National Biography* and was the father of Virginia Woolf. Graham Storey, among other distinctions, edited the letters of Charles Dickens. Pride of place among notable figures in the Hall's literary history must nevertheless go to Robert Herrick (1591–1674), a poet of gentle wit and not just the name of a building on the Wychfield site. Herrick's poetry makes light of some of the divine questions so ponderously drawn out by Aylett, and he is described in *The Norton Anthology of English Literature* as 'the happiest of English poets'. His poetry has some of the playfully profound illumination offered by Emily Dickinson, mixed with hints of that arch affability and personism later perfected by Frank O'Hara:

Delight in Disorder
A sweet disorder in the dresse
Kindles in cloathes a wantonnesse :
A Lawne about the shoulders thrown
Into a fine distraction :
An erring Lace, which here and there
Enthralls the Crimson Stomacher :

A Cuffe neglectfull, and thereby
Ribbands to flow confusedly :
A winning wave (deserving Notes)
In the tempestuous petticote :
A careless shooe-string, in whose tye
I see a wilde civility :
Doe more bewitch me, then when Art
Is too precise in every part.

(from *The Poetical Works of Robert Herrick*,
  ed. F.W. Moorman [Oxford: Clarendon, 1915], p. 28)

For all its historical determination to stick to the punishments of law and physical exercise, a touch of this wild civility informs the hidden delights of Trinity Hall's contributions to literary history.

Drew Milne read English as an undergraduate at Trinity Hall, 1982–85; and as a PhD student, 1986–90. Having worked at the Universities of Edinburgh and Sussex, he has since 1997 been the Judith E. Wilson Lecturer in Drama and Poetry, Faculty of English and a Fellow of Trinity Hall.

THE OLD LIBRARY
PETER HUTCHINSON

What *is* that curious narrow oak door, about two and a half metres above the colourful herbaceous border on the southern side of the Old Library, half-hidden in summer by the creeping roses? A fascination for every fresher, this was originally a private means of access for the Master, to whose Lodge it was connected by a walkway on top of a wall. The doorway was bricked up in the 1740s and the walkway was demolished, but the door itself was preserved and replaced at some point in the late nineteenth century – a clear example of that period's respect for the past, and now an essential stop for every tour guide.

The library itself contains around six thousand books and occupies the upper storey of a simple but imposing building;

Chained volumes: the Old Library bookstacks.

constructed of clunch faced with fine red brick, it has a stepped gable and a wide four-light window dominating Latham Lawn. The interior is perfectly balanced, giving a pleasing sense of space: at right angles to the side windows are six pairs of carved wooden bookcases with lecterns (and accompanying benches on each side), divided by a grand aisle which displays the broad oak beams used in the flooring. Yet for all this craftsmanship, the College has no early records of one of its finest buildings, and even the date of its construction is unknown. Warren, in his famous 'Book' which

Elizabethan Charter. Dating from 1559 and presented to the College in the first year of Elizabeth's reign, it reaffirms land rights and establishes other legal rights following the dissolution of the monasteries.

provides so much detail on virtually every aspect of the College, can only inform us that it was built 'about the latter end of Queen Elizabeth's time'. It is, however, featured on a plan of Cambridge from 1592, so we may be comfortable in assuming that it was conceived around the period of the Armada, and that the magnificent beams used in its construction were possibly from the same forests that provided the timbers for Drake.

The library's major source of attraction is obviously its chained books. Bateman, in his statutes, had given orders for the manuscripts he presented to the College to be kept in a 'safe place' and for those of the 'Doctors of Civil and Canon Law' to be chained. The Fellows were clearly adhering to these principles in their design for the library, for they not only ensured a large number of books could be supplied with chains, but also that the locking mechanism of the rods to which the chains were attached was operated by *two* keys. Amazingly, the mechanism is still in perfect condition today.

Ironically, however, it is most unlikely that more than a handful of books were actually supplied with chains. Although two still remain (Erasmus's *Adagia* of 1523 and Faber's *Paraphrases in Aristotelis philosophiam naturalem* of 1512) – and there are others which provide evidence of having been secured at some point – the printing press had been invented by Gutenberg some 150 years before, and it must have been evident to at least some of the Fellowship that the very concept of a chained library was already obsolete. So too the requirement to read books in the library itself. The lecterns, and benches for reading, severely reduced the space for storage of books, and for that reason the library needed to expand, in due course into various other parts of the College. By 1721 Warren recorded no fewer than 2,338 books and pamphlets,

so in the 1740s the original main door was sealed in order to provide the extensive shelving which now covers the eastern end. A door then created (from the Chetwode Room) still survives, and the present main door, constructed from nineteenth-century timbers, was installed in 2001 following renovation of the room below. That renovation had brought out a fascinating aspect of the library's construction: originally built, as was then common for Cambridge libraries, at a height above the flood level, it had no heating. But heat from a chimney breast and from warm air rising through the gaps in the floor timbers did ensure some warmth and circulation. With the renovation of the room below – and the sealing of all gaps – there was suddenly heavy condensation and the need for urgent action. Small electric heaters have therefore had to be installed, as well as dehumidifiers, strange modern objects among the some of the oldest library furniture to survive in Cambridge.

Prior to the building of the library, books were kept in a small room adjacent to the chapel, and the need for a separate building may well have become acute in 1588, when William Mowse, former Master, bequeathed his substantial library of law books. Acquisitions came mainly through benefactions or bequests in those days, and the treasures of the library can be traced to a handful of major philanthropists: Bateman himself, Mowse and Thomas Eden (whose collections form a major part of our pre-1640 legal volumes), Robert Hare (a passionate local bibliophile), and numerous others. Among the manuscripts given to the College by Hare there is the History of St Augustine's Abbey of Canterbury (*c.*1420), which contains elaborate chronological tables and facsimiles of many lost Anglo-Saxon charters (which is why it is still consulted today); an early fifteenth-century French translation

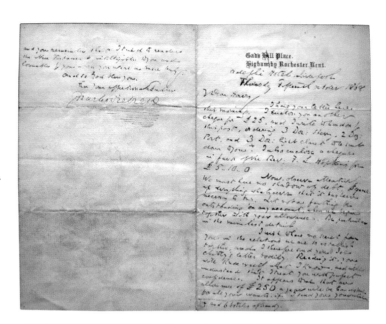

Right: *Letter from Charles Dickens to his son, dated 1868.*

Bottom right: *Diderot's* Encyclopédie. *First Paris 'Neuchatel' folio edition.*

of Boethius's *De Consolatione*, a volume packed with lively (occasionally salacious) illustrations; and Roger Dymok's late fourteenth-century diatribe against the 'Lollards' (the followers of John Wycliffe, who was responsible for the first English translation of the Bible). This copy, containing much rich colour and gold leaf, was presented to Richard II and was at one stage owned by the first Master of Christ's. Among the printed books given by Hare, there is a 'Schoeffer Bible' (a Latin Bible printed in Nuremberg in 1472), and a copy of the *Nuremberg Chronicle*, a 'history of the world' lavishly illustrated with brightly coloured woodcuts and printed in 1493. Our oldest manuscript is a life of St Martin (*c.*1050), while other important volumes include the first complete edition of Milton (1695), the two volumes of Samuel Johnson's *Dictionary* (1755), Chambers' *Cyclopedia* (1728), and Diderot's complete *Encyclopédie* in thirty-five volumes. The most striking of our curiosities is a letter from Charles Dickens to his son (who was an undergraduate at the Hall), which urges diligence and the avoidance of debt, but which also promises several dozen bottles of sherry, claret and port. Of books there is no mention!

Peter Hutchinson, Reader in Modern German Studies, studied modern languages at Caius, graduating in 1968. He returned from a lectureship in Scotland to Cambridge in 1974. He joined the Hall as a Fellow in 1986, and since then has acted in a number of roles, including Director of Studies in Modern Languages, Tutor, Vice-Master and Librarian.

THE CASE OF DR PHILIP NICHOLS, BOOK THIEF
JACKIE HARMON (2003)

Dr Philip Nichols previously of Brasenose College in Oxford arrived at Trinity Hall in 1723 to take up a position as one of two presbyter Fellows. (The other being that early archivist of Hall matters, William Warren). The Master, Sir Nathanael Lloyd, had elected him *jure devolutionis*, after the incumbent Fellows failed to reach a majority vote on any of the other six candidates.

Imprimerie, Tremperie et Lavage des Formes.

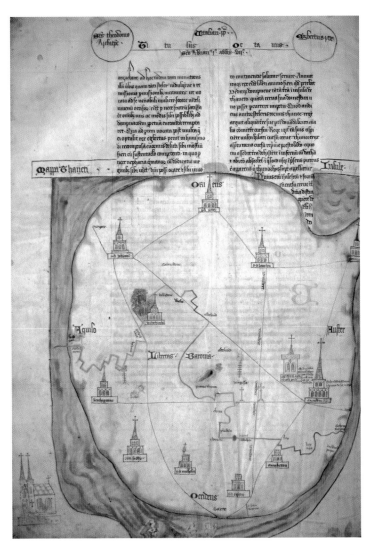

Above: *Ms1. History of St Augustine's Abbey of Canterbury from the fifteenth century.*

Right: *Ms12. An illustration showing a scene from the Trojan Wars, also from the fifteenth century. Both manuscripts are found in the Old Library.*

Of Nichols's early Hall career little is said in *Warren's Book* and it was only in January 1731 when the librarian at St John's noticed several books missing from his stock that the scandal became common knowledge. Nichols, it transpired, had been selling books at London auctions, presumably in an effort to fund his somewhat dubious lifestyle. (Not only was he in debt but reportedly he was sleeping out of College with a woman of the town).

Subsequent enquiries amongst library staff led to the discovery of further missing volumes not only from St John's but from Trinity Hall itself, the University Library and one of the town bookshops. We can only infer from this that they too had found their way into London to be sold.

Lloyd, being absent from the College (as was Nichols) at the time of the discovery, delegated the investigation and a search of Nichols's rooms to Warren. This Warren did, finding not only books belonging to a number of libraries but also the tools of Nichols's trade – fourteen keys (including one to St John's library), a pair of pincers and a steel file. Much later, Nichols was to admit to having picked Dr Chetwode's lock and it was certainly true that Chetwode had been relieved of eight volumes of Rushworth's *Collections* at some point.

By June Warren was in possession of all the evidence and again contacted Lloyd (still absent) for further instructions as he was keen to see the matter resolved before term ended on 9 July 1731. Lloyd sent further instructions.

To be fair, Nichols, who had been traced to London and had confessed all, was given the opportunity to answer the charges at a Governing Body meeting on 7 July. Unsurprisingly, and perhaps fearing the worst, he did not appear. The College gave him two further chances before Lloyd (finally in residence again) held a ceremony of expulsion on 4 August. This College decision was followed up by a grace two days later in which the University stripped Nichols of all his degrees. By October the miscreant had fled the country.

Was Nichols repentant? It appears he was, if surviving evidence is to be believed and, in a letter to Lloyd dated 15 October 1731, he refers to himself as 'this exiled infamous creature' and implores the Master to pray for him. An enclosed list gave the titles of all the books Nichols could recall stealing and, somewhat belatedly, his confession to having also disposed of several pieces of the College silver. Whether the Master was amenable to the exile's request is unknown.

As a direct result of the Nichols affair there was a general tightening of library security both in the colleges and at the University. It should perhaps be noted here that, along with all his illegal acquisitions, Nichols had in his possession a legitimately borrowed book that was seven years overdue!

At Trinity Hall Sir Nathanael dealt with the aftermath in two ways. Firstly, keen to distance himself from the whole affair, he indulged in a little 'track covering' by making it clear to Warren that *he* had never liked the look of Nichols and had only taken him on the recommendation of a fellow advocate (name withheld). Secondly, and to finally draw the matter to a close, he wrote a letter to the Trinity Hall Fellows in which he promised *never* to use his right to appoint by devolution again.

Jackie Harmon read humanities at the Open University, graduating in 2002. She joined the College in March 2001, working in the Tutorial Office, first as Tutorial Administrator and then as Tutorial Officer. She is now studying for a Master of Studies in local and regional history.

RONALD FIRBANK
AMIR BAGHDADCHI (2003)

'The world is so dreadfully managed, one hardly knows to whom to complain.'

When the slim and fluttering figure of Ronald Firbank (1886–1926) sauntered for the first time into the Front Court of Trinity Hall, where he was to take up residence for three years from October 1906, he had yet to conquer the craft of writing novels, but had thoroughly mastered the art of acting like a novelist. His arrival struck the Cambridge literati, all six or seven of them, with envy and awe. Here was an undergraduate who had already had a book

published, *Odette d'Antrevernes* – a slim volume which, naturally, no one had read, and which, probably because no one had read it, was presumed to be the last word in literary chic. His age was baffling; he was only a first year, and yet everything about him was *fin de siècle*, dandyism and decadence, Beardsley and button-holes. And when Lord Alfred Douglas, no less, fled to Cambridge, it was with Ronald Firbank that he dined. A.C. Landsberg, also at Trinity Hall, found him 'terribly feminine, sophisticated, cosmopolitan, and elegant!' One gathered in his room to hear him giggle and talk literature and rattle off the names of Parisian celebrities one hadn't heard of, but tried very hard to seem as if one had.

In very much the same way, the cult of Firbank – for no one is indifferent to the novels of Ronald Firbank – flourishes today: here is an author writing experimental prose in the era of Joyce, Woolf, Eliot, and Pound, yet somehow standing removed and *recherché*, an impossible orchid adored only by a coterie of connoisseurs. After his death the public soon forgot him; while to paragons of style, like Evelyn Waugh and Joe Orton, he became an acknowledged and unrivalled master.

Not that Firbank much cared for the public. He was much too busy furnishing his room, to which he probably regarded himself as simply one more exquisite ornament. His friends remember how, in a drab square chamber, on the chapel side of the main court (in what is now the MCR), Firbank contrived to make a pleaure dome:

He was happiest in the curtained and shaded twilight of his rooms, that were always full of flowers and lit by candles in carved and gilt Italian altar candle-sticks. There he would sit with his back to the light, surrounded by old silks and photographs of his mother in court dress and innumerable little tables covered with books and statuettes (reproductions for the most part of little religious Gothic figures and of Pompeian and Tanagra things)… and, once, an Egyptian bronze statuette which he spoilt by having an opal set into it "as a propitiatory offering".

Ronald Firbank's room in 1907 (F2, now the MCR).

"Oh, I don't remember," – and a laugh. "Well, was the ball round or egg-shaped?" "Oh! I was never near enough to it to see that!'"

He made up for it with parties, sometimes in others' rooms, like the member with the roulette wheel, but most often with lavish entertainments in his own. He would spend hours on the menu (which, in the end, would be whatever the Trinity Hall chef chose to make), and on the guest lists and flowers. When Rupert Brooke came to dine, Firbank strewed heaps of white flowers in every room. That he was a misfit at Trinity Hall there is no doubt; but there were plenty of others, and Firbank's College friendships endured for years.

However, true to the Hall's reputation, Firbank left without passing a single examination. But, as he was set to become a great novelist, he was naturally occupied with forming his style. His method of writing was calculated equally to produce gems of wit and to waste vast amounts of time. He would write on both sides of small blue postcards, sometimes filling a single one with one sentence in large loopy handwriting, and accumulating these on his desk in confusion. Orton's delight in the outrageous scrap of conversation comes direct from Firbank, who revelled in stringing together the chatter of a drawing room to ridiculous effect, as in this scene from his second novel, *Valmouth*:

Remarkably, Firbank's room was never ragged by practical jokers. It was, somehow, considered off-limits. Indeed, apart from the room of one undergraduate who had thoughtfully installed a working roulette wheel in his, perhaps no one's room was respected more.

To say the truth, Trinity Hall was not an intuitive choice for Firbank. The Hall was, of course, in those days Head of the River, supreme and undisputed, and any time not taken up with rowing was given over to hunting and racing. Next, as Vyvyan Holland remembered, 'any energy left over after our athletic duties were performed was devoted to a thoroughly inattentive study of the Law.' One day Holland found Firbank, who was always sickly and weak, dressed in a sweater and football shorts: 'I asked him what on earth he had been doing: "Oh, football," he replied. "Rugger or soccer?"

…'Heroin.' 'Adorable simplicity.' 'What could anyone find to admire in such a shelving profile?' 'We reckon a duck here of two or three and twenty not so old. And a spring chicken anything to fourteen.' 'My husband had no amorous energy whatsoever; which just suited me, of course.' 'I suppose when there's no room for another crow's-foot, one attains a sort of peace?' 'I once said to Doctor Fothergill, a clergyman of Oxford and a great friend of mine, "Doctor," I said, "oh, if only you could see my – Elle était jolie! Mais jolie!… C'était une si belle brune…!"' 'Cruelly lonely.' 'Leery …' 'Vulpine.' 'Calumny.' 'People look like pearls, dear, beneath your wonderful trees.'

Firbank had a genius for leaving things out. As one of his characters remarks, 'I think nothing of filing fifty pages down to make a brief, crisp paragraph, or even a row of dots.'

Coming down from Cambridge in 1909, Firbank made two unexpected announcements. First, while he was at Cambridge, he had converted to Catholicism, a move which surprised everyone, including the Catholics. Second, he wanted to become a Swiss Guard, so splendid were their uniforms. His application, however, for this position met an impediment, as he was unable to answer, to the Vatican's complete satisfaction, the initial question: 'Are you Swiss?'

For the rest of his life Firbank became a recluse, but one almost incessantly on the move. Whether in London, or Paris, or Rome, or Madrid, or Vienna, or Constantinople, he was alone, at the Opera, in cafés, in small apartments, always writhing and giggling if one got near him, and giggling by himself at nothing in particular. His books came out steadily, mystifying the public, enraging some critics, but quoted and read and whooped over by all the literati. The line about a 'pause just long enough for an Angel to pass, flying slowly' is justly celebrated. His never performed play, *The Princess Zoubaroff*, won immortality for the following introduction:

> *Nadine*: My husband.
> *Blanche* [genially]: I think we've slept together once?
> *Adrian*: I don't remember.
> *Blanche*: At the opera. During *Bérénice*.

Perhaps even more notorious is this complete chapter from *Inclinations*, when Miss O. Brookomore discovers that her friend Mabel Collins, with whom she is desperately enamoured, has run off with an Italian Count:

> 'Mabel! Mabel! Mabel! Mabel!
> Mabel! Mabel! Mabel! Mabel!'

Yet the orderly mind that produced such lapidary wit was permanently in a state of disorder. Firbank excited comment when he was sober, and seemed to find life impossible.

Then, in a twist so ridiculous he giggled about it no end, there suddenly became a vogue for Firbank in America. The pleasure did not last; his health deteriorated; his last completed work, *Concerning the Eccentricities of Cardinal Pirelli*, in which a police dog is baptized, was rejected by publishers. Finally, Firbank succumbed to pneumonia in Rome, in 1926, at last fulfilling his desire of never turning forty by dying at thirty-nine. As if his ghost were responsible for the funeral arrangements, Firbank was buried by accident in the wrong cemetery, the Protestant one in Rome, just down from Keats and Shelley. He would have giggled tremendously.

The painter Augustus John, as intimate a friend of Firbank's as any could be, commented that 'in his life, as in his books, he left out the dull bits and concentrated on the irrelevant.' His books have indeed survived, as camp and cult favourites, and a lasting measure of literary style. They continue to divide critics, and they should. As W.H. Auden said, 'the novels of Ronald Firbank are, for me, an absolute test. A person who dislikes them… may, for all I know, possess some admirable quality, but I do not wish to ever see him again.'

After reading classics at Michigan and Berkeley, Amir Baghdadchi came to Cambridge from San Francisco, where he was a freelance writer and theatre critic. He is currently a postgraduate student at Trinity Hall, researching for a PhD in eighteenth-century English literature.

Thomas Thornely on aesthetics

… The aesthetic craze never got much of a hold in undergraduate circles, though a few nincompoops here and there showed signs of being influenced by it. I remember my College gyp's strongly-worded disgust at the new-fangled ornaments and knick-knacks, with which some of the cult were beginning to adorn their rooms, instead of being content with the two sculptured gladiators, the

Robert Herrick, frontispiece to The Hesperides, *1648, British Library.*

pair of bullock's horns, the College shield, and photographs of winning crews, which had sufficed for less sophisticated generations. His special aversion was Japanese fans, which he thought marked the lowest depths of degradation and effeminacy, and the fact that he and his peers were expected to dust these abominations gave added point to his indignation.

From Cambridge Memories, *1936. Thornely was an undergraduate in the 1870s.*

CHARLES CAVANAGH (1970)

I was at the Hall from 1970–74, and was one year President of the Hesperides Society, a literary club which had been organised before the war, but which came and went from time to time depending on which dons were willing to encourage it. Graham Storey, who was then Vice-Master, was its guiding light in our time.

The club met twice in each of the first two terms, usually in the Vice-Master's rooms, for wine and the presentation of a paper by some eminent scholar. Lively discussions ensued. In the final term

of the academic year there was both a 'poetry breakfast' wherein members read their favourite poems to the group, and a formal dinner held in Dr Eden's Room. The quality of speakers was very high, including such figures as Pevsner, Needham, Sparrow and Maugham. The dinner speech in 1974, by Revd David Isitt, was in fact about the work of Ronald Firbank.

JOHN WELLS (1983)

My poem, *College Library,* was written in the Elizabethan building, on a sheet of loose-leaf A4 that would otherwise have become part of an essay on the Norman Conquest. Much of my working life has been spent in the University Library, where one of the duties is to discourage readers from eating and drinking while reading the books. The UL is a place where an undergraduate of two weeks' standing can fill out a fetching-slip and be handed a first folio of Shakespeare, as I discovered in 1983, but it has never aimed at being homely. The College library, on the other hand, served as an extension of members' own rooms. No doubt the regulations prohibited food and drink, but they were not enforced out of hours: once the librarian had locked the glass-fronted office and departed for the night, essayists would bring in whatever refreshments they needed to see them through. The proximity of the bar, just up the brick steps and past the cherry tree, abetted the practice with coffee and fruit juice, and Greene King. There were occasional sticky rings on the table-varnish, but outright spillages were rare. In comparison, at least, an orange is not too grave a danger to a book.

College Library

Every brain is soaked
In a different dye: Hegel,
Tapeworms, pistons or sonatas;

But a girl skins a bright orange,
And sends the smell of her fruit
Into all our heads.

William Bateman, Bishop of Norwich and founder of Trinity Hall.

From Bishop Bateman to law on-line

06

THE LAW TRADITION

LEGAL STUDIES AT TRINITY HALL BEFORE THE VICTORIANS
JOHN LANGBEIN

Trinity Hall is the only college in either Oxford or Cambridge that was founded exclusively for the study of law. For its first five centuries, however, the law that was studied at Trinity Hall was not the English common law, but rather the common law of Europe, also called the *ius commune* or the civil law. Trinity Hall was the Cambridge outpost for the study and transmission of this European or 'civilian' law. Only in Victorian times, as part of the larger university reforms of the nineteenth century, did Trinity Hall develop its modern character as a general-purpose college with a pronounced strength in English law.

The legal systems of all the modern Continental states trace back to the law of classical Rome. In the sixth century, as the Roman Empire was crumbling, the emperor Justinian caused an extensive body of sources from classical Roman law to be compiled and preserved. These materials were rediscovered at the end of the eleventh century and rapidly became the basis of study and instruction in the universities of the North Italian city states. Across the twelfth and especially the thirteenth centuries, university-trained lawyers brought the vocabulary and the conceptual structure of Roman law into the legal systems that were then developing in the secular states and in the church.

The Roman church was in many respects the most important institution of governance in the later Middle Ages. The church drew upon the Roman sources in developing the canon law, which came to be studied in the Italian universities alongside the civil law.

The study of this Roman-canon law spread in the thirteenth century to universities in France and Spain, then north to the German states and Holland in the fourteenth century.

The English universities shared in this European-wide movement towards university study of the *ius commune*. By the second quarter of the thirteenth century, both Oxford and Cambridge were teaching it. Unlike the experience on the Continent, however, in England the *ius commune* did not achieve primacy in shaping the national legal system. By the time the Roman-canon learning reached England, the English common law had already been moulded in an indigenous tradition that limited the relevance and thus the influence of the civilian materials.

The English legal tradition was shaped in court practice rather than by university study. The bearers of the English common law were pleaders and judges, as opposed to professors. Oxford and Cambridge were the wrong places to learn such a legal system. Novices studied English law by coming into association with the practitioners, hence by observation and apprenticeship as opposed to formal instruction in the schoolroom.

When Trinity Hall appeared on the scene in the middle of the fourteenth century, the principle was already well settled that the two English universities would not teach English law – that is to say, they would not teach the English common law. As late as the 1880s, Dicey was still echoing this tradition. In his inaugural lecture at Oxford he observed: 'English law must be learned and cannot be taught…. [T]he only places where it can be learned are the law courts or chambers.'

The main reason that the English universities continued to teach Roman-canon law is that it had prevailed in several English jurisdictional enclaves outside the common law. By far the most important employer of Oxbridge-trained civilians was the English church. The medieval church is in many respects best thought of as a coordinate government, in the sense that it performed many of the functions that we now expect the secular authorities to undertake. The church was the ministry of health, the ministry of education, and the ministry of human services. The church, not the state, ran the hospitals, the orphanages, the almshouses, and the schools.

The church also operated law courts, both to deal with internal matters, and as forums for certain classes of secular jurisdiction. The ecclesiastical courts kept exclusive jurisdiction over the law of marriage and over the probate of wills in England until 1857. Other important enclaves were the High Court of Admiralty and the courts of the two universities. Civilian-trained personnel were also employed as ecclesiastical administrators and in the royal service as diplomats.

The founder of Trinity Hall, William Bateman, was Bishop of Norwich from 1344 until his death in 1355. He was born about 1298 and studied Roman-canon law at Cambridge. In the late 1320s Bateman was active at the papal court, where he served as an administrator, judge, and diplomat. In 1329 he was appointed a judge of the papal Rota, the highest court of the church, and for a time he was a chaplain to the pope.

Bateman established Trinity Hall, in his words, 'for the promotion of divine worship and of canon and civil [law] science… and also for the advantage… of the… commonwealth and especially of our church and diocese of Norwich.' He had rather a long-winded name for the place: he called it 'The College of Scholars of the Holy Trinity of Norwich.' (The name got trimmed down to Trinity Hall in the sixteenth century.) Bateman's statutes required every Fellow of the College to agree to promote the interest of the church of Norwich. The Fellows had to promise

to act professionally (that is, as lawyers) always for and never against the church of Norwich or its bishop.

We see, therefore, that Bateman envisioned Trinity Hall not just as a training ground but also as a captive supply station for civilian legal talent for his diocese. The likely reason is that in 1348–49 the Black Death (which broke out in central Europe in 1347) crossed the channel and swept England. It was the worst epidemic of plague in Western history. Between a third and a half of the population of England died within a few months.

The resulting dislocations affected every corner of life, leading to wage and price controls (the so-called Statutes of Labourers), and to the suspension and reordering of many civil obligations. Whole villages and their parishes disappeared. Customary obligations, including the church's claims to tithe support, were thrown into doubt.

We can well imagine that, as the church attempted to cope with the challenges of helping to restore civic life, Bateman found himself shorthanded in his roles as diocesan administrator and ecclesiastical court keeper. In founding Trinity Hall, Bateman was attempting to restock and to lock in a supply of canon-law expertise to replace the plague-decimated ranks.

If this emphasis on church law and church administration strikes us as an odd mission for a Cambridge college, we must remember that in a deep sense Cambridge University in its entirety, and Oxford as well, were not much more than seminaries. We actually have some data on this: as late as the middle of the eighteenth century, 76 per cent of Cambridge graduates entered the church.

Bateman arranged for Trinity Hall to acquire its present central site, which had belonged to the Priory of Ely. (Bateman acquired it in exchange for a rectory elsewhere.) Thus, we can say with some confidence that law has been continuously studied and taught on this site for 650 years.

If I were to divide the history of Trinity Hall into epochs, I would treat the first epoch as the period from the founding down to the reign of Henry VIII. I would regard the English Reformation as launching the second epoch, a period that endured until the university reforms of the nineteenth century, which I would treat as commencing the third epoch, which endures to the present day.

Because Trinity Hall was so centered on the canon law, the Reformation shook the College with special force. The canon law of Rome was, after all, the law of the papacy. Among the steps that Henry VIII took to sever the English church from the papacy was his prohibition upon the teaching of the Roman-canon law. He suppressed it. Henry was by no means hostile to the civilian legal tradition. Because he now had to staff national courts for the newly-reformed Anglican church, Henry undertook in 1540 to reinforce the English civilians, by establishing the Regius Chairs, one each at Cambridge and Oxford. The Cambridge Chair was held at Trinity Hall several times from its founding until the Interregnum; and from 1666 to 1875, all twelve holders of the Regius Chair were Fellows of Trinity Hall.

Across the sixteenth century Trinity Hall reoriented itself in three ways: from Norwich to London, from the canon law of Rome to the civil-law enclaves of England; and from academia to the practice of law. In his history of the College, Charles Crawley put his finger on what caused these transitions. '[T]he fellows, having no longer license nor motive for the formal study of canon law, soon came… to be mostly laymen practising the civil law….'

For two centuries, from the 1560s to the 1760s, Trinity Hall became in effect the sponsor and *alter ego* of the principal London professional organisation for the practice of civil law, called the 'College of Doctors and Advocates of the Court of the Arches,' or Doctors' Commons for short. Doctors' Commons was the civilian counterpart to the Inns of Court. It had been organised in 1512 as a society of London practitioners active in the Court of the Arches (the principal ecclesiastical court), but included practitioners from the Admiralty, the lesser ecclesiastical courts, and other civilian courts.

Doctors' Commons resembled the Inns of Court in that it provided chambers and a common table, but Doctors' Commons did not gain that absolute control over admission to practice or

John Langbein, Sterling Professor of Law and Legal History at Yale University.

preferment to judgeships that characterized the Inns of Court on the common law side. Still, Doctors' Commons dominated the professional life of the civilian branch of the legal profession in England. Indeed, some of the civilian courts convened their sittings in the hall of Doctor's Commons, including the Admiralty, the Court of the Arches, and the Prerogative Court of Canterbury.

In the 1560s, in connection with a relocation of the premises of Doctors' Commons to a site owned by the Dean and Chapter of St Paul's Cathedral, Trinity Hall took over the leasehold and the sponsorship of Doctors' Commons. Trinity Hall remained the landlord to Doctors' Commons for the next two hundred years. And from 1552 to 1803, every Master of Trinity Hall was a member of Doctors' Commons (except for one, John Bond, who served during the turmoil of the Interregnum). In the seventeenth and eighteenth centuries, more than a quarter of the Fellows of Trinity Hall were members of Doctors' Commons. Fellowships in Trinity Hall appear to have become in many cases Cambridge sinecures for London-based advocates practising in Doctors' Commons.

Membership in Doctors' Commons was limited to advocates, who were the equivalent of barristers in the civilian world. Not all Trinity Hall civilians became advocates. Some acted as proctors, which was the attorney- or solicitor-equivalent role. Working as a proctor could be a training station on the way to becoming an advocate, or it could be a life-long career. In the period from 1560 to 1640, for example, in the Vice Chancellor's Court of Cambridge (the University's own court, which dispatched a good deal of Cambridge-area commercial business) the Fellowship of Trinity Hall supplied the proctors who conducted 80 per cent of the court's business.

In its second epoch, therefore, Trinity Hall became primarily a society of practising civil lawyers. It kept this character for three centuries – from the Reformation to the mid-nineteenth-century reform of the universities. During this second epoch of Trinity Hall, education of any sort, even in the civil law, appears to have been a sideline at best. Trinity Hall looked more like a law firm than a law school. We know that the Regius Professor gave a few public lectures, but just how the civilian tradition was handed on to new recruits in this period is something of a mystery. One suggestion, which has echoes in the way that would-be barristers were commonly apprenticed to solicitors in order to learn the common law in the seventeenth and eighteenth centuries, is that novice civilians at Trinity Hall practised as proctors en route to becoming advocates.

Trinity Hall dominated the civilian world of early modern England, but across the eighteenth and especially the nineteenth centuries, that world imploded. The civilians steadily lost business as the ecclesiastical courts lost jurisdiction. Chancery took over ever larger portions of the administration of decedents' estates. The development of commercial law in King's Bench under Lord Mansfield in the second half of the eighteenth century came at the expense of the Admiralty. Finally, in the 1850s, the secular jurisdiction of the civilian courts was eliminated, and Doctors' Commons was abolished. Probate and admiralty jurisdiction was transferred to the common law courts, and Trinity Hall was out of work.

This demise of the civilian courts and of the civilian legal profession occurred just at the time when the reform of Oxford and Cambridge was getting underway. Only in this epoch did Trinity Hall develop its modern character as a general-purpose college with a pronounced emphasis on the study of English law.

John H. Langbein is Sterling Professor of Law and Legal History at Yale University. He came up to Trinity Hall in 1964 where he studied for his LLB and then PhD. He also holds degrees in economics from Columbia and in law from Harvard.

Jacobean Constitutional Controversies and the Hall
Clare Jackson

Dr John Cowell was elected Master of Trinity Hall in 1598. Having entered King's College in 1570, Cowell had been a Fellow of King's from 1573 to 1595 and had been appointed the University's Regius Professor of Civil Law in 1594. As Regius Professor, Cowell

The Chapel ceiling, showing the arms of the benefactors, including Dr Eden and Bishop Bateman.

energetically aimed to restore the authoritative pre-eminence commanded by the civil law in ancient Rome and medieval Europe by emphasising the shared similarities between the English civil and common law traditions. While serving as the University's Vice-Chancellor for two annual terms from 1604 to 1606, Cowell published his *Institutiones Juris Anglicani* ('Institutes of English Law') in 1605, arranging English law according to the system of legal codification employed in Justinian's *Institutes*. Two years later, Cowell compiled an alphabetical legal dictionary entitled *The Interpreter, or Book containing the Signification of Words* providing definitions and brief commentaries on various terms in English law.

Although Cowell's *Interpreter* initially seemed to be a legal manual directed towards a limited readership of practising lawyers, the volatile political atmosphere of Jacobean England rendered the Master of Trinity Hall's lexicographical enterprises highly controversial. When the English Parliament reconvened for the first time since the book's publication in February 1610 to debate the contentious issue of financial subsidies to the monarch, one MP, a common lawyer named John Hoskins complained about the contents of Cowell's dictionary. For as well as incurring the professional jealousies of those numerous common lawyers who were MPs and resented Cowell's citations of civilian authorities, particular objection was taken to four of Cowell's definitions: those of 'king', 'parliament', 'prerogative of the king' and 'subsidy'. Cowell had certainly entered thorny constitutional territory in attempting to impose conceptual clarity. For while most early-seventeenth-century Englishmen acknowledged the monarch as the ultimate source of political authority in the country, most were also simultaneously accustomed to regarding Parliament as the supreme source of English legislative authority. For his part, Cowell had simply drawn attention to the irreconcilable tension that subsisted between these two viewpoints by stating, in the entry on 'parliament', that 'of these two one must needs be true: that either the king is above Parliament, that he is above the positive laws of his kingdom, or else he is not an

absolute king'. Moreover, while Cowell's definition accepted that English monarchs conventionally legislated with parliamentary consent, he pointed out that this custom was only 'a merciful policy' that could be disregarded if a monarch wished, for 'simply to bind the prince to or by these laws, were repugnant to the nature and constitution of an absolute monarchy'.

Formal investigation of Cowell's *Interpreter* was referred to the House of Commons' committee of grievances. At a joint conference between Members of the Commons and of the Lords, the Attorney-General, Sir Henry Hobart, attacked Cowell's claim that a monarch could legislate outwith Parliament as 'a presumptuous novelty' that threatened the '*lapis angularis*' (cornerstone) of the English system of government. As Commons MPs petitioned King James I for the right to initiate legal proceedings against the beleaguered Master of Trinity Hall, one contemporary diarist observed that if royal permission was granted, 'it is thought they will go very near to hang him'. On 8 March, however, James himself intervened by conveying his own personal displeasure at the book's contents at which point the Commons abandoned their own enquiries. Denouncing 'the insatiable curiosity' of the times that encouraged scholars who 'never went out of the compass of cloisters or colleges' to 'wade by their writings in the deepest mysteries of monarchy and political government', James condemned Cowell's *Interpreter* in a royal proclamation issued on 25 March 1610. The edict also banned the book from being sold or read and ordered all extant copies to be surrendered to the civil authorities.

Interestingly, although James's proclamation reproved Cowell for seeking to define certain constitutional terms, it avoided censuring any specific political precepts. Hence although Hoskins and several other common lawyers had initially sought to gain a tactical advantage against James by drawing attention to the extreme character of Cowell's absolutist claims, it was ultimately the king himself who derived the greater tactical advantage by ensuring that any potentially destabilising scrutiny of the royal prerogative was prevented at a time when royal finances were under review. For as James was keenly aware, the very strength of his monarchical authority lay in its historic ambiguity. Any attempt to define the royal prerogative in the early seventeenth century could only serve to circumscribe it. Hence, as James later insisted in a speech in 1616, 'the absolute prerogative of the crown: that is no subject for the tongue of a lawyer, nor is it lawful to be disputed'. Ironically, far from supporting the common lawyers in their outraged defence of Parliamentary legislative supremacy, James had himself summoned Cowell on two separate occasions to question him on 'some other passages of his book, which do as well pinch upon the authority of the king'.

Following James's intervention, Cowell retreated to Trinity Hall. He resigned his Regius Chair of Civil Law in May 1611 and died in October that year during a medical operation. Buried in the College chapel, Cowell bequeathed his Cambridge house to Trinity Hall to provide the residence for a Lecturer in Logic who was to lecture at least four times a week in the Michaelmas and Lent terms from 6am to 8am, before lecturing on Aristotle's *Ethics* in the Easter term. Despite being suppressed, Cowell's *Interpreter* proved enduringly popular and was republished without alteration in 1637, 1658, 1684, 1701, 1708 and 1727. James had perhaps been aware that official prohibitions were rarely effective, having previously issued a similar proclamation in 1609 ordering the return of all copies of his own polemical treatise, *Triplici Nodo*,

following the discovery of numerous typographical printing errors. In the event, only 15 of the 800 copies sold were returned.

Clare Jackson became Staff Fellow, Lecturer and Director of Studies in History at Trinity Hall in October 2000. Before that, she was a Research Fellow at Sidney Sussex College, where she also obtained her PhD. She is the author of Restoration Scotland, 1660–1690. Royalist Politics, Religion and Ideas *(2003).*

TEL: AN APPRECIATION
GEOFFREY LEWIS (1949)

Dr T. Ellis Lewis, universally known as Tel, was the most kindly and unassuming law don there ever was. I remember John Willie Morris (Lord Morris of Borth-y-Gest) beginning his speech at a Trinity Hall Association dinner, at which Tel was guest of honour, by saying: 'Should Doctors tell? Our Doctor is Tel.' His pupils will think of him always dispensing an unending stream of fino sherry in his rooms on O staircase, under the row of shields and above the lower gate to Garret Hostel Lane. You could go and see him at any time and have a chat. Everyone did because it was such a pleasure. I do not recall him as a great lecturer or supervisor, but it did not seem to matter. His speciality was the law of torts, an unruly subject composed of a disparate series of civil wrongs which defy all efforts to be welded into a coherent whole. Tel sometimes tried. It was not a great success. I was supervised by Tel with Anthony Buck, later a notably uxorious Tory MP. Buck was not interested in the study of law. Tel realised this early, and our sessions were devoted to sherry-drinking, with forays into the realm of torts which became more spaced out as time went on. Tel was endlessly patient, never censorious, responded always to an appeal for help. But like a good Welshman, he enjoyed above everything the chance to swap anecdotes, of which he had an endless supply.

Tel was a Welsh boy through and through. At the time of the Varsity rugby match, he acquired a hatful of tickets for

Twickenham and handed them out to his undergraduate friends. In this way he assembled around him in the stand a large Cambridge claque from South Wales. He had been born in 1900 in Abergorlich, a Carmarthen village. Then he went to school in Pontardawe in the rugby-worshipping *Under Milkwood* country. He took his law degree at Aberystwyth and became a research student at Caius. In 1927 he wrote his PhD thesis on the history of the doctrine of precedent. For this he was supervised by Sir Percy Winfield, who at once realised his quality. Tel succeeded Winfield as Cambridge lecturer on tort and he later edited several editions of the celebrated textbook, *Winfield on Tort*. He became Squire Law Librarian in 1931 and then, to the untold advantage of the College and all who read law there, he was elected a Fellow of Trinity Hall in 1932. He taught here for 35 years. In 1944 Tel married Ann White, a delightful lady of robust temperament who seemed to enjoy the company of his pupils as much as her husband. Their home was as informally and bibulously hospitable as the rooms on O staircase.

He died content in Cambridge on 22 October 1978, mourned and loved by a huge circle of former pupils and friends.

Geoffrey Lewis studied law at Trinity Hall from 1949–52. He was a partner in Herbert Smith 1960–90. He has published several biographies, including Lord Atkin *(Butterworth, 1983);* Lord Hailsham *(Jonathan Cape, 1997) and, to be published in 2005, a biography of Sir Edward Carson.*

JAMES SUNNUCKS (1946)

After three years of mental stagnation in the Navy I found it difficult to concentrate on legal studies, but we were lucky to have as supervisors Cecil Turner, Ellis Lewis and Trevor Thomas. The former made it clear that it was unnecessary to attend any lectures on criminal law and emphasised that he would teach us all we needed to know, which proved to be correct. In illustrating the maxim *res ipsa loquitur,* Turner asked my supervision group what

Caricature of Tel, drawn on his retirement.

they would infer if they saw me writhing on the floor and purple in the face. My fellow student Nicholson answered that he would assume that I had just eaten a College lunch. This was not an entirely satisfactory answer as Turner was the College steward. Supervisions with Tel were sometimes puzzling but frequently ended with a glass of beer and somehow the law of real property all fell into place long before any exams. I seem to remember my first supervision with Trevor Thomas involved him for some reason wearing the uniform of a flight lieutenant. Michael Hickman was being 'supervised' despite his rank as a wing commander. Similar situations were frequent and most of the third-year men seemed like schoolboys.

David Thomas.

Handing on the torch
David Thomas

My legal career at Trinity Hall began in October 1959. I had come up to Queens' two years earlier to read English, straight from school, unlike most of my undergraduate contempories who were ex-National Servicemen. Having completed Part I of the English Tripos, I thought I might try my hand at something else, and decided to read Part II of the Law Tripos. My Director of Studies at Queens', Geoffrey Wilson, arranged for myself and other 'change-overs' to be supervised in criminal law by J.W.C. Turner. Although by this time he had long passed the retirement age, Turner was still one of the leading scholars of criminal law in the country. He was editor of Kenny's *Outlines of Criminal Law*, which had been the principal student textbook on criminal law for longer than anyone could remember, and also of the two-volume *Russell on Crime*. I remember clearly my first visit to his room in Latham Court. Together with three other Queens' change-overs I shuffled nervously into the distinguished man's presence. We were immediately offered a rather tatty school exercise book and were directed to sign our names. 'I've got the autograph of every man I've ever taught,' he told us. 'I've got High Court Judges, Lords Justices, an Attorney General or two. There is only one piece missing from my collection.' He looked at us each in turn. 'I haven't got a convicted murderer.' So far as I have been able to tell, those who were present on that occasion have disappointed him in that ambition. He was a stimulating supervisor and my lifelong interest in the study of criminal law owes much to the hours we spent with him. He sat with his back to the clock on his mantlepiece and seemed to be unaware of the passage of time. We were never quick to point out that our allotted hour had passed, and would remain in his company as long as he would tolerate us.

I was never personally taught by Tel, but I well remember Trevor Thomas's lectures on the law of personal property. It is the mark of a great lecturer that he can make an apparently dreary subject come alive, and Trevor Thomas certainly did so, breathing life into the rules for the passage of property under the Sale of Goods Act 1893 and inspiring a disproportionate interest in the law of gift. In the more than forty years since I went to these lectures, I have never had to deal with a case of *donatio mortis causa*, but if I had, I would have been ready to do so, thanks to him. His final lecture in the course, dealing with the law of fish Royal, bird Royal, flotsam and jetsam, was a masterful set-piece.

Having completed Part II of the Law Tripos with a measure of success which surprised both myself and my Director of Studies, I returned to Cambridge for what was then known as the LLB. I was taught the law of town and country planning by a young Fellow of

Trinity Hall, Tony Bradley. I then left Cambridge for an assistant lectureship at the London School of Economics, where I remained for nine years before returning to Cambridge in January 1971.

The fact that at that time I came to Trinity Hall was a happy accident organised by John Collier. By the end of the 1960s, Trinity Hall was short of law Fellows. Turner himself had died in 1968, Tel had retired from active teaching although he was still seen at College social events, Trevor Thomas had moved on, first to St John's College as Bursar, then to the University of Liverpool as Vice-Chancellor. Tony Bradley was by now Professor of Public and Constitutional Law at the University of Edinburgh. John Collier had come to the Hall in 1966, and it fell to him to bring together a new team of law teachers. My own arrival at Trinity Hall came about because John Collier was at that time secretary of the Institute of Criminology Appointments Committee, which appointed me to the quaintly-named post of Assistant Director of Research. He came straight out of the Appointments Committee meeting, rang me up and asked if he could put my name forward to the Governing Body as a candidate for a Fellowship in law. I readily agreed and after a few minor formalities I became a Fellow in January 1971. One term earlier, David Fleming, then a recent graduate, had taken up a Fellowship, and together we formed the new team which would endeavour to discharge the formidable task of carrying forward the College's distinguished tradition of teaching in law. We never lost any opportunity of reminding our colleagues that the original intention of the founder was that the College should exist exclusively for the study of law (albeit not of the kind we taught!). We were reinforced from 1973 by the arrival of Peter Wallington, a former student, who was succeeded by Tony Oakley. Keith Ewing, a former graduate student of the Hall, was a member of the team from 1983 until he was appointed to a chair at King's College, London, in 1989.

Since the early 1970s, the content of the law has changed beyond recognition. Established subjects have expanded and wholly new subjects, in particular European community law and European human rights law, have established themselves on the syllabus as essential parts of the law student's knowledge base. There is much more to learn. By the time I returned to Cambridge, I had begun to establish myself as a specialist in the neglected field of sentencing law. In 1970, the whole of the statutory law relevant to sentencing probably amounted to about forty sections of legislation contained in the Criminal Justice Acts of 1948 and 1967. In the two Parliamentary Sessions 2001–02 and 2002–03 alone, Parliament has added to the statute book more than 300 sections of legislation dealing with sentencing, accompanied by voluminous schedules and to be followed by innumerable statutory instruments. The undergraduate studying law is spared the full details, but what were once relatively simple problems of principle have become encrusted with conflicting case law and it takes a lot longer to master them. Methods of studying law have also changed. Electronic databases of various forms are now one of the principal resources for the law student and researcher alike. To access a relatively recent statute, it is not necessary to walk to the Law Library, find the relevant volume and thumb through the pages. Two or three clicks of the mouse will usually bring up the relevant section, and a Google search will quickly find that statutory instrument which not so long ago meant searching on hands and knees in a series of boxes on a low shelf in the Squire. Traditional law reports also are less important in the life of the law student or the teacher. Most current case law can be accessed from one of the various commercial databases, and copied and pasted into an essay or article. It is now rare to receive a handwritten essay from an undergraduate; most arrive by email.

Despite these changes, the daily routine of the law student has not changed much in the last thirty years. Academic study still revolves around lectures and supervisions. The College remains as fully committed as ever to teaching undergraduates in small groups, usually of four, providing them the opportunity to discuss legal issues with their contemporaries and their supervisors. Academic demands on undergraduates are undoubtedly higher

A group of Hall judges: Sir Donald Rattee, Judge Blofeld (not Trinity Hall), Lord Justice Croom-Johnson, the Rt Hon. Lord Oliver of Aylmerton, the Rt Hon. Lord Justice Millett (later Lord Millett of St Marylebone), the Rt Hon. Lord Nicholls of Birkenhead, Lord Justice MacDermott and Judge Sheerin (not Trinity Hall).

Hall men have often accounted for up to a quarter of Law Lords. Photograph taken at the inauguration of Nigel Chancellor (centre) as High Sheriff of Cambridgeshire, 1996.

now than thirty years ago. For those who aspire to a career in the law, whether as barristers or solicitors, an Upper Second is more or less essential, and they are no easier to get now than they were in the past. Commitment to academic study is high, but this does not get in the way of other aspects of undergraduate life.

The most outwardly noticeable change in the daily life of a law student is that all Faculty-related activities take place in the new Law Faculty building designed by Lord Foster and situated on the West Road site. No longer are lectures spread around the City, some in the Old Schools, some in Mill Lane. The new building experienced some problems in its early days, but these have now been resolved and the Faculty has settled into its new accommodation. All lectures take place in the same building, in modern lecture rooms immediately below the Squire Library.

There was some reluctance on the part of some members of the Faculty to leave the Old Schools, where law had been taught to generations of students, but there can be no doubt the new building is a vast improvement. The East Room, although a beautiful room, was hopeless to lecture in. I well remember standing on the podium peering into the darkness on a late winter afternoon trying to see if any of my audience, most of whom sat as far away as possible, were still awake. By an accident of the lecture timetable it fell to me to give the very last law lecture in the East Room, and I was disappointed that the occasion was not marked in some way. I had no regrets at the move. The new building brings the Faculty together, its modern styling emphasising the fact that law is concerned with issues of the moment.

Trinity Hall is spoken of by many as 'the law college'. We have, of course, to acknowledge that there are other colleges in the University which teach law very successfully, and also that law, although still an important subject in College, is by no means the only or dominant subject. The College's record in law, however, remains outstanding for what is still a small college. However one evaluates the success of our law graduates, we can take pride in their achievements. One measure of the College's importance as a breeding ground for lawyers is the number of members of the higher judiciary who are members of the College. We have always been well represented among the Lords of Appeal in Ordinary (most recently by Lords Millett and Nicholls); two recently appointed Lord Justices, Thomas and Hooper, are Hall men, and our High Court judges seldom fall below nine or ten in number. While the list of Queen's Counsel still appeared annually, it was rare not to find several Hall men in the list. We are still waiting for our first female silk, and may have to wait some time while the uncertainty over the future of the office of Queen's Counsel remains. Numerous other Hall lawyers have found distinction as solicitors, achieving partnerships in some of the largest and best-known firms in the country. Not all of our law graduates have chosen to practise law; others have achieved distinction in many fields, including journalism and education.

Just as the end of the 1960s saw a changing of the guard in the College's law Fellows, so have the last few years. Tony Oakley took advantage of the early retirement scheme to turn to full-time practice at the Bar, John Collier retired in 2001 after 35 years' service to the College (and was delighted to receive a large number of cards from his magic boys and girls on his recent seventieth birthday); I retired from the Fellowship in September 2003. David Fleming continues in harness, but a new team of young law teachers has filled the places we have vacated. Angus Johnston, whose special interests lie in the field of European law, John Armour (company law) and Matthew Conaglen (property law) will carry forward the teaching of law to a new generation, aided and abetted by Brian Cheffins, Professor of Corporate Law. We are confident that the future of law teaching at the Hall is secure, and that the founder's purpose in establishing the College will continue to be observed.

David Thomas read English and then law at Queens' College from 1957–61. He taught at the London School of Economics from 1961–70, and returned to the Institute of Criminology in 1971. He was elected a Fellow of the College in 1971, and was at various times Graduate Tutor and Vice-Master. He retired in 2003, and is now an Emeritus Fellow.

Penny Moreland (1982)

Reflecting on how my time at College had been helpful and relevant to my subsequent career required a mental sea change: I had, to date, thought of my undergraduate years only as tremendous fun.

On first considering the situation, I saw little or no relevance. After reading law at Trinity Hall, I went to Bar School, and then to pupillage in Newcastle-upon-Tyne where I've practised ever since, exclusively in crime for the last ten years. I've never been asked to represent a defendant who has injured one of a troupe of performing slaves, or advise as to any offence committed when someone has attached their handle to someone else's dish, so Roman law has been no help. Frankly, my grasp on certain subjects was at best tenuous even twenty years ago… I think immediately of the rule against perpetuities… and thankfully I've not found much call for that kind of thing. Even the criminal law I learnt has changed in many respects, thanks to frequent successive reforms, the adage 'leave well alone' not forming part of any government's policy so far as the criminal justice system is concerned.

However, I learnt some important lessons at College, for example, the value of a concise argument persuasively presented. This I learnt from Mr Collier, having handed in my first essay to him. 'Miss Moreland,' he said, 'I could not have been less impressed if you had stood on the other side of a field waving a bunch of damp daisies at me.' I still have the essay: he was quite right.

From some rather tense supervisions I learnt to consider an argument thoroughly before committing it to paper: writing an essay in haste and including a thought that seemed like a good idea at the time led to some uncomfortable moments trying to defend the indefensible. This is known to the Newcastle Bar as a Peterborough point. Grounds of Appeal are drafted in high dudgeon and submitted, which by some chance get past the single judge: only halfway to London on the 6.30am train does the inherent weakness of one's argument become apparent, far too late to avoid the inevitable pasting from the full court.

This highlights both the geographical and metaphorical distance between Newcastle and Cambridge. Newcastle is the northernmost outpost of the Bar and regarded as remote even by barristers from the southern end of the North Eastern circuit. The last time a High Court judge was appointed from the ranks of those who had practised in Newcastle was over twenty years ago: by contrast, whilst I was at College there was a party to celebrate the appointment of the tenth High Court judge who had studied at Trinity Hall.

There is in Newcastle a real risk of isolation and the Cambridge connection reminds one there is a world south of the Tyne.

There are no real coal faces left in the North East, but on a wet Monday in February, slogging it out in Court 10 over some particularly lurid example of human depravity can truly feel like the coal face of the Bar. Nothing I learnt or experienced at College could have prepared me for the reality of a criminal practice, nor was it ever intended to. How to handle the irascible judge, the schizophrenic defendant, the truculent witness or the unreasonable opponent are survival skills learnt generally by making the kind of mistakes that make you cringe to recall them fifteen years later.

Similarly, how to make the rules do what you want them to do and achieve a satisfactory solution to an intractable problem is a skill born of experience. But knowing the rules and, more

importantly, respecting them comes first: pragmatism is a good thing but only when tempered with an application of the principles and a recollection that the case in hand does not stand alone but fits into the framework set out during Part I of the Tripos.

Those of us who have gone on to practise in criminal law are, I suspect, aware of the privilege of having had that framework first set out for us by Dr Thomas, who made it all seem so straightforward. Only experience shows what great learning is required to achieve that particular feat.

Mine has not been the most obvious career path from Trinity Hall, but I recall my time there with tremendous affection and gratitude. In truth, Trinity Hall made me the lawyer I am, in ways that I can't identify and express, as it did all of us who went on to practise in so many different ways. I acknowledge that debt: whether the Hall wishes to accept that attribution is another matter!

Penny Moreland read law at Trinity Hall 1982–85. She is now a member of the Bar in Newcastle-upon-Tyne, practising in criminal law. She was recently appointed a Recorder.

LAW AND THE NEW DISCIPLINE OF CRIMINOLOGY
ALISON LIEBLING

[The Cambridge Institute of Criminology] owes its birth to the initiative of R.A. Butler, an outstanding Home Secretary, and it took root in an ancient University and within a traditionally minded Faculty of Law. It was brought into being to raise the status of criminology and through teaching and research to extend its influence in the Universities and in government.

(Radzinowicz, *The Cambridge Institute of Criminology: Its Background and Scope*, London: 1988).

Modern criminology grew out of two separate enterprises: a government-inspired series of empirical inquiries aimed at the increasingly efficient and equitable administration of justice, and a search for satisfactory explanations of the causes of crime. Trinity

Hall has a special relationship with this academic discipline and has for many years had more than a handful of MPhil and PhD students studying criminology annually as well as a number of prominent criminologists, such as David Thomas, amongst its Fellows. Cecil Turner (Fellow, 1926–68), a 'first class and tireless teacher' in law, was one of the founders of the Cambridge Institute of Criminology. It was Cecil Turner who first invited Leon Radzinowicz to 'come to Cambridge and help me to expand the study of crime and punishment' during the late 1930s.

Leon Radzinowicz came to England interested by the English probation and borstal systems. English criminal policy was regarded by many at the time as 'unique'. In his *Adventures in Criminology*, Radzinowicz described the borstal system as an 'infant prodigy' of criminology and penology. It 'stood out as the most impressive and the most successful achievement in applied penology the world had seen and is likely ever to see again'. He had intended to return to Poland, but instead, he eventually became the first Director of the Cambridge Institute of Criminology, established in January 1960.

In 1940, a few years after Radzinowicz arrived in Cambridge, Cecil Turner persuaded Cambridge University's Faculty of Law to establish a 'Committee to Consider the Promotion of Research and Teaching in Criminal Science'. Soon after, the Faculty established a tiny Department of Criminal Science, in 1941. It was housed in the old Squire Law library. Radzinowicz and Turner led this department together. During the late 1950s, the government approached London and Cambridge Universities with a suggestion that there should be an interdisciplinary university-based Institute of Criminology. Cambridge responded with enthusiasm, and our Institute of Criminology was established. The next year saw the introduction of a new postgraduate course for the training of criminological researchers and scholars, now the MPhil in Criminology. A considerable number of the established first generation of criminologists, in the UK and internationally, began their careers at the Cambridge Institute of Criminology. We also teach two part-time Masters courses for senior professionals in criminal justice, an undergraduate course in the Law Tripos (Sentencing and the Penal System) and an undergraduate paper in the Social and Political Sciences Tripos (Crime and Deviance). The department has grown considerably in size (to eight established posts, several externally-funded lecturers and many research positions) and we share a high mutual respect with the Law Faculty, perhaps especially since some early reservations about the respectability of the social sciences have started to fade. Many of our interests overlap and we are, due to our research activities, especially high performers in the Research Assessment Exercise. At the time of writing we are looking forward to a new purpose-built department ready for occupation in the autumn of 2004.

Alison Liebling is a University Reader in Criminology and Criminal Justice and Director of the Cambridge Institute of Criminology's Prisons Research Centre. She studied for her first degrees at York (BA Politics) and Hull (MA Criminology). She became a Fellow of Trinity Hall in 1991.

Dialectic and expression

07

HISTORY AND ARTS

THE HISTORY OF HISTORY AT THE HALL
JONATHAN STEINBERG

Nobody records College memories. New Fellows replace the old and the old forget to tell them the most important things because the most important things are taken for granted. Facts slip out of the collective consciousness. Nobody knew in 1996 what everybody knew in 1920 that the ground floor rooms between P and Q staircases had been built inside an obsolete lecture room. Tristan Rees Roberts, the architect of the Jerwood Library, was amazed when he found it. I feel guilty about this cloud of oblivion. As the senior College historian from 1966 to 1999, I ought to have recorded the collective memory and done something to keep a proper archive of my time at the Hall. I will try to make amends by reflecting on the study of history at the Hall, some ways in which it changed and more in which it did not.

In May 1965, I got a note from Mr C.W. Crawley, written on small Trinity Hall note-paper in his slanting, pointy hand. 'Dear Steinberg' it began and to my surprise continued by offering me a Fellowship when he retired on 30 September 1966. I called on him in his rooms in L staircase and he explained that the College, which was not rich, had to consider the finances of a new appointment carefully. Apparently I had been quite high on the list of unsuccessful applicants for an Assistant Lectureship that May and might be thought a reasonable candidate for a future vacancy. Were I to get a post in the next round, I might arrive at Trinity Hall on 1 October 1966, largely at the University's expense. In 1993 when I reviewed College committee papers in order to write a memorial to

Charles Crawley, I discovered that I was the Fellowship Committee's third choice.

A few weeks later, on 14 June 1965, the Master, Sir Ivor Jennings, wrote to explain that the basic emolument of a Staff Fellow who is also a University teaching officer are as follows:

Fellowship dividend	£ 350
Ancient allowances	£ 50
Education staff basic payment	£ 75
	£ 475

The Master added that the Fellowship Committee had agreed to offer me an additional £425 a year 'for a period of three years or until you obtained a University appointment, whichever first occurred.'

I had literally not set foot in the Hall until that meeting with Charles Crawley. It looked cosy but shabby. Trinity Hall reminded me of an agreeable old gentleman, who had known better days. Later I learned how true that was, when I came across a *Financial Times* article on college finances which put the Hall just above Girton and Magdalene in endowment income. Yet there was something deeply charming about 'that poore society'. I said yes.

Charles Crawley and I had nothing in common, not religion, style, background (Charles was Winchester and Trinity; I was at a New York progressive school and Harvard) nor interests. Yet we shared, I think, a deep love and commitment to Trinity Hall. Neither of us could have remotely foreseen in May 1965 that between us we would be history Fellows at the Hall for most of the twentieth century. Charles began as a twenty-four year old in 1924 and I retired at 65 on 31 December 1999. Charles had been 'hanging around Trinity', as he put it in an interview I taped with him, wondering what to do with his life, when Henry Bond, the Master, wrote to him. Charles lived to a great age and regularly attended the undergraduate History Society. He would sit sleeping in the deepest chair in the Chetwode Room with his pipe and curvature of the spine, looking like an elderly human pretzel.

Charles Crawley only wrote one book: *The Question of Greek Independence; a study of British policy in the Near East. 1821–1833* which was published by Cambridge University Press in 1930. He edited a volume in the Cambridge series on Modern Europe and some papers of John Capodistrias, but otherwise did almost no professional scholarship for more than thirty years. He taught, administered, attended Governing Bodies, chaired committees and became an icon to generations of Hall undergraduates. In his retirement he wrote the delightful *Trinity Hall : the history of a Cambridge college, 1350–1975*, which the College published privately in 1976. In the government-imposed Research Assessment Exercises to which all academic departments must now respond he would have been recorded as 'research-active: nil'. Charles Crawley, a great College asset, would have become by the 1990s a University liability. In future no young man or woman will take Charles Crawley as a role model. No faculty will dare to carry research-inactive persons. The 'good college man' has gone for ever. And that is undoubtedly the single greatest change in the history of history at Trinity Hall during my 33 years.

I had arrived at St John's College, Cambridge, a few years earlier to get a PhD, a qualification still regarded by older dons as a new-fangled German invention. I remember that my beloved *Doktorvater* Sir Harry Hinsley once told me, 'black MA is the gentleman's gown'. A PhD was a degree only pedants and Americans obtained. There was no graduate school at all and no training in methods of research, theory or historiography. A potential scholar just 'got on with it' in that time-honoured English

way. Graduate students scarcely knew each other, had no meeting room, no status and not much money.

The day I arrived in Cambridge, 1 October 1961, I found one of those notes from Harry Hinsley that began 'Dear Steinberg', a usage now obsolete, asking me 'to take thirteen pupils' (also obsolete – 'to take' meaning 'to supervise') for American history. Frank Thistlethwaite, the Fellow who taught US history at St John's, had gone off at short notice to become Vice-Chancellor of the new University of East Anglia. Among those pupils was Peter Clarke, until recently Master of Trinity Hall. I knew no American history but had the right accent and a store of diversionary anecdotes. I survived and so did the pupils. Ignorance in those days was not thought to be a bar to supervising a subject. The great Herbert Butterfield, Regius Professor and Master of Peterhouse, always insisted that Fellows of that college teach all the subjects in the Tripos. When Roger Lovatt, a direct contemporary of mine, refused to teach American history, Butterfield allowed him to engage me to teach at Peterhouse but it had to be concealed, lest it set an unwholesome precedent. I had to teach in the Small Parlour where nobody would notice my shameful presence.

The next few years were the best years to enter the academic profession in Britain in the entire history of the United Kingdom. Ten new universities opened up between 1961 and 1968 and literally dozens of dons in Oxford and Cambridge left to be vice-chancellors and heads of exciting new, socially relevant, departments and institutes. There were jobs for us all. I got my PhD in 1965, nearly got a Faculty job that year, got one the following year and arrived at the Hall as a new Fellow on 1 October 1966 at a cost to the College of a few hundred pounds. I was never interviewed for either the University or College post.

During the tenure of my College job, the subjects historians study changed but it is not easy in an account such as this to summarise them. Historians tend to be too busy to reflect either on their own methods or the status of the discipline. The past is 'out there', getting bigger all the time and the small crew of quarry-workers in the great mine of human experience has more than enough to dig up. Indeed, in modern historical research the sheer volume of human communication, multiplied since 1900 by mechanical and electronic means of reproduction, has produced an overwhelming and rapidly growing mass of potential evidence. Volume alone becomes an obstacle to research. The archive of only one German bank, Deutsche Bank AG, Frankfurt/Main, from 1870 to 1945, runs for 9 kilometers. The personal files collected by the State Security Office in the German Democratic Republic, the infamous Stasi Files, cover more than 180 kilometres and there are an additional 200 kilometres of files on organisations and groups. The Lyndon Johnson Presidential Library houses several millions of his papers. Who can 'know' all this material?

One answer for the historical profession has been division of labour. In 1924 Charles Crawley taught the entire Tripos. By 1999 nobody did that any more. There has been an expansion of specialised journals, now augmented by even more specialised on-line enterprises. Historians literally know more today but about much less than Charles Crawley did and write very much less attractive prose.

History at Trinity Hall over the years has moved ever more obviously to the University and away from the College. By 1969 the Faculty of History had a building and much of my professional life was spent in James Stirling's inverted green house on the Sidgwick Site, though as a vestigial 'good college' type I never claimed an office there. The building put an end to the ancient wanderings of Faculty office-holders from college to college and created a modern hierarchy of function with junior members allotted precisely 12 feet by 10 feet of office space to perform their duties. The building gave the Faculty a corporate identity and reduced the role of the colleges as teaching institutions.

In the mid-1990s I was chair of the Faculty Board of History, and that meant *ex officio* chairing the History Degree Committee, the Faculty Appointments Committee, the Teaching and Learning Committee, the Appraisals Committee, the Equal Opportunities Committee, the Graduate Students Committee, the Faculty Planning Committee and representing the Faculty on the Council of the School of Humanities and Social Sciences. Chairing the Faculty Board of History bears only tangential similarity to the chair of an ordinary history department. An American private university like Harvard or Penn is a capitalist corporation run by Trustees with a chief executive officer as President. It has vertical lines of command and a very strong authoritarian temper. As 'Chair' (the genderized term for my office here) of the Department of History, I feel like the regional plant manager of some multi-national company.

When I arrived at the Hall in October 1966, there was another Fellow in History, Nicholas Richardson, perhaps the cleverest colleague I have ever had. He was in place, senior to me, and should have been offered the job of Director of Studies as a matter of course. The then rather elderly and conservative Fellowship could not cope with Nick; I doubt if today's would either. He was always badly behaved, especially in the evening as alcohol poisoned his tongue. I have horrid memories of High Table dinners as he sliced chunks off the stolid egos of less agile colleagues in Trinity Hall, innocents who happened to be slow-moving targets when the black mood took him. Many of these people never forgave Nick for the pain he caused them.

He was a brilliant historian. In 1966 he published *The French Prefectoral Corps 1814–1830* with the Cambridge University Press, a superb little monograph, now long out of print and forgotten, but part of the permanent intellectual furniture of my work. I never lecture on France or the growth of the modern state without citing it and I must have used the quote about the prefects conveying Napoleonic commands to the periphery of France *avec la rapidité du fluide électrique* hundreds of times.

In 1976 Dr Sandra Raban of Girton arrived to become a Staff Fellow in history. From the first day she and I established a harmonious partnership. For years she directed studies and I was tutor or vice versa. I cannot recall a single serious case of disagreement or friction and the admissions interviews and assessments were uncanny. We might occasionally disagree in the exact ranking of the individual candidate but rarely anything beyond that. It is hard to imagine two people more different in background, habits, subject of study, method, style, etc. but we just got along. Sometimes I think Bishop Bateman put something in the water to make sure that his quarrelsome canon lawyers would not fight all the time and forgot to take it out.

During the 1960s and 1970s historiography occupied itself with 'forces and factors' and not with human agents. It seemed odd, even at the time, that the twentieth century, which had been overshadowed by larger-than-life human beings – Hitler, Stalin, Mussolini, Mao, Roosevelt, Churchill, De Gaulle, Gandhi – should have spawned a generation of historians who rejected biography as a tool. Perhaps the one had caused the other. In addition, a kind of diluted Marxism mixed with prejudices about 'history from above' went with the new universities and their radical student activism to create an attitude which led its holders to condemn the personal, the biographical and the political as reactionary by definition. 'History from above' meant 'politics from above'.

Gradually new subjects – demography under the auspices of the Cambridge pioneers in family reconstruction, the new contextual approach to the history of ideas associated with Quentin Skinner, the history of daily life, the history of women and gender, the history of the self – emerged. New theoretical structures – the realisation that history rests on 'texts' and that 'texts' are themselves not transparent panes through which an unproblematic past can be observed – altered the ways we approach the subject. The collapse of the Communist bloc certainly accelerated the discrediting of all 'systematic' theories of social causation, especially those, which relied on impersonal factors like class. In the 1990s, biography returned as a major tool of historical analysis.

All these changes plus an increasing division of labour and the multiplication of journals and electronic substitutes made the profession less homogeneous, more fragmented and less amateur. Yet history teaching at Trinity Hall has not changed all that much.

Supervision, the one-on-one tutorial, continues to be used, though how my successors arrange it may have changed. College still 'teaches' and undergraduates still learn in personal face-to-face encounters. Here at Penn where I lecture to big audiences, I have less chance to do that kind of intimate teaching but when I do, I realize how extraordinarily powerful a teaching tool it remains. The interaction of tutor and pupil creates in the learner an alternate way of knowing. The *Oxford English Dictionary* defines 'conscious' as 'knowing something with others, knowing in oneself' and that, I think, has always been the aim of the history supervision: to make the student 'conscious', to develop that critical awareness which makes the past the laboratory of the present. That was the one constant element in my teaching during the thirty three years and one term that I was a Fellow of Trinity Hall. How often I succeeded the supervisees must say, but then what is success? Leslie Stephen shrewdly observed that institutions take credit for producing people they have not managed to suppress. So I suppose my students would have found their own route to self-knowledge without my ministrations.

Recently I had to introduce a distinguished English historian, who gave a talk at the Annenberg Colloquium in European History at the University of Pennsylvania. He happened to be a former student, though not from the Hall. It occurred to me that I might still have his supervision reports from Michaelmas 1982, among the private notes I made on all my supervisions. I did. When I read them, two things occurred to me: How little the man differed in style and temper from the boy and how many hours of human interaction those ragged supervision notes represented. Some students came back to life the moment I saw the notes; others not. The Trinity Hall people mingled with the 'outsiders'. Part I students and Part II students were on adjoining pages. I am glad I never threw those notes away. I use them when unexpectedly some former student suddenly decides to change his or her life and needs an academic reference. I used them to introduce the visiting lecturer and impressed my colleagues and the graduate students with the

Jonathan Steinberg, Vice-Master 1990–94.

fact that this famous figure had once been my student. I hope supervision survives yet a while. It offers individual teaching in a world less and less willing to spend time or money on individual things. Supervisor and supervisee become persons to each other and sometimes in time friends. There must have been more than three hundred Hall men and women who read history during my time there. I owe them much and I hope they feel that I gave them something worthwhile. I thank that remote Trinity Hall Fellowship Committee of 1965 for deciding to offer me a job. From first to last it was a joy and privilege to be a Fellow of 'that poore society'.

Jonathan Steinberg is now Walter H. Annenberg Professor of Modern European History at the University of Pennsylvania.

Colin Hayes (1962)

When I arrived at the Hall I was quite unprepared for the asperity of Cambridge history. Warning bells sounded in my very first supervision. My essay on some obscure hill folk and their role in early English economic history was a splurge of absurdly florid passages, penned well after midnight. I was quietly pleased with it. My tutor received it with a series of ruminative noises, a prolonged tapping out of the pipe, and then the judgement: 'If you don't mind me saying so, I fear it's rather too well written.' If the essay was long on form, it was very short indeed on substance. He continued: 'I think it would be a good idea for you to go to Miss Wood-Legh for medieval history.'

Katherine Wood-Legh lived in Owlstone Road and was an authority on medieval chantries. She took several students from the Hall. The house was gloomy and ascetic, warmed only by a small gas fire, and the silence was profound. She was blind. Every three weeks for my first year I would cycle there in a state of acute apprehension. Miss Wood-Legh would sit on one side of the puttering fire, head bowed, eyes closed, hands folded in her lap. I sat on the other and read aloud what I had written. It soon became clear that her concentration and powers of detection were total. She could recall every single word. A woolly thought stood little chance, a sloppy one none at all. Portentous statements were despatched without ceremony. With a sinking heart one realised that a sentence wasn't going to stand up; I would press on, trying to accelerate through the next soggy patch, but the lights always turned red. 'Stop, please! Now, young man, what *exactly* do you mean by that?' Worse still, evasive tactics were useless; she could tell when I had deliberately changed a word or missed something out. This was not a game.

Apprehension, yes; fear on occasion, pain at times, but admiration and affection too. Miss Wood-Legh lived for her students as well as for her subject. And it wasn't all graft and severity. I remember this quiet, middle-aged spinster, to my intense surprise, launching into a feisty dissertation on the Roman

Catholic church, contraception, guilt and confession, not subjects on which I was able to make any useful contribution. She was a splendid teacher, and later was one of the original advocates for the foundation of Lucy Cavendish College.

My second and third years took me for modern European history to a very different person, for whom supervisions *were*, or so it seemed, a game. Nicholas Richardson had just been elected a Fellow, coming from Peterhouse with a doctorate on the French prefecture of the early nineteenth century. He had attractive rooms, painted out in white, on the ground floor of Front Court.

Nicholas was the antithesis of Miss Wood-Legh: young, sharp-featured, suede jacketed, chain-smoking, restless. There were hints of some mysterious military service in North Africa and of a girlfriend in Paris. He was obsessed with French chic in all its forms and was passionate about the language. He had a coterie of colleagues and pupils who enjoyed an esoteric vocabulary. Acquaintances were either a 'hellhound' or a 'japer', both epithets impossible to define. I suspect I was a japer, whatever that was.

Supervisions were startling. First, the invitation to read widely, voraciously, and miles from the subject. Why on earth did he tell me to read Eric Ambler as an insight to my first assignment? I never did discover. Then the appointed hour to discuss one's essay, often adjourned or even re-scheduled until after Hall. Out then would come the drum of fifty Players Medium and the bottle of College sherry, to be shared and consumed by close of play, which could be well into the small hours. The interrogation would begin, first about the subject and one's essay and what one had read, then about oneself; relentless, probing, peeling away all one's attempts at self-defence, relieved only by visits to the Buttery for more sherry. Or the discussion would take off suddenly at wild tangents. His favourite recordings were played and re-played as the smoke thickened and alcohol took hold: the French singers Sylvie Vartan and Marie Laforet, or an interminable, sonorous defence plea by some tragic hero of his called Tixier-Vignancourt. The atmosphere would become maudlin, then combative, then darkly aggressive,

then destructive, and finally – if Nicholas knew he had gone too far – apologetic.

But behind this mischievous façade there lay nevertheless a dynamic and deeply serious approach to history. Nicholas forced us to engage with the subject he loved, to ask the right questions, to research carefully, to be accurate with facts and to argue coherently. In a word: to think. He too was a teacher and he wanted his students to succeed.

Richardson always maintained that he was denied a Fellowship at Peterhouse because his thesis contained a joke, thus subtly acknowledging Trinity Hall's liberality in electing him.

NIGEL THOMAS (1955)

Charles Crawley was very wise and a delicious tease. He and his wife invited me to a freshers' tea. As we relaxed afterwards, he fixed me with a musing eye.

'Thomas,' he said, 'Nigel Thomas… Your headmaster, ex-Hall man, terrible character! He turns up here and sits opposite me just like a travelling salesman in prospective entrants. He opens his brief-case and takes out a file. "That one," he says. I look at it and say, "No, I think not." "Well, this one, then." Again, I say "No." He takes out several more, one after the other, and all of them I decline. Do you know, after a while, my sales resistance is a bit low! Yes, Thomas,' he mused, gently suggesting that, had my name been 'Alexander', I would have been consigned to outer darkness somewhere else.

JOHN PHILIP JONES (1950)

I came to the Hall to read law, because I had a family legal practice I could have joined. But the first thing that Charles Crawley told me (as he told most other aspirant lawyers), was that it was best not to focus my total attention on law, but to read another subject first. Economics was a good choice, because it offered a one-year Part I, which meant that I could spend two years on Part II of the Law Tripos.

Michael Noakes
1966

Charles Crawley taught history at the Hall from 1924 and was an Honorary Fellow until his death in 1992. 'An icon to generations of undergraduates.'

Once I had embarked on Part I of the Economics Tripos, I got caught up in the subject. Not only did it help me understand some of the strange things that were happening in Britain during the 1950s (inefficient and stagnating production allied to constant problems with the management of the economy), but it also brought me into direct contact with the intellectual power of the Economics Faculty. Unfortunately Trinity Hall had no economics Fellow at that time and my director of studies was Peter Bauer (later Lord Bauer), Fellow of Caius. The economics dons were all stepping out from under the shadow of Maynard Keynes, who had died in 1946, and they were on the way to building the Cambridge economics department as the pre-eminent centre of learning in the world for the study of both micro and macroeconomics. (This had alas all changed within a decade, as many of the greatest talents quit either to retire or to go to other universities.)

Charles Crawley represented everything that was and is good about British education: that what matters most is brains, that brains are best developed by studies in the liberal arts, and that an educated individual is a rounded individual.

EXCERPT FROM THE ADDRESS GIVEN BY GRAHAM STOREY AT THE FUNERAL OF CHARLES CRAWLEY, 12 OCTOBER 1992

I was a tutorial pupil of Charles's in 1939; and no one could have been kinder or more helpful. He was the gentlest of men – though he could be sharp when the occasion demanded it – but the characteristic hesitant manner showed not only an inherent modesty, but a belief that judgements should not be sudden but be carefully and meticulously worked out. And this – together with his absolute integrity and experience of the College and its ways – made him an invaluable member of the Governing Body for over forty years, the last sixteen of them as Vice-Master. We so rightly made him an Honorary Fellow in 1971.

Charles Crawley gave this advice for what I think were three reasons. First, he believed in the value of breadth as well as depth in a person's education. Second (a connected point), he thought that a progressive career demands what Americans call left-field thinking: a degree of unorthodoxy that no amount of narrowly-focused study can provide. Third and not least, he thought that to study two subjects is more fun than to concentrate on one. There is less danger of staleness. I took Charles Crawley's advice and it determined the course of my life.

As a young Fellow, he learnt to fly and held a pilot's licence. I sometimes like to think of Charles and his former Trinity friend, Dr Simpson – who also had a licence – hovering in the air all those years ago together over Marshall's air-field.

He had a keen interest in the cloak and dagger world behind the scenes of history. This I discovered when he asked me to take with me on a Greek holiday the manuscript of his book on Capodistrias: the Colonels were in power and Capodistrias was much too liberal for them. So I was given strict instructions how to find his Greek publisher, in Constitution Square, within a few yards of the Govet's HQ – I am glad to say that the book was published.

He was a formidably good squash-player. I remember that in the 1950s the Fellows rashly challenged the undergraduates 1st team and Charles, then nearing 60, was the only one who won.

But Charles was not only a devoted Trinity Hall man; he was a devoted family-man too. His wife, Kitty, played a great part in entertaining, both undergraduates and Fellows' wives, and had herself an instinctive feeling for any undergraduate in trouble. Their summer parties in the garden of Madingley road, where they lived for fifty years, and their Sunday lunches were memorable.

Establishing legal principles in Victorian literature
Jan-Melissa Schramm

Indigenous English law was added to the curriculum in the nineteenth century with the demise of Doctors' Commons and the secular jurisdiction of the ecclesiastical courts that had dominated legal education at Trinity Hall in the medieval and Renaissance periods. Spanning this time of great transition was the career of the renowned jurist Henry Sumner Maine; he won an exhibition to study classics at Pembroke College in 1840 and his long association with the Hall began when he became a tutor here in 1845. He was appointed Regius Professor of Civil Law in 1847, a post which he held until 1854. He was called to the Bar in 1850, and in 1852 he became the first reader in Roman law and jurisprudence at the Inns of Court. *Ancient Law* (1861) – a proto-sociological study of the development of law deeply indebted to the methodology of Charles Darwin's *Origin of Species* (1859) – established his national reputation, and Maine was then persuaded to work in the administration of English law in India. His subsequent career included periods of service as the Vice-Chancellor of the University of Calcutta and the Corpus Christi Professor of Jurisprudence in Oxford. He returned to the Hall as Master in 1877, and before his death was again elevated to a chair, this time here in Cambridge as Whewell Professor of International Law.

One of the most interesting features of Maine's professional life was his abiding commitment to both journalism and legal education. Yet it was his intellectually productive friendship with two brothers that shows the vigour of nineteenth-century moral and political discourse. James Fitzjames Stephen entered Trinity College in 1847; his younger brother Leslie followed their father to Trinity Hall in 1850 (he became a Fellow four years later), and, together with Maine, the young men were to become particularly influential in the realm of nineteenth-century letters. Maine and Fitzjames Stephen met in 1845 – in the course of a shooting accident at Filey, according to Leslie in his *Life* of his brother. Maine sponsored Fitzjames Stephen's entry to the Cambridge Apostles in 1847, and both men went on to write for the *Morning Chronicle* and the *Saturday Review* (indeed Fitzjames Stephen was to succeed Maine on the legal council in India). All were interested in the relationship between forensic fact and techniques of rhetorical persuasion – in Leslie Stephen's words 'the same principles which underlie the English laws of evidence are also applicable to innumerable questions belonging to religious, philosophical and scientific inquiries' (the *Life*). Although Fitzjames Stephen never yielded to his impulse to abandon law for literature, he did go on to serve as a conduit for the importation into Victorian literary thought of legal standards of proof and evidence which impacted significantly upon the formulation of some of our most influential conceptions of narrative realism. This

Opposite: *Detail from* Senate House Hill, Degree Morning, 1863 *by Robert Farren, showing Leslie Stephen. The painting was bought for the College by the Master, Thomas Geldart, in 1872. He is also depicted, as are Henry Fawcett and Henry Latham, later also Master.*

was, after all, the period in which George Eliot could write of her narrative technique that 'my strongest effort is to… give a faithful account of men and things as they have mirrored themselves in my mind. The mirror is doubtless defective; the outlines will sometimes be disturbed, the reflection faint or confused; but I feel as much bound to tell you as precisely as I can what that reflection is, as if I were in the witness-box narrating my experience on oath' (*Adam Bede*, 1859). This deft linguistic appropriation of testimonial responsibility tells us much about the ethical agenda of each profession in the period. Yet it also implies a real sense of discursive competition; for Fitzjames Stephen, this rich interdisciplinary exchange also indicated some of the ways in which authors of realist fiction should be held to account before the court of public opinion; he was deeply critical of Charles Dickens and the language of sentimentality – and his assumptions that fiction must deal only with evidence engendered much debate in the Victorian periodical press. Whilst Leslie was to become famous as editor of the sprawling *Dictionary of National Biography*, a post he would hold for nine years, Fitzjames Stephen's most influential contributions to literary criticism was the pithy article 'The License of Modern Novelists' (1857), which called for a restriction of the ambit of the authorial imagination in the interests of ethical representation. Leslie in his *Life* of his brother tells us that Fitzjames Stephen attended various Christmas festivities at Trinity Hall, firstly as his guest, then later as Maine's: it is tempting to imagine that some of their conversations at High Table were of law and literature and contemporary conventions of narrative realism. They perhaps thereby founded the Hall tradition that was later to be so ably extended by the work of Graham Storey and his publication of Charles Dickens's letters.

Jan-Melissa Schramm practised as a lawyer in Australia before undertaking her PhD in English Literature at Pembroke College, Cambridge. She came to Trinity Hall as a Fellow in English in October 2000.

ECONOMICS: THE DISMAL SCIENCE
GEOFFREY HARCOURT

I was Trinity Hall's first teaching Fellow in economics (1964–66). (Marshall's predecessor, Henry Fawcett, was a Professorial Fellow in the nineteenth century). Evidently, every time the election of an economist as a teaching Fellow was raised at the Governing Body, Louis Clarke, a much-loved but very conservative old chap, would say, 'What's that, what's that, a Communist?'

'No, Louis, an economist.'

'Same thing, same thing.'

And so the matter stalled until he died. I was in my early thirties and in Cambridge on my first study leave from the University of Adelaide for the academic year 1963–64. To my amazement, Joan Robinson asked me to apply for a three-year University Lectureship in the Faculty of Economics and Politics, to which I was appointed the day after President Kennedy was assassinated, to start in October 1964. Sir Ivor Jennings was then Master; he had chaired the Faculty Appointments committee for the lectureship. Evidently he suggested to the Governing Body that I be 'looked over' for a teaching Fellowship. I passed (probably not with honours) the requisite knife and fork test at High Table and I understand my election was clinched by Charles Crawley, the Vice-Master, saying that, 'Even if it is a disaster, it will only be a short-run disaster.' Thus it was that in October 1964 I started what was probably the happiest and most productive period of my academic and personal life, teaching economics in the Faculty and at the Hall, and living in Newnham with Joan and our children. During my time two really outstanding economists/philosophers were undergraduates, John Broome and Peter Hammond, but I can take no credit for either since they started life at the Hall as mathematicians and only started economics right at the end of my stay.

I greatly admired Sir Ivor as a person, not least because of the following episode. I was interviewing candidates to read economics; there was a young chap I immediately liked enormously and so we chatted on after the formal interview was over. In the course of this I

evidently referred to the then Tory member for Cambridgeshire as 'a wet fish'. My high opinion of the candidate was not shared by the Senior Tutor and so he was not offered a place. One day soon after I came into lunch and saw Graham Storey and the Master in conversation. They called me over and showed me a letter from the candidate's father that either had come directly to the Master or had been forwarded by the candidate's headmaster. It said in part: 'I told my son when he came up for interview that he was not to get into any discussion on politics. Imagine my horror when he told me that he had been interviewed by a Dr Harcourt, a *socialist* and an *Australian*'(!). He then reported my comment on the member for Cambridgeshire and concluded by saying that he was not at all surprised that his son was not admitted to the Hall to read economics. I told the Master what had happened. He said, 'Right, I'll deal with this,' and he wrote a letter which must have made both the

father and the headmaster curl up with embarrassment. I was most impressed by this support for it would have been so easy for him to have thrown me to the wolves, as it were.

When I was elected a Fellow, Trinity Hall was renowned for having one of the best cellars in Cambridge, not least because of the Louis Clarke bequest. I had, however, been advised by our GP not to drink alcohol. After six months or so as an abstemious Fellow, witnessing the great wine my colleagues drank, I changed my doctor. From then on, I enjoyed even more than before, our Tuesday night Fellows' Nights. I remember that Geoffrey Kirk was the outstanding conversationalist at these gatherings and that it was wise not to leave the Combination Room before him if you wished to avoid being the subject of his rather wicked sallies. Howard Purnell, the distinguished chemist, was Steward and I noticed that the special occasions when we were allowed to sample wines from

Professor Sir Ivor Jennings,
Master 1954–65.

Michael Noakes
1964

inclined to be sceptical of the other 'culture's' evaluations of their proposed candidates. In particular, I put forward enthusiastically a most distinguished economist (who subsequently won the Nobel Prize); I found out that the Fellows had been checking up on me by asking people in my Faculty whether I was over-icing the cake. One Research Fellow in engineering went so far as to look at one of my candidate's books (not anywhere near his best) and, on finding a mathematical mistake in an appendix, suggested that he was not of the necessary calibre to be our Master. I became so upset at this lack of trust that I actually wrote a letter of resignation from my Fellowship.

Luckily, wiser heads prevailed, I was persuaded to forget it, a meeting was called at which it was said it was silly to have dissent amongst a friendly Fellowship over a Master not yet elected and from now on we would accept in good faith the judgements offered on candidates, regardless of the discipline of those who offered them. This was a most satisfactory outcome that also showed the strength and value of a collegiate Fellowship with a fund of goodwill and wise elders of the tribe.

I also enjoyed playing cricket for the College team and being John Nurser's doubles partner – I don't think he reciprocated as I usually volleyed into the net the winners his play had set up. I played squash with Roy Calne who inevitably beat me 9.1, 9.1, 9.1 – and then analysed why he lost a point in each set. But he also operated on me in 1965 and proved a considerate as well as fabulous surgeon; I did watch his knife and fork work at High Table with great interest before the op.

Geoffrey Harcourt joined Trinity Hall as its first teaching Fellow and Director of Studies in Economics from 1964–66. He endowed a prize in economics at Trinity Hall, which bears his name, and returned to Cambridge from Australia in 1982–90 as University Lecturer in Economics and Politics.

the Louis Clarke bequest increased greatly in number, so much so that one night Howard announced that we were to drink the last of Louis's splendid cellar. With exquisite timing, Howard asked us to charge our glasses and drink his (Howard's) health to celebrate his election as Professor of Chemistry in the University of Wales and his return to the land of his fathers.

Sadly, Sir Ivor Jennings died of cancer while I was a Fellow and we embarked on a Mastership election which soon threatened to make C.P. Snow's account look like kindergarten stuff. Basically, a two-culture split emerged. Some of the natural scientists were

GRAHAM STOREY: AN INTERVIEW
NIGEL CHANCELLOR

On 23rd November 2000 the Queen visited Trinity Hall as part of its 650th anniversary celebrations. Arguably, the highlight of that visit was the opening of the Graham Storey Room, created from what had been the library before the Jerwood. In the same year Graham Storey received an honorary doctorate from the University of Cambridge for services to English Literature. He had been awarded the OBE in 1997.

These accolades crowned a formidable academic career which established Graham Storey as one of the foremost authorities on the works of Gerard Manley Hopkins, the Shakespearean critiques of A.P. Rossiter and, above all, the character and works of Charles Dickens, revealed in the monumental twelve-volume edition of the author's letters, published from 1965. But, to many generations of alumni this career of outstanding scholarship lay concealed behind the self-effacing charm and candour which Graham presented without preference to staff, students and Fellows of the College over almost fifty years, and especially during his ten years as Senior Tutor, from 1958 to 1968. Graham came up to read classics in 1939, but was then called up for the Army and spent the war as an artillery officer. Like many others of his generation he returned to complete his undergraduate studies in 1946, at the age of 24. These extracts are taken from a conversation I recorded with him at the end of 2003.

NC: When you came back after the war, did you resume reading classics?

GS: No, I read a great deal during wartime and when I returned to Cambridge in 1946 I decided to read English for Part I and then changed again to law for Part II. I was lucky enough to be awarded a First in both parts of the Tripos. After I graduated, I moved to London where I studied law in the Middle Temple and was subsequently called to the Bar.

NC: How did you become a Fellow?

GS: I let it be known that I wanted to return to Cambridge to pursue an academic life teaching English, in spite of my recent training in law. I was actually offered a teaching Fellowship at both Caius and Trinity Hall but had no hesitation in accepting the offer from the Hall.

NC: What was the size of the Fellowship when you joined it in 1949?

GS: Twelve! Which sounds very few compared to the fifty or so we have today. But, there was a determination amongst the twelve that we should try and restrict the Fellowship to this size for as long as possible with everyone sharing the workload. The tutorial committee remained at four for many years.

NC: I remember you once told me that this practice extended into a debate on whether in the absence of a Master there was any reason to appoint one at all, when the job would be done quite adequately by the Fellows in rotation.

GS: Yes, that was Geoffrey Kirk's idea, but in the end we felt we had to appoint one. When Ivor Jennings replaced Henry Dean, Louis Clarke was heard to remark that Jennings was 'decidedly pink' in his politics. I remember that his election produced a particularly violent reaction from Dean. Jennings was not considered to be 'a good College man' particularly amongst members of the Aula Club and some of the older members of the Association, although Jennings was a very distinguished Master. He made and unmade various constitutions, as a constitutional lawyer and travelled widely in doing this. I was on the admissions committee at the time. Apart from law the other strong subject at the time was English which was growing gradually in popularity. I was Director of Studies for English and we had some very good students.

NC: Turning to your own writing, when did you start on your life's work on Dickens?

GS: I had been teaching for a few years when I was asked to join Humphrey House, distinguished art historian and later Professor of the Courtauld Institute, who was then collecting and editing Dickens's letter in Oxford assisted by his wife, Madeline. After Humphrey died, Madeline moved to Cambridge and we then worked together to produce twelve volumes of the letters. The critic Christopher Ricks briefly worked with us in the early days of the project but he soon resigned. My interest in Gerard Manley Hopkins also stemmed from Humphrey House, who was working on the Hopkins papers and journals. When he died, I took these over and completed the work.

NC: Who were the other influences on your academic life?

GS: Undoubtedly Lionel Elvin, who was the first teacher of English at Cambridge, and the Shakespearean critic A.P. Rossiter whose lectures were published and edited by me.

NC: When you were the Admissions Tutor, what were the characteristics that you looked out for amongst applicants for a place?

GS: In those days the Association and the Aula Club would be promoting candidates who could be described as 'good Hall men' though I wouldn't necessarily go to the wall for this rather bland characteristic. I looked for intelligent, interesting and self-motivated young men to join the College. The Association and Aula Club were strongly influenced by solicitors.

NC: After law, what were the other popular subjects to read at Trinity Hall?

GS: We gradually accepted more students to read scientific subjects but it was a slow process, and classics continued to be popular at that time. But there was a decision after the war to accept more scientists and engineers, and with that decision the whole admissions system as we now know it was created.

NC: Did public schools continue to dominate the intake of students in the College after the war?

GS: Yes, and it is notable that of the four College tutors after the war three were products of public schools. I was probably the only one who hadn't been to one of the smart establishments. It would have been unthinkable then to have increased the numbers of students from schools that were not public schools.

I became Admissions Tutor quite early on, but as Charles Crawley was the Senior tutor for a long time, I only succeeded him on his retirement in 1958. As Senior Tutor he had a considerable influence over admissions, but not for graduates, whose numbers were much smaller than they are today. There was a different system of admissions for graduates.

I knew Charles's style of working having already been a tutor for a number of years. I admired him, he gave the impression of a distinguished scholar who dealt with everyone in the College with great courtesy and good manners. The four tutors including the Senior Tutor worked very closely together. When I succeeded him in that role, he took on exclusive responsibility for graduates as their Tutor.

NC: How did Charles Crawley get on with Dean as Master?

GS: I think Charles found Dean something of a handful and difficult to get on with but he was far too polite to say so. Thankfully, his quiet diplomacy and the co-operation between the four tutors helped to maintain a good equilibrium in the College. Trinity Hall never in my experience had the sort of infighting experienced regularly in some colleges, like Christ's and Gonville and Caius. Nor was it seen as necessary to have a President. Issues between the Fellowship and the Master were dealt with by the Vice-Master.

NC: Dean was clearly a powerful figure in Trinity Hall, having been Master for 25 years, but how would you rate him by

Graham Storey at the palace of Estói on the Algarve, with a bust of Shakespeare, 1987.

comparison with other Masters of Cambridge colleges at the time?

GS: You're right! Dean would stalk into the SCR as a man who demanded the deference due to great distinction which, of course, he hadn't.

As to his standing within the University, it was said that Dean could only converse on two subjects, 'Rowing and the College silver', and that just about sums him up. He was very set in his ways, and those ways were rather narrow.

NC: Why didn't this dogmatism cause more problems than appears to have been the case?

GS: Because, on the whole, the Fellows tended to ignore Dean. If any serious problems arose they turned to Charles Crawley who handled Dean with masterful diplomacy.

In many ways, the Storey years at the Hall represent a continuation of the scholarship and quiet authority so closely associated with the Senior Tutorship of his predecessor and close friend Charles Crawley.

It was a period in which the affairs of the College were discreetly but firmly dominated by a small tutorial committee united in their dedication to high academic standards, a benign regard for the Hall's traditions of sporting prowess and active encouragement of the benefits to be had from dining and good fellowship. From this central position of influence and control, a dominating Master such as Henry Dean was simply a hazard to be circumnavigated, never the driving authority in the College. Subsequently, the frequent absences of Ivor Jennings from the College, in pursuit of constitutional change, left the governance of the College still firmly in the hands of the Senior Tutor and his colleagues.

Nigel Chancellor came up in 1990 to read history, after two earlier careers as a soldier and an industrialist. He stayed on at the Hall and took his PhD in 2002. He was appointed High Sheriff of Cambridgeshire for 1996–97, and elected a Fellow Commoner of the College in 2003. He is a teaching Fellow in history and a College mentor for postgraduates.

The Hall at War

1939 TO 1945

08

BERT STEARN

The war upset everything. I shall never forget that first Monday morning when war broke out: three quarters of the staff were away on holiday and my telephone didn't cease ringing the whole morning; undergraduates ringing up – what'd they gotta do? Parents ringing up, who'd got freshmen coming up – what'd they gotta do? Dons ringing me up, asking me, 'What'd you like me to do?'

We hadn't made any arrangements whatever for any blacking out, for any sand-bagging or anything when war broke out. I knew what was happening with all the colleges because our Master, Henry Dean, was Vice-Chancellor for the two years preceding the war, so it was all worked out that this College could have the RAF men, St Cath's would have Queen Mary College and Trinity would have two ministries, Caius would have the Royal Courts of Justice. But we hadn't done any arrangements for anything as far as the College itself was concerned. What would have happened had war broken out during term time I just shudder to think! I had my seamstress come in that morning; I said 'Go into the town and buy as much black-out material as you can buy, wherever you can get it'. We had to organise sand-bagging and the Kitchens and the Porters' Lodge, which was to be the nerve centre, and we built an air-raid shelter at the end of the bicycle shed which was down beside Q staircase, where the terrace is now… and the gardener's potting shed, his greenhouse and about half a dozen lavatories. We knew that the Air Force were coming in. There were initial training wings, chaps coming from schools into the forces and they were doing their six weeks 'drilling bashing' and they took over Q

staircase and P staircase, South Court, with the exception of F2 and F9, which I had as furniture stores, and G1 and G2. One of those we made into a first aid room, but other than that, they took over H staircase. We kept O, Q4 here and L, where Mr Crawley was, the Front Court and A and S staircases. At the end of the war, the furniture which the Air Force chaps had had wasn't fit for anything! A lot of it they'd chopped up for firewood during the war. We had chaps coming back and no furniture anywhere. I tried to beg, borrow, buy furniture all over the place to furnish the rooms for the men coming here.

When the RAF came in, being service places, they would post a sentry on the door, here, the front door, with fixed bayonets. We all had a pass with our photographs on it, our signature, everything. Mrs Dean, the Master's wife, went into the town shopping one day and forgot her pass. And the sentry refused to let Mrs Dean back in! The Master's little grandson at that period was three years old, and this sentry went marching backwards and forwards with his gun. John got a stick and about ten yards from him walked up and down like this. The gardener and I stood there and chuckled!

We had fire-fighting from the beginning of the war. The Kitchen staff and the gyps looked after the fire-fighting the mornings. Then I had a squad under me in the afternoons. We had a fire-fighting pump put down on the terrace. So with a long tube into the river, and pipes laid so that we could throw when the extension from the hydrants was put up. We could throw water not only here, through Caius, we could pour our water on that Caius building, on the Market Square. It was never used, as it happened, because we didn't

Undergraduates filling sandbags, 1939.

have that many air raids. We had a room up on A staircase for fire-watching. It was a set and the porters took it in turns to be up there fire-watching. One night, some of the men put a bicycle up on the spire over the cupola, and the porter didn't hear it. He must have been sound asleep! So they decided they'd have some undergraduates as fire-watchers. Mr Crawley and I used to make a roster up every week of the chaps to do the fire-watching during that week. Then in the vacations, we had a number of overseas students here, who were stuck here during the war and who couldn't get home.

Bert Stearn joined the Hall staff from the University Registry as Tutor's Clerk in 1929. He retired in 1970.

R.G. Gibbs (1941)

In College, a fire chief was appointed for a time and was responsible for various pieces of equipment and also the hoses, which were run out from time to time. The fire-watchers became familiar with the various roof tops, and it proved possible to communicate with their opposite number on Clare. This only involved a quite short leap from one college to another.

There were a few nightclimbers in the Hall. *The Night Climbers of Cambridge* by Whipplesmaith had been published just before the war. In fact King's chapel had been climbed but there were far easier exercises elsewhere. On one occasion the south face of Caius was scaled, and the occupant of the turret set of rooms was roused

Trinity Hall students being trained to use fire hoses, 1939.

It is perhaps difficult now to realise how very dark was the blacked-out Cambridge at night. This allowed an adventurous few to enjoy climbing unseen over College and University buildings. One of the infrequent bombs to fall on Cambridge landed one night not far from Trinity Hall. Two of us climbed out of College and, guided by the sound of diesel-powered rescue lights, made our way beyond Trinity Street and the Round Church to a scene of devastation – a totally collapsed house. We saw a badly injured man being pulled from the wreckage on a stretcher. There was nothing we could do. Later Lord Haw-Haw announced on German radio that Petty Cury had been bombed.

MICHAEL WHEAR (1941)

Fire-watchers at the Boathouse enjoyed a fire laid by Jackson the Boatman, but by morning any water on the floor was frozen. Fire-watching in College meant a deck chair in the cupola over the screens with one army blanket. On one occasion I did three nights running as punishment by Charles Crawley. I had forgotten I was on duty and went out. I climbed back in after hours via the buttress in Garret Hostel Lane but Crawley was still up.

JOHN OSBORN (1941)

My life was very much bound up with CU OTC, and training with some who joined the Army whilst I was doing a second year at the University. There were many air bases near Cambridge, and I had occasion to meet many from the US Air Force as well as the RAF. People I had met one week did not come back the following week because they had been shot down on a bombing mission and their fate unknown. There were many pacifist undergraduates, especially those reading natural sciences with me. My recollection is that genuine pacifism was treated with tolerance in discussions in College. One exception was when one summer evening those connected with the OTC, including some returning to Cambridge on leave, were having a drink outside King's College. They were accosted by a group of unkempt pacifists, who by way of retaliation were thrown

by tapping on his window. After hospitality, the climbers had no difficulty in finding their way back to College by different routes. At about this time, a bicycle appeared on the weather vane on top of the cupola. The Senior Tutor, Charles Crawley, soon found two steeplejacks to take it down and the weathervane was mercifully undamaged.

ARTHUR FERGUSON (1941)

Cambridge was the better for being almost empty of cars. On Sunday mornings, tin-hatted young cyclists in Home Guard uniform hastened to Midsummer Common where the 7th Cambs (Mobile) Battalion assembled. Made up almost entirely of undergraduates and dons, we relied on bikes for mobility, and I carried a Lewis gun across my handlebars.

Bomb damage to the Union Society after a raid in which incendiary
bombs were dropped on the Bridge Street area in 1942. The Union
library was completely destroyed and three people were killed.

golf clubs slung over the shoulder. Golf at Mildenhall involved a train journey with a cycle, as it was needed at the other end. One friend from the Hall lived at St Ives and had a grass tennis court. On more than one occasion I remember cycling a round trip of over thirty miles with ladies from Newnham and Girton for afternoon tea and tennis.

John Osborn read natural sciences between 1941 and 1943. After War Service in the Royal Signals, he joined the TA as a battery commander. He resigned his commission in 1955 and from 1959 to 1987 was Conservative MP for Sheffield's Hallam Division. He was knighted in 1983.

WILLIAM BALLANTYNE (1940)

I recall it as a pretty wild time…. We were out climbing pretty well every night. We lowered Charlie Chan, Captain of Fencing, from the room. Charlie and I with other friends were both in the CU Air Squadron and fenced for the University. I flew with him briefly in 1944 but he later killed himself in a de Havilland Mosquito. At the foot of the Senate House we met a Clare man who had just finished painting the giant crater in the Senate House grounds in Clare colours.

My next-door neighbour in College was normally clad in a scarlet silk dressing gown, breakfasted off Sobrani black Russian cigarettes and black coffee and used to entertain a beautiful married lady in his room. The rowing men regarded him as a bit of a bounder, but he was a splendid man; he did not return from the war.

We all vehemently opposed, in a lively meeting at the Guildhall, a peace faction which was preaching against the war. We dunked its leader in the fountain in the Market Square, an act of which I am still ashamed. Then in 1941 we dispersed. Some for good. I think a letter from the tutor, Revd Angus, written to me while in the RAF is worth quoting (see over).

When I returned to the Hall in January 1946 after five years as a pilot, life was very different. I was allowed to take Parts I and II of

into a tank of water. This was one of many, providing emergency supplies of water for fire-fighting purposes. I remember following a wet trail to well beyond St John's Road, where I was in digs.

We arrived at Cambridge by train and went home by train each term. Because of petrol rationing, journeys away from Cambridge by car were few and far between. A round of golf at the Gog Magog course involved nearly a ten-mile cycle ride with a bag of

Revd Charles Angus in 1937, Reader in
Greek philosophy and Vice-Master 1934–50.

REV. C. F. ANGUS.   TRINIT

Dear Ballantyne,   21 June

        There are two very differ
questions which need an answer r
urgently:
        (1) the Porters found in your
a Hore Belisha beacon, and we wa
explanation of how it came to be
It may be a serious offence, but
was a silly thing to reomve it in
first instance, it was almost sil
to leave it behind when you went s

        (2) There has arrived from the
Joint Recruiting Board the usual f
for me to fill up with regard to yo
past and future, but it is tiresome
it should have come only when you w
gone, for there are some questions
I can only answer satisfactorily if
know what you would like the answers
be. For instance "Other Activities
I should mention that you fence, but
there anything else you would like s
and did you hold any offices at scho
"Particular service" - which do yo
                                    want?
"post graduate employment" - what
                you intend or ho

                    Yours sincerely

                        C. F. Angus

the Law Tripos combined with only two terms to do it. Life since Cambridge has been colourful. That is another story, but I have never in my life worked as hard as during those two terms.

William Ballantyne read law from 1940–41 before War Service in the RAF. He returned to finish his degree in 1946. He became a solicitor specialising in oil concessions and worked in the Middle East. He transferred to the Bar in 1977 and now acts in international litigation and arbitration in the commercial law of the Middle East.

MAURICE SMELT (1943)

In 1943 the Hall was different in a million ways because the war distorted everything. The dons were few and generally oldish. The Latham buildings were billets for the RAF. There were rations – delivered weekly to one's set by Benny or Mrs Pawley: 2oz butter, some tea in a cone of tissue paper, sugar, marge. There were austere shilling lunches at the British Restaurant in (I think) Jesus Lane. There was fire watching on rota on the roof of the Library when, there being no fires to watch, one played bridge or chess. There were weekly parades for those of us destined for the Army: RSM Hosegood was the Army pistol champion, and he could shoot the pips out of cards without even looking. There might or might not be any plugs in the bathroom, because people (not me, not me!) stole them to make sure that they at least could have a bath whenever they wanted. And there was coal heaving.

Each set was entitled to a hundredweight of coal a week. The coal was piled in sacks along the wall behind C and D staircases, and we all paired off to help each other carry a sack on a stretcher up to the coal holes outside our sets. All of us, that is, except Ingvarsson. He just picked up a full sack in one hand and a minute later was back with an empty sack. Legend had it that this mighty Icelander, a sheriff in his own country, had sailed single-handed from Iceland to do postgraduate work at the Hall in law: well, he had to get from Iceland somehow, and how else during a war?

It would be fanciful to imagine Salvador Resendi, the other foreign postgraduate law student, sailing single-handed from Mexico. If you wanted to forget the war he was the man to help you, for he never (then or later) let anything get in the way of a good time. He eventually satisfied honour by dashing off a thesis for Dr Gutteridge, comparing the law of trust in England to its counterpart in Mexico, and paid me a decent sum to turn it into proper English – which I did. It was extravagantly boring (is all the law like that?) and I earned every penny.

I read history. Among my lecturers were George Kitson-Clark (ripe and rotund), Canon Smyth (quiet and malicious), and Kenneth Pickthorn (all too hypnotic). By way of amusements there were plenty of cinemas, pubs with weak beer, dances at the Dot. And then there was that nice girl from Girton, but fat chance I had at my age, and anyway Girton – too far. However we did meet for chaste tea with buttered muffins in my rooms, and we spoke of anything except what was certainly on my mind, and (who knows?) perhaps on hers too.

A freshman in 1943 was either unfit for War Service, or already enlisted and on a Short Course, or very fresh indeed. I was one of the latter, and went up when I had just turned seventeen – a boy acting the grown-up, not always convincingly, and often with terrible props. I blush to remember that my first cigarettes were ultra-posh Marcovitch to lend me sophistication, and my pipe was a Dunhill to make me old and wise. All my aspirations to *savoir faire* were sharply tested at my first Eden Feast, which was also the first time I put on a dinner jacket and found I couldn't manage the tie. I rushed down to the blacked-out courts praying for deliverance, and bumped into an angel thinly disguised as Charles Crawley. 'Don't worry,' he said, tied my tie, explained that the trick was to shut one's eyes and think of shoe laces, and we made our way into chapel. It was then I saw that his own tie was not at all *à la* Fred Astaire – and did he care, and did anyone even notice, and did it make a blind bit of difference to anything? I realised at once that his advice not to worry could be usefully extended to cover all my age-conscious anxieties, and a few other anxieties as well.

After the war Cambridge was suddenly full of old undergraduates and young dons and, thanks to that generation of the demobbed, 1948–50 might claim to be a golden age – most obviously in sport. With men in their twenties to call on, the University cricket team had no fewer than four England players, including the Hall's David Sheppard; and half the Rugby blues of the time were internationals, including the Hall's Hugh Lloyd-Davies. But the main advantage of the strange demography was that undergraduates were keen to make up for lost time, and old enough to appreciate the pleasure of doing so.

For my own part I remember a Hall that was politically active. Cyril Salmon had been a wartime President of the Union, and was followed in this period by Clem Davies, and Denzil Freeth. Michael Aylmer was another Union luminary, a wit and mimic who used to do imaginary conversations between Charles Crawley and Winston Churchill, in which Crawley quite rightly came out on top. He did a famous take-off, from the lectern in a Mill Lane lecture room, of Kitson-Clark, who suddenly appeared at the door half way through the act: Michael, being blind, was unaware. Kitson loved it, never said a word.

I also remember a Hall that was not always on its best behaviour… as when, one evening, I was trying to shift a ladder to help someone climb in and invited a shadowy figure in the dark to give me a hand.

'Do you know who I am?' he said. Alas, it was Shaun Wylie.

'Yes,' I said, 'but do you know who I am?'

'If you put the ladder back,' he said, 'I will forget you're Maurice Smelt.'

Maurice Smelt came up in 1943 to read history. After War Service he returned to graduate in 1950. He pursued a career in advertising before turning to commissioned writing. He lives in Cornwall and is Chairman of the Morrab Library in Penzance.

ALBERT SLOOTS

Up to the war, there had been a lot of regulations.... During the war of course, a lot of these things slipped a bit.... Undergraduates had to be in by a certain time and were not allowed out except with permission. All around the College wall were spikes and broken glass to prevent students from breaking out or breaking in. This was all right before the war, because the boys up before the war were mostly eighteen when they came up. They had been brought up to behave... but just after the war we had undergraduates of mature age.... Instead of being nineteen years old, they were twenty-six years old.... These were mature men who had fought a war.... Some had been in prisoner of war camps and broken out and some had invaded and so on. Thus, these bits of glass and spikes on top of the wall would be nothing to them. Nothing. They leapt over them as though they were smooth walls. So the College authorities decided 'We are not going to have this,' and they put two rolls of barbed wire all round the College wall. They took a fair number of days to put it up. The night it was finished, or I should say, the following morning, it was all piled up on that round lawn in front of the Master's Lodge. As big as a mountain. To these ex-soldiers it was just a joke. So it never went up again.

Albert Sloots joined the Hall staff as Pastry Cook in 1939. After War Service he returned to the Hall in 1946 as Kitchen Manager. He retired in 1980.

STANDLEY BUSHELL (1943)

One had sort of ghastly fears of ending up in a paddy field with a Japanese bag inside one in those days because that was a period of despair. Despair is a strong word, but the prospects for an eighteen or nineteen year old in 1943–44 were pretty grim.

When I arrived in 1943, virtually every part of the College beyond the screens towards the river was occupied by the RAF. They had some of their squads here for the early stages of their training, and one could see and hear their parades outside Q and O staircases as one went through for one's rations allocated from the Buttery.

The duties in terms of one's service days amounted to about two days a week, a fair amount of old-fashioned square-bashing, but for the naval people, lectures on and demonstrations and practicals in signalling and navigation and the sort of activities one would have expected for prospective Naval Officers.

Girton was always a long way out. It was easier to ask a lady into tea here.... There was a cake shop at the bottom of Pembroke Street, opposite the University Press, which did a special kind of cake that we used to queue up for and, if lucky, that added to the wealth of one's offerings to those one did invite to tea and, of course, one stuck into bread with sort of substitutes for butter. Peanut butter was a tremendous substitute in those days. The things we did with peanut butter and powdered egg were quite something.

Obviously, the bicycle was all essential, even more so than now. The Cruising Club kept going in a very scratchy way. In order to sail we cycled up to Waterbeach and back. Indeed, later on, although there was a railway line from Cambridge to St Ives, when the Cruising Club did have its own premises and a small fleet of boats on a somewhat narrow but pleasant location at St Ives, there were times when we cycled to St Ives and back to sail on a Sunday.

The College in 1945 then took a dramatic change as a result of the end of the war in Europe and the start of the return of the ex-service chaps, some of whom had left early in 1939, others had served or taken part here for a year or four terms before going into the services, others never even having started. They wanted to be involved in the sport and all the activities. More and more gyps were coming back, replacing the bedders who had helped to keep things going. The Kitchen staff became stronger, and, rations permitting, the food got better. Hall was restored to its former position in the diary of each day and once more there were two halls instead of one. During 1945, things got better when the RAF moved out, so that the half of the College nearest the river was brought back into use. College concerts restarted in 1946 or 47 and musical societies, history and law societies and all the other societies which are taken for granted got back into full swing.

Not only the distinction between grammar school boys and public school boys diminished. Those coming back from the services were anxious to throw off the mantle of their commissioned rank and come back as civilians. The manner in which they had been obliged to mix in the services had so changed them that the social distinctions were of little consequence to them. One always had the feeling that they were judging the fellows on their merits and not where they came from.

Standley Bushell read history between 1943 and 1947. He gained a half blue in sailing and was Captain of the Trinity Hall Hockey Club. After a brief career as a schoolmaster, he became a solicitor, qualifying in 1956. He joined local Norfolk firm, Emmett and Tacon, where he became Senior Partner.

Fabric, treasures and tradition

09

THE INHERITANCE

TRINITY HALL : THE BUILDINGS

TRISTAN REES ROBERTS (1967)

My family and I had driven up on our first visit to Cambridge to decide which college should head my application list. After walking for an hour around the colleges, we decided it had to be by the river. Almost by accident, we walked through the gate from Garret Hostel Lane into Latham Court. The court was bathed in sunlight: students lay on the grass or sat on the Memorial Terrace wall. The lawn was enclosed by the warm terracotta and gold of the surrounding buildings, overlooked benignly by the Old Library. I had not even seen Front Court at that point but my decision was instant: this was the college. At my interview with the Senior Tutor, Ernest Frankl asked why I had chosen Trinity Hall. I explained that it was simply the most beautiful college. Tears came to his eyes and our interview was concluded, successfully – as it turned out – for me. I was reminded of this first impression when I later came across Henry James's own reflections:

'If I were called upon to mention the prettiest corner of the world, I should draw a thoughtful sigh and point the way to the garden of Trinity Hall…. The trees are of prodigious size; they occupy half the garden, and are remarkable for the fact that their giant limbs strike down into the earth, take root again and emulate, as they rise, the majesty of the parent stem. The manner in which this magnificent group of horse-chestnuts sprawls about over the grass… is one of the most heart-shaking features of the garden of Trinity Hall.'

Far left: *Chestnut Walk, Fellows' Garden, 1880s.*

Left: *The old entrance gate which was relocated from South Court to Garret Hostel Lane* (below) *in 1873.*

So what is it about this particular collection of buildings that inspires such affection? Possibly it is their human quality, and their simplicity – unencumbered by the more awe-inspiring splendour that greater architects such as Gibbs or Hawksmoor might have imposed. Possibly the site has always been too small for a ruthless sweep of the architect's pencil and rubber. Even great and famous architects like Alfred Waterhouse and Sir Giles Gilbert Scott, who built on the site, have rarely designed anything more modest, whilst the façades of Essex and Burrough have a naïve quality to their classicism which is both charming and endearing.

In his history of the College, Charles Crawley regretted the scale of Salvin's entrance building of 1852 which added a storey to the earlier building destroyed by fire. I personally regret the 1952 rooftop extensions to both the 1889 Latham building, and the 1926 Bond building, but it is important to add that these overzealous attempts to house as many undergraduates as possible on this tiny site have not spoilt the College's essential quality. The challenge facing any architect trying to add to the site is to make as much use as possible of the very small spaces and to integrate the different eras.

David Loggan's plan of the College, 1688.

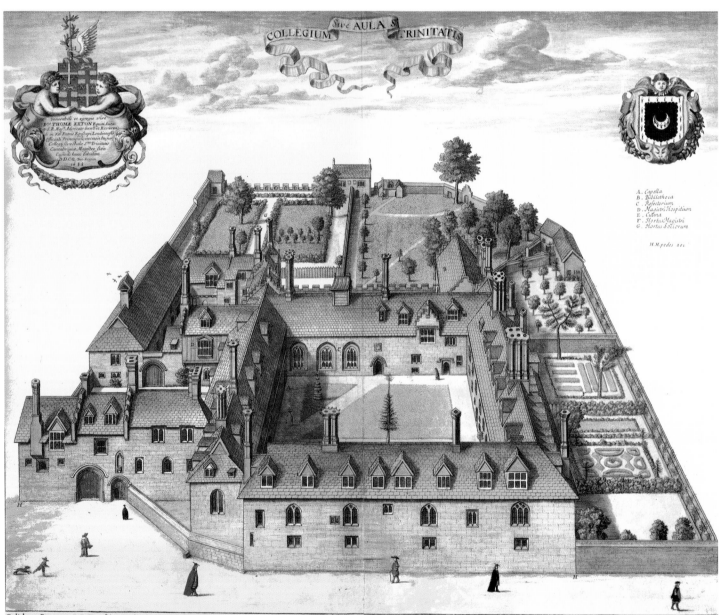

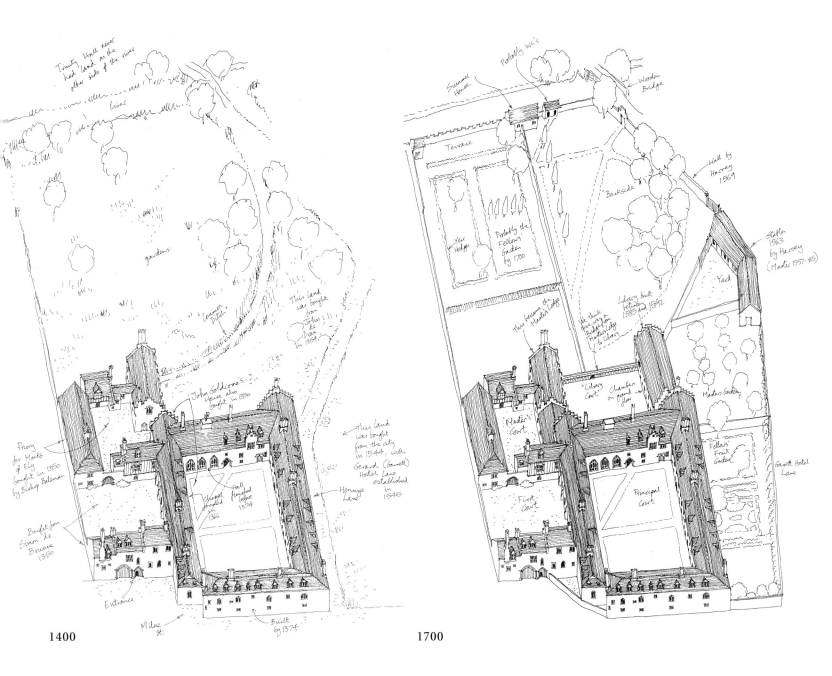

1400

1700

Having worked on the buildings of Trinity Hall for over ten years now, I have became familiar with various sources of historical information. One of the most important is Willis and Clarke's *Architectural History of the University of Cambridge and the Colleges of Cambridge and Eton*, (1886). This work describes in great detail the various transactions, remodellings and rebuilding that developed into the College of 1350. The Royal Commission survey of the City of Cambridge (1959) and Charles Crawley's history of the College (published 1976, re-issued in 1992) were also very useful to me. These books – together with the aerial views of John Hammond (1592), of

David Loggan (1688) and of Geoffrey Clarke and David Roberts in 1975 – were an excellent guide to the growth of the College.

However, I must admit – rather shamefully – to finding it extremely difficult to retain a three dimensional picture in my head of what had been built, or to visualise the form of the College at various stages of its development. Therefore, I have attempted here to 'freeze frame' various chronological views of Trinity Hall. To begin the series I have chosen the year 1400, fifty years after the College's foundation. Next – after centuries of building and consolidation – we see the College as it looked in 1700, just after Loggan's engraving.

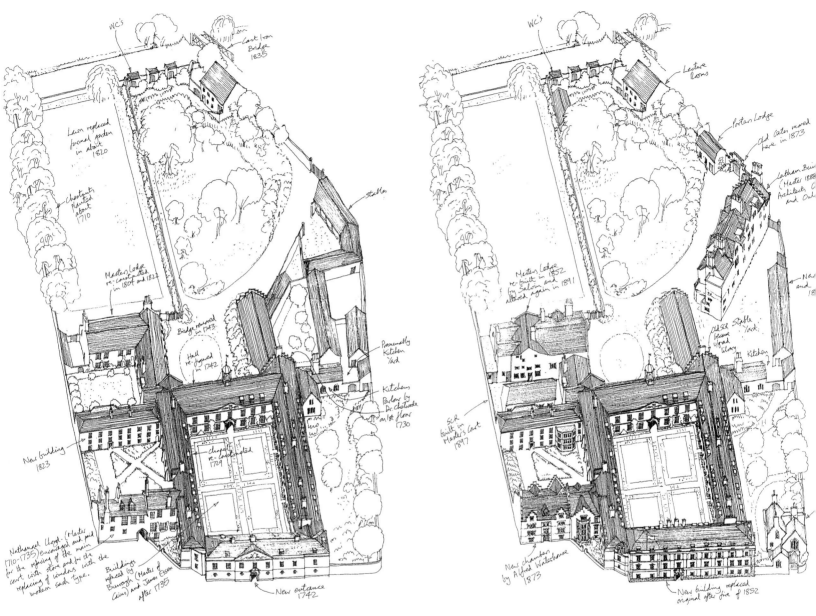

1850

1900

During the eighteenth century the Master, Nathanael Lloyd (1710-35), began a programme of modernisation which changed many interiors and façades, but did not have a great effect on the fundamental form of the College. He commissioned Burrough and Essex to reface Front Court in the classical style in 1735 and also converted the chapel. Soon after his retirement both the hall and the entrance buildings were re-figured into the classical style with the main College entrance moved to where it is now. The next major new building in the Hall was what is now H stair, which was built in 1823.

In 1852 a fierce fire razed the entrance building (staircases D and C). This began a century and a half of intensive reconstruction

where little has been untouched for long. First Salvin, famous for his work on castles, rebuilt the entrance building. He also remodelled the Master's Lodge, which began to resemble what we see now. Soon after this, Waterhouse replaced the quaint medieval gateway with what is now F and G staircases. The old gate was preserved and moved to where it is now, by O stair. The Latham Building was completed in 1890 by Grayson and Ould of Chester.

Twenty years later, the same architects built Q stair (the Thornton Building), while Sir Giles Gilbert Scott built S stair in the 1920s together with A stair, moving the JCR from Q stair to under the Old Library. In 1965 Trevor Dannatt replaced an 1897

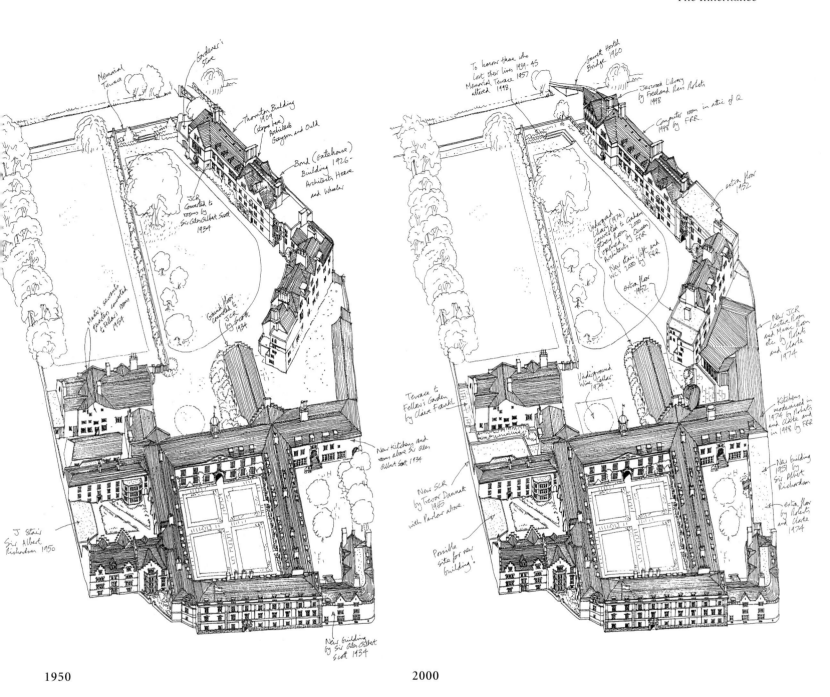

1950

2000

SCR which had filled what must have been a charming Master's Court. In 1975 Roberts and Clarke replaced all the old stables, garages and outhouses along Garret Hostel Lane with a large new car park, lecture room, music room and JCR above opening onto a first-floor courtyard, Cherry Tree Court. The JCR under the Old Library was converted into the undergraduate library. The library remained there until 1998 when we built the new library on the river, replacing a small store-room. Finally, in 2000 we converted the room under the Old Library into the Graham Storey Room and built the new cloakrooms, lift and stair building to link these rooms with the public rooms above.

The millennium seemed an appropriate point at which to end this survey of the College's architectural development. I hope the accompanying illustrations will give an idea of how the College has evolved organically – almost like a village – a factor which contributes a great deal to its charm.

Tristan Rees Roberts studied architecture at Trinity Hall from 1967–73. He set up the Freeland Rees Roberts partnership with Henry Freeland in 1981 and their work for the Hall includes the renovations to the Boathouse, the new Jerwood Library, the Graham Storey Room with the lift and stair link and the new Wychfield pavilion.

College Silver
Vasant Kumar, Silver Steward

Trinity Hall has one of the finest collections of silver in Great Britain, numbering over 260 catalogued items, pairs or sets, from the fourteenth century to the present day. The attraction of owning silver down the centuries has been – for any collector – based on several factors, including the metallic lustre and aesthetic qualities of silver, the craftsmanship of the silversmith and the intrinsic value of silver simply as bullion. Silver in Trinity Hall has come to be treasured for two main reasons: its historical associations and as the work of an eminent maker or designer. Use of silver as ceremonial plates and as attractive and durable table silver has also played an important role. There are records of sales of College silver in 1624, between 1672 and 1696 and in 1704 but these were carried out for purchase of replacements.

In England, most pre-Reformation plates vanished by 1535 and silver bullion was debased by adding more copper. What survived this period was looted during the Civil War from 1643 onwards. Given this historical context, the Hall's pre-Commonwealth possessions, numbering 22, are priceless indeed, especially when you consider they are all associated with important donors – perhaps one of the reasons why they have survived.

1

2

3

Our most prized possession, the Founder's Cup (Item 1), donated by Bishop Bateman, shortly after founding the Hall in 1350, was acquired by the Bishop as a gift from the pope at Avignon. The Cup depicts the arms of Etienne Aubert, Pope Innocent VI, under the base of the beaker and repeated on the cover.

Dr Thomas Eden's Tankard of 1635 (Item 2) was donated to Trinity Hall to commemorate his Mastership. As a result of his strong Parliamentary credentials and close acquaintance with Oliver Cromwell, the Hall escaped the purges of people and plates during the Civil War. This object is characterised by its heavy weight and by the simplicity of design both arising directly from the loss of craftsmanship in the turbulent centuries and from a

4

5

sudden influx of silver in England after the defeat of the Spanish Armada.

The real strength of our collection lies in the articles we possess made by the leading silversmiths of the late seventeenth century and the Georgian era, representing a triumphant period in English silver art, inspired by new ideas from elsewhere, notably from France and the Low Countries. One such example is the cup (Item 3), made by the master craftsman Paul de Lamarie, who came from a Huguenot family and worked as a London silversmith. He was the leading exponent of the Rococo style and has been described as the most outstanding silversmith of all times. Trinity Hall has silver made or designed by the following eminent and prolific silversmiths of the eighteenth century: Anthony Nelme – a great proponent of Restoration silver, Huguenot design and the Queen Anne style; Robert Hennell – who belonged to the second generation of a family of five generations of London silversmiths; Paul Storr – of 'Warwick Vase' fame, which was auctioned to Warwick Castle in 1985 for £1 million, and the pioneer of the English Regency style; Peter Archambo, Louis Mattayer, Pierre Platel and David Willaume – some of the early Huguenot craftsmen of great influence; and Joseph Bird, John Café, Ebenezer Coker, James Gould and Edward Wakelin – some of the most famous candlestick-makers of all times.

Trinity Hall continued its tradition of patronage of silvercraft in the twentieth century by commissioning a piece from Omar Ramsden in 1904 who led the revival of Art Nouveau by rejecting machine-produced silver. The College has acquired, either by donation or by commission, wonderful silver articles made by the great craftsmen of the twentieth century, represented by Leslie Durban, Gerald Benny, David Mellor, C.N. Lawrence and, most recently, Alex Brogden. Item 4 is a display of the jug, made by C.N. Lawrence and donated to the College by the Trinity Hall Association to mark the 650th anniversary of the founding of the Hall. A number of silver pieces in our collection have been crafted by C.N. Lawrence in contemporary idiom using hammered finish and textured surface.

The fluted silver vessel (Item 5) commissioned by the College to commemorate the millennium coinciding with the 650th year, was made by Alex Brogden, in a uniquely post-modernist style, moving beyond form reflecting function to form being a stylised abstraction of the flow and growth of natural forces. The technique is unique and relies on lost-wax casting, electroforming and carving of each individual flute on the surface.

The College is proud to share its heritage and the College silver is on display frequently throughout the year every year, for example, on General Admission day for our students and their guests; at the Annual Gathering of the THA; for benefactors; for Fellows and their guests; on High Table and for charity events organised by College members.

R. Vasant Kumar joined Trinity Hall as a Fellow in 1999 after studying material sciences in India and Canada. He is a Tutor, Director of Studies in Natural Sciences (Physical), Member of the Admissions Committee and the College Silver Steward. He is a Senior Lecturer at the Department of Material Sciences.

Lunch celebrating the 650th anniversary of the founding of the College, attended by Her Majesty Queen Elizabeth II, 2000.

WINE AND FEASTS
COLIN AUSTIN, WINE STEWARD

'All things in moderation' is a maxim I had learnt from the Ancient Greeks and for nearly quarter of a century I had been the most virtuous of teetotallers. My election to the Fellowship in 1965 opened up new horizons. How could I resist the temptation of tasting liquid gold? Louis Clarke, whose portrait and bust now adorn the SCR, had bequeathed his wine-cellar to the Fellows. This meant that on Fellowship Nights we often had a chance to sample such gems as a fine old Cognac predating the First World War or even an 1896 Croft. Here too were healthy supplies of 1934 Lafite, Latour and Mouton, a 1947 Cheval-Blanc, some 1949 Krug, and a choice 1953 Beerenauslese. Those evenings were magic and worked wonders for my research: I felt divinely inspired when I returned to my books on Greek comedy.

Alas, all good things come to an end and the fabulous bequest eventually vanished like a dream. When I became Wine Steward in 1973, a fresh start had to be made. The Bursar, Stuart Abbott, very kindly issued me with an official permit to go hunting for bargains at the prestigious auction houses. Wine in those days was meant to be drunk and enjoyed and even a modest Château d'Yquem was not beyond our means for a special occasion. Unscrupulous investors – the curse of wine lovers – had not yet hijacked the market and sent prices spiralling out of control.

My *annus mirabilis* came in 1976. To begin with, an enormous pit had been excavated between the Master's Lodge and the Old Library to accommodate a brand new cellar for my latest acquisitions from Christie's. I still keep in reserve the last two bottles of my very first purchase: a double-magnum of 1966 Gruaud-Larose (with the proud label: *Le Roi des Vins – Le Vin des Rois*) and a 1971 Niersteiner Orbel Trockenbeerenauslese. Then at the end of the same year came my turn to deliver the Eden Oration in chapel. I performed this in Latin and from memory (as stipulated in the Will) and it seems I was the first (and last) Fellow ever to do so in elegiacs (with a sprinkling of Greek). Non-classicists were given the text as they entered the chapel: they could follow at least the marginal notes written in Old English. Waxing lyrical, I sang the praises of women and wine: women, both students and Fellows, had recently been admitted for the very first time.

When John and Danielle Lyons came to the Lodge in 1984, it was a fitting gesture, I felt, to welcome them with not one but two First-Growths – 1971 Lafite and Mouton – and when they left in 2000 we toasted their retirement with a 1970 Latour.

In my job as Wine Steward I am ably assisted by Sara Rhodes, the first woman butler in Cambridge. Wine is hardly her 'cup of tea', but she never says no to a glass of 1963 Croft or Dow, especially on her birthday. Her deputy, Simon Pike, doubles up as Cellar Master. He nurtures our treasures with exemplary discretion.

Trinity Hall originally had two main feasts a year: Dr Eden's Supper in early December (in commemoration of benefactors) and the Feast of St Edward King and Martyr in mid-March (to entertain supervisors who help with the teaching). As numbers grew, the time came when personal guests could no longer attend the December celebrations. To compensate for this we upgraded the Guest Night in Easter Term to a new 'Bateman Feast'. To mark its inauguration in 1986 I composed a Latin epigram which is now printed on the menu and which I recite every year before the Dean says Grace. The couplet reads:

Conditor o Bateman nunc te celebrare quotannis
ecce iuvat dapibus: pocula Avennica erunt

'Bateman, our Founder, see how it pleases us to celebrate Thee With a Feast every year and cups of wine from Avignon.'

Below: *The arms of Norwich impaling those of the founder with an ermine bordure, underneath a bishop's mitre.*

Bottom: *The College arms (a full 'achievement' with helmet and crest).*

This is a reference to the fourteenth-century papal court in Southern France, from where Bishop Bateman had brought back the Founder's Cup. For the main course at the Feast I normally select a Chateauneuf-du-Pape or other fine wine from the Rhône valley.

Besides these three gatherings, the College has other occasions to share its nectar – notably the Midsummer Guest Night (formerly 'Ladies Night') in early July for Fellows and their wives or partners and friends. And for past alumni, a Reunion Dinner, preceded by champagne in the Fellows' Garden, is always a mystic and memorable moment. Joseph Risino, the Manciple, is then in charge of proceedings, which he conducts like a maestro, supported by his young and lively team of helpers. Wine is the Hall's hidden asset – an elixir which bewitches all.

Colin Austin, the College Wine Steward, was born in Melbourne in 1941, grew up in Australia, Scotland and France and studied classics at Cambridge (Jesus College), Oxford and West Berlin. His dream in life was to wear the maillot jaune and win the 'Tour de France'. Instead he fell back on his other love and became a University Professor, specialising in Ancient Greek comedy.

The Arms of Trinity Hall
Andrew Senior (1987)

Walking around College, or indeed anywhere in the centre of Cambridge, coats of arms are visible on nearly all of the older buildings. In general, we give little thought to these displays, thinking of them as merely anachronistic architectural decoration; but each coat of arms represents an association, and by recognising the arms we can read a little more into the history in which Cambridge buildings are steeped.

In Trinity Hall there are arms all around the College buildings, mostly the arms of the College itself, but also those of former Masters and benefactors. In the economical, French-tinged language of heraldry, the College arms are described, or

blazoned, as 'Sable, a crescent within a bordure Ermine'. Ermine represents the fur – white with black tail spots, while sable is the colour black, considered to be a colour not a fur in heraldry. Repetition is avoided in blazons, so ermine applies to both the crescent and bordure. Sometimes, as below, the arms are displayed in a full 'achievement' – with a helmet, crest and mantling. The mantling is a cloth backdrop, usually in the principal colours

of the arms. The crest of Trinity Hall is 'On a wreath of the [principal] colours, a lion sejant [sitting] Gules [red], holding in its right paw a book Sable leaved and clasped Or. [Gold]'

The College arms are derived from those of the founder, Bishop Bateman of Norwich, which are 'Sable a crescent Ermine within a bordure engrailed Argent', argent being the metal silver, often depicted as white. Engrailed describes the scalloping of the border's edges. Since the arms are very similar to those of the College, they are often confused, as they have been above B staircase in Front Court. The founder's arms are there shown on the same shield as ('impaling') the arms of his office – the Bishopric of Norwich. Currently the border is painted with ermine spots that are not in the original carving, creating a hybrid between the arms of the founder and the College.

The arms of Bishop Bateman were derived from those of his father and elder brother, which Warren's book about Trinity Hall gives as 'Sable a coat sylver and Sables thre cressants ermyn with a Scochion engrailed,' but beyond that, the origin of the arms is unknown.

Left: *South Court.*
Below: *The Fellows' Garden and entrance.*

sometime after 1933 leaving a long border as you see it today. The plants were all lifted during the winter 2003/4 and replanting has been carried out to improve the range and variety. The early colour and interest is provided by the paeonies, lysimachia, aconitum and iris with a backdrop of climbing roses on the wall of the library. Later on in the season rudbeckias, fuschias, dahlias, cannas, hollyhocks and echinaceas are some of the plants which provide a colourful display.

Fellows' Garden: The main border contains a mixture of herbaceous plants, shrub roses and bulbs with a selection of shrubs and climbers trained on the wall. The larger horse-chestnut trees near the boundary with Clare provide shade in the summer and are underplanted with a display of spring bulbs. The over-mature horse-chestnut trees are nearing the end of their 'useful' life, necessitating the need for some redesigning and replanting of this area in order to maintain the process of a growing, developing garden.

Wychfield: The plan (see opposite) shows the layout of the garden areas around and within the new development. Between the two main 'strips' of buildings there will be a 'green lane' leading through to the tree belt, of lawn with shrub borders near the buildings planted in an informal way with the ground-cover planting punctuated by specimen plants. The Round Court will comprise of a circular lawn

THE GARDENS
ANDREW MYSON, HEAD GARDENER

South Court: This courtyard garden was redesigned and planted in 1994 to give a series of planting beds defined by low box hedging. The beds are planted with a mixture of shrubs, herbaceous and bulbs. The sheltered nature of this court provides the opportunity to grow wall shrubs, which require some protection from the cold.

Library Border: This area is dominated by the large magnolia grandiflora with its glossy leaves and sweetly scented flowers. The border is full of traditional herbaceous plants, which provide a colourful display throughout the summer months. Originally the border was split into two, divided by the entrance to a ground floor doorway facing the Master's Lodge. This was done away with

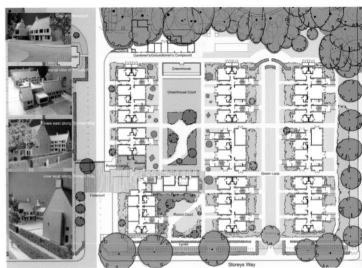

Left: *Wychfield's gardens today.*

Below: *Plans for new development at Wychfield, prepared by RH Partnership.*

with stepping stone paths with a 'rich' and 'full' planting of shrubs and herbaceous plants.

The Greenhouse Court will comprise of a glasshouse at one end, with the perimeter of the court planted with a complex selection of plants and trees to provide a secluded area within the court. Two paths will be created to link the new area with the existing gardens at Wychfield and further planting and development along their routes will provide a pleasing transition from one area to the next.

Andrew Myson, Head Gardener, started his horticultural career 25 years ago at Cambridge University Botanic Garden. He has worked in several private gardens, set up and ran a garden design and construction business. He then worked as Senior Gardener for the National Trust at Cliveden for nine years before becoming Head Gardener at Trinity Hall in April 2000.

WYCHFIELD DEVELOPMENT
CHRISTOPHER PADFIELD, GRADUATE TUTOR

The plans above show a major development at Wychfield, which should be ready for occupation in October 2006. Lying between the belt of mature trees to the south of our own beautiful Wychfield gardens, and Storeys Way with its famous arts and crafts houses by Baillie-Scott, quality of design has been paramount. Our architects – Cambridge-based RH Partnership – have designed modern buildings that fit naturally into a garden landscape, and that reflect the qualities of the domestic architecture opposite. One of their

inspirations was to create a 'green lane' that provided both a quiet pedestrian-only street between the terraces of houses, and transparency through to the trees, for those passing on the street. Inside the houses, care has been taken to ensure that the detail of the staircases and the ample common areas promote a sense of quality, community and inclusiveness – there is, for example, generous provision for disabled students and visitors, fully integrated within the hub-space of the houses.

For the College, this development provides solutions to many pent-up difficulties. Our accommodation on Central Site requires updating, with additional kitchens and bathrooms; the new development allows us to move perhaps forty undergraduates to Wychfield, thereby freeing rooms on the Central Site for first-year undergraduates, and providing additional teaching rooms. It will allow us to restore the number of graduate students we take, which has recently had to be cut due to the scarcity of accommodation, and to house a greater proportion of them. Importantly, it will also allow us to convert the splendid Wychfield House itself to provide desperately needed flats for young Fellows. This has become a determinant in the recruitment of new blood to the Fellowship, as young academics find it increasingly unfeasible to rent accommodation within reach of the city centre. Finally, together with the pavilion that is already under construction, the development consolidates and improves our provision for sports (fieldsports, tennis, squash, gym), and for the gardeners and groundsmen who care for this beautiful space.

Conformity and rebellion

10

Geoffrey Howe (1948)

At the risk of sounding disloyal, I have to confess that when, in October 1948, this twenty-one year old 'came back' from the Army (Royal Signals, mainly as a lieutenant in Kenya and Uganda), it was to Cambridge (no more and no less) that I was going up. Trinity Hall was my specific destination – but only because it was the Oxbridge college at which I had been lucky enough to secure a (minor) scholarship. I knew little about the place, except that my Winchester housemaster had, with obvious relief, proclaimed it 'the right college for you, at the right University.'

In the three years of discovery that were to follow, I was able to learn just how right he was. For the Hall did indeed turn out to provide exactly the right opportunity for me to take legal studies seriously – but not obsessively. And for so much more besides. One in three of the undergraduates were reading law. That numerical predominance seemed somehow to grant us lawyers an *entrée* into almost every clique in the College – and thus, indirectly at least, in the University as well.

So we found ourselves 'networking', long before the word had been invented. And the Hall itself, almost exactly three hundred strong, was just about the ideal size, as Hall men very quickly discovered – not the remotest suggestion of women in those days – for the extensive cross-fertilisation of camaraderie.

Not unusually, I imagine, my two closest friendships were with the two lawyers, with whom I successively shared rooms, Gordon Adam (L3) and Dick Stone (E5). In later life I acted as best man for each of them – and Dick for me. Like other Hall lawyers, we relished the intimacy of supervision by that remarkable trio – J.W.C. Turner, Trevor Thomas and T. Ellis Lewis (and not least, the generosity of Tel's hospitality). So too, we enjoyed the gently persuasive wisdom of Micky Dias – baffled though we were by the strange oversight that denied him a Fellowship of the Hall.

The Welshness of the Hall's legal establishment was (unsurprisingly) reflected in the rugger club. Despite my birth in a house which overlooked the Aberavon Rugby ground, this was by no means a forte of mine. No more was any other form of athleticism. A brief and undistinguished first year in the Hall's Fourth Boat quickly gave way to politics. In those declining years of the Attlee government, the Conservative Association had more than 1,000 members – about one fifth of the undergraduate population. The other parties were not far behind, with the Hall well represented across the board.

Not least, perhaps, because the Hall was a small college, it had a great sense of mutual solidarity. Following the example set by the Master, Daddy Dean, and the Senior Tutor, Charles Crawley, on his sit-up-and-beg-bicycle, the lawyers and the politicians supported the oarsmen on the towpath; and the rowers and the rugger club provided a formidable block vote when the politicians needed it. Dick Stone and I were only two of the five Hall men who chaired the University Tories in my time (Denzil Freeth, Peter Jenkin-Jones and Tony Buck were the other three); Greville Janner and Edward Greenfield were similarly propelled into the chair of the Labour Club. And we were almost equally supportive of each other in

Union elections and debates. (Ted Greenfield also did his fluent best to give us encouraging coverage in *Varsity* and the *Cambridge Review*.)

My father found it hard to forgive my failure to get a First in my final year – though for me it was excused by the amazing diversity of my Cambridge life. Quite a lot of it I chronicled in a weekly column I produced for Oxford's *Isis* magazine – most notably, I recall, Julian Slade's striking May Week productions, *The Lady May* and *Bang goes the Meringue*. For all of us, his *Salad Days* became a life-long reminder of the times on which 'we said we'd never look back'.

Back in the Hall itself, social life was lively enough despite the theoretical constraints: College gate was closed at 10 o'clock, your time of entry being recorded after that time.

Arrival after midnight (without a late pass) meant that you were gated. Happily for most of my last year, however, it was possible to 'climb in' because the glass-topped Garret Hostel Lane wall had been thoughtfully provided with builder's scaffolding on each side. Despite that careless (or was it thoughtful?) gesture, however, I did manage to find myself once gated for one week – most inconveniently the week in which I was due to preside, as Chairman, over the Conservative 'Ball of the Year' (with Ivy Benson and her All-Girls Band *and* Humphrey Lyttelton – on separate floors – at the Dorothy Restaurant). The merciful Charles Crawley was prevailed upon to suspend my sentence for the one night.

Later that year, in my last week at the Hall, I failed – inadvertently but miserably – to repay that kindness. The Hall Law Society (of which I was Chairman) held its end-of-year AGM – and someone proposed an 'emergency' resolution. This was prompted by news (just in) of a sharp reduction in the proportion of would-be lawyers amongst those being admitted to the Hall in October 1951. Passed, as it was on the nod, I was thereby required to write to the Master, no less, a letter of protest, deploring this affront to the Hall's long-standing tradition as a law college. I duly did so – and months later, at the first meeting of the Governing Body in the new academic year, Professor Dean produced the letter and called on Charles Crawley, as Senior Tutor responsible for admission policy, to explain this lapse. The snag was that no-one – least of all myself – had thought to advise the Senior Tutor that any such letter was on its way. I don't think I was ever forgiven for what Crawley regarded as a personal affront. I feel guilty even to this day – and never forgot the lesson.

If only I had thought of taking advice on the point from any one of the special champions of the Church Militant, who sought to look after our moral welfare at the Hall. The first I remember was our Baptist Fellow, the Revd C.F. Angus, who had conducted my (very gentle) *viva* during my scholarship exam. I consulted him only once, just before I went off to debate at Aberystwyth University the motion that 'This House deplores the Churches' attitude towards divorce'. What exactly, I asked him, was the attitude of the Baptist church to this important question? After a long pause, he replied: 'You know, I don't believe we've got an attitude'.

I should, no doubt, have done better with Tony Tremlett, whose room (like Angus's) was on E staircase, below Dick Stone and myself (Tony frequently complained of the clatter of high heels on the stone stairs, never, we felt, entirely convinced by our testimony about the frequency of Conservative Committee meetings in our set). It was said that he was reluctant to accept a Fellowship, since that would have required him to report offences confessed to him by undergraduate confidants. We remained in touch for some years, during his subsequent service at St Stephen's, Rochester Row.

After graduating in law, Geoffrey Howe was called to the Bar by the Middle Temple in 1952. He was elected a Conservative MP in 1964 and has held many parliamentary and government posts, including Solicitor General, Chancellor of the Exchequer, Secretary of State for Foreign and Commonwealth Affairs, Leader of the House and Deputy Prime Minister. He was created a life peer in 1992. He became an Honorary Fellow in 1992.

GREVILLE JANNER (1949)

By my eighteenth birthday, I was an Army conscript. Six months later, I was the youngest War Crimes Investigator in the British Army of the Rhine, working voluntarily at weekends in the Bergen Belsen Displaced Persons Camp. At twenty, I emerged from a uniform into non-uniform… from the forces to the unenforced… from post-war imposed discipline into the choice of freedom of Cambridge in general and Trinity Hall in particular. It was bliss. I shared a room with Edward Greenfield, an Army friend who later became a distinguished music critic. The double room was at the top of a staircase, looking down on the lawn and across to the Cam. Our military experience prepared us for the primitive arrangements. The lavatories were in sheds by the river. The College provided us with chamber pots. One morning, I found our gyp emptying the contents into the washbasin. Yuk!

Still, Ted and I led a contented Box and Cox existence. For him, it was early to bed and early to rise. For me, it was late night chats, discussions and gallons of coffee and wine, and very late mornings.

For a small College, the Hall was remarkable and unique for its energetic participation in University activities. For many, it was rowing and rugby. For me, politics and athletics.

I found that skipping morning lectures was inevitable and that many of the lecturers had been good enough to publish their works, so that I could read their wisdom during the day. And I was blessed with the help and friendship of a great Hall don, Dr T. Ellis Lewis – known to us all as Tel. He came from a pit village and had lost fingers on one hand in an accident. When I approached my Finals, having spent most of my years on extra curricular joys, I was petrified. 'What am I going to do?' I asked him. 'How can I become a barrister if I get a Provisional?'

'Don't worry, Boyo,' he said to me. 'I can't help you with the tort paper, because I set it. But let's do some question-spotting on the others shall we?'

We did. And I emerged with a 2ii. Enough in those days to get me into Bar school and, even better, as a route into another energetic but unacademic year at Harvard Law School.

Hall regrets? No women – at least, not undergraduates. Otherwise, and especially for ex-servicemen like me, post-war Trinity Hall was a blessing – hugely enjoyed at the time and appreciated for ever after.

After National Service, which included time served as a War Crimes Investigator, Greville Janner came to Trinity Hall to read law. He then took up a Fulbright Scholarship to Harvard before joining the Middle Temple in 1955. In 1970 he was elected a Labour MP and created a life peer in 1997. He has published many books and is an expert on Jewish affairs. He is also a member of the Magic Circle.

LOUIS CLARKE AND THE POST-WAR FELLOWSHIP
GRAHAM STOREY

Louis Clarke, Director of the Fitzwilliam Museum, was one of the best-known Cambridge eccentrics of his day: very rich (and very generous to the College), an Edwardian Tory, with a fund of anecdotes told in an almost incomprehensible eighteenth-century voice, very successful in making his friends give pictures or money to the Fitzwilliam, wearing generally a cloak green with age; he lived in Leckhampton House on Grange Road, with six acres of garden; had his own taxi from Marshall's for coming to the College; but towards the end of his life bought what he called 'a motor', so that Hawkes, his butler (who doubled with being a gyp), could drive him to the bottom of his garden.

Governing Body meetings took place every other Tuesday of Full Term; they generally began at about 9pm, after the Tuesday night dinner, and could easily go on until midnight. I remember few agenda papers; but they were hardly necessary, as the Master spent the entire day before the meeting calling on each Fellow to make sure he would vote on any important issue the way the Master wished. Such calls, of course, played havoc with supervisions. The

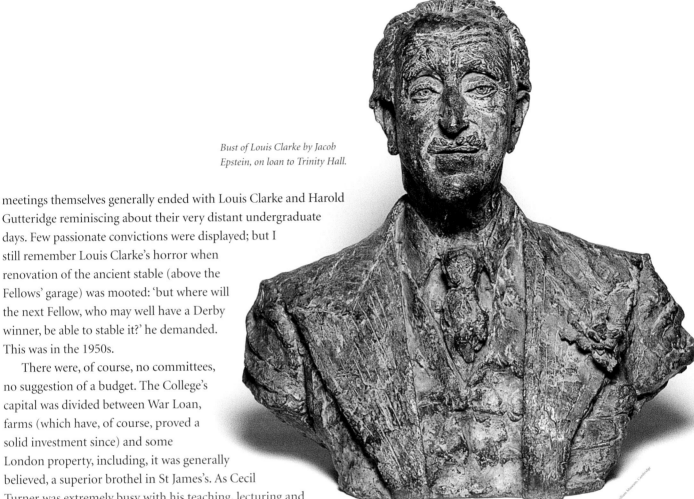

Bust of Louis Clarke by Jacob Epstein, on loan to Trinity Hall.

meetings themselves generally ended with Louis Clarke and Harold Gutteridge reminiscing about their very distant undergraduate days. Few passionate convictions were displayed; but I still remember Louis Clarke's horror when renovation of the ancient stable (above the Fellows' garage) was mooted: 'but where will the next Fellow, who may well have a Derby winner, be able to stable it?' he demanded. This was in the 1950s.

There were, of course, no committees, no suggestion of a budget. The College's capital was divided between War Loan, farms (which have, of course, proved a solid investment since) and some London property, including, it was generally believed, a superior brothel in St James's. As Cecil Turner was extremely busy with his teaching, lecturing and writing (his editions of Kenny's *Criminal Law* were famous), a good deal of the financial running of the College was left to the formidable Chief Clerk, Mr Dickinson, who inspired Fellows and undergraduates alike with terror. A running battle went on for years between him and the considerably more humane – if less tidy – Tutors' Clerk, Bert Stearn.

Once or twice I was requested to accompany the Master to the University swimming sheds on the river, where Dean set out at full speed for Grantchester, while I paddled astern, I hoped invisible, and had to wait – getting extremely cold – for his return. 'Ah!' he said on one occasion, 'as my old housemaster used to say, you can't make a boy's character in the summer.' With the background of those two formidable Trinity Hall muscular Christians, Frederick Denison Maurice and F.J. Furnivall (both highly distinguished in other ways too), that, I think, went to the heart of Dean's ethic.

From a memoir by Graham Storey in the College archive. (See also Nigel Chancellor's interview with Graham Storey, chapter 7).

BOB ELY (1950)

At cricket, I was a poor performer but an avid enthusiast. So I took out Life Membership of the CUCC for £5. This allowed me to sit on the roof of the pavilion at Fenner's to watch matches. The Hall's Bursar, J.W.C. Turner, who was Treasurer of the CUCC, would also sit up on the roof and reminisce. He had played for Worcestershire in his day and knew well Frank Chester who was then as famous as an umpire as David Shepherd is today and a similar character.

Clearly life was too restricted and by unusual means I was able to get a copy of a key to the Side Gate. As I had the room beside the Main Gate, which is still covered in wisteria, I would leave the key on the outer window sill for anyone whom I felt had a deserving cause! Some time after I went down a less-than-deserving cause carelessly unlocked the gate as a porter stood near. The idyll was at an end!

I stayed up for the Long Vac term which was always more relaxed with many social events. One of these was the bowls match, undergraduates versus the College servants. We thought this was an old man's game – after the war their average age was high – but it might be fun. After all, we were fit and quite sporty. We were very soundly trounced but worse was to come. Next day the College servants were trotting round as usual and laughing at us. We were stiff as boards. Bowls uses muscles that other sports do not!

Just after the war there was not a vast amount of entertainment and so a bridge four was a pleasant way of spending an evening. One such took place in Frank Kirk-Cohen's rooms on our staircase. Apart from Frank there was the late David Dickinson, my room mate, Ramon Subba Row and Alan Blandford, all of whom were pretty distinguished in their later careers. My own role was as observer, coffee-maker and drinks pourer as my bridge was a bit like my cricket – I was better at watching than playing. The group met once or twice a week for 2–3 hours after dinner. On the last night of our second year, Alan and Frank's last, they played all night till breakfast – I just managed to keep awake.

From the JCR Suggestion Book circa 1951:
(We had had bashed beans, butter beans, broad beans, dried beans by the truck-load.)
Suggestion: 'That we are far too full of beans!'
Reply: 'Some form of appeasement will be tried.'

Overheard in Hall:
'Let's look at the carte to see what they have done to the horse.'
And after a somewhat doubtful and strong-smelling dish:
'Bugged hare be juggered'.

HARRY GUEST (1951)

Varsity, Granta, the *Silver Crescent* and *delta* accepted pieces of mine and then Michael Bakewell, Ronald Hayman, Karl Miller and I founded *Chequer* – parodied wittily after its appearance by Mark Boxer in *Granta.*

Poets I associated with included Thom Gunn (last met in cowboy boots outside Charing Cross Station), Philip Hobsbaum and Peter Redgrove – we would read poems into his massive tape-recorder, the first I'd seen. We were privileged to meet George Barker, Vernon Watkins and Angus Wilson, all of whom hobnobbed with no trace of condescension. Nicholas Tomalin gave a tea party for E.M. Forster who stretched arthritic hands to the gas fire and chuckled naughtily about the titles Henry Green gave his novels.

For the Preston Society, I played the sinister count in *The Duke in Darkness* and the bishop in the first English production of Cocteau's *Bacchus*, directed by Ronald Hayman. I translated and produced Cocteau's *Antigone* for the Mummers and sent a roneoed copy to the poet, who responded to this callow undergraduate with characteristic charm: '*Dis-moi ce que le public de Cambridge a pensé de notre travail.*'

In retrospect, I admit to working less hard than I should have but am endlessly grateful for those three rich years at the Hall, for enlightening supervisions with Dr Bolger, Ronald Gray, Ray Kelly, Miss Mitchell and Douglas Parmée and for warm friendships which have lasted for more than half a century.

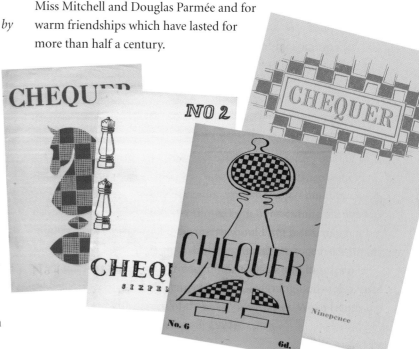

From Harry Guest's poem **Autobiography**:

And then I talked three years away
wandering round Cambridge, where for
the last time all the cares I had
were of my own making; where I
learned something of Montaigne and Kleist,
heard Bartók, Jelly Roll, Bechet,
and marvelled at Pauls Klee and Nash.

Arguing from ignorance with
friends about Buñuel; falling
very drunk into the snow; on
the narrow college bed making
such satisfactory love with him
or her as the late suns dropped to
silence behind invisible
clock-towers; Parmée on Rimbaud;
tea in punts; Peter Hall's Saint's Day;
sandwiches at The Mill for lunch;
the viscous smell of the Cam. And
the chestnut-spikes in front of King's
alone announcing time.

Published in *Arrangements*, (Anvil Press, 1968)

NORMAN SANDERS (1953)

In 1954 I shared rooms with Philip Mickman, sadly no longer with us, who was then the youngest person to have swum the Channel. He swam it at the age of seventeen from France to England in a shade under twenty-four hours, and again in the other direction the following year in somewhat less time. He came up in 1952 at a time when Dr Dean was Master. Dr Dean was an avid swimmer, but by then was well over seventy years of age and needed supervision. In the absence of any volunteers, Philip's task upon arrival at the College was to accompany the Master in the Cam at 7am each day. He took this as an order. He told me that the Cam was much colder than the English Channel, but he carried out his duty with exemplary regularity until medical instructions put a stop to them.

MICHAEL LUCAS (1954)

I do not remember any 'social apartheid' existing in Hall based on that old public school versus grammar school chestnut. Social cliques seemed to form around one's financial status so one tended to mix with people with a similar budget and range of interests.

I particularly remember a 'skeleton in the cupboard' when Micky Baynes, one of the stalwarts of the Boat Club, was rusticated after an acrimonious run-in with our beloved Daddy Dean. This unfortunate situation had something to do with keeping a car in Cambridge – which one was not supposed to do. I remember Micky coming into hall in something of a rage, walking across the tables – as we normally had to do in those days – and occupying one of the inner benches for dinner. Ironically, a few days before the Lent Races of 1956, he smashed his TR2 sports into a tree on the Cambridge to London road and was killed instantaneously.

The whole psychological environment for me, at least during these three years, was somewhat monastic, even austere: I had spent two years doing National Service in the Army and having to report into College by a certain time at night was to me rather infantile. So most evenings after a party we had to climb in. This was OK and not very difficult, until one evening, Mark Tully (one of our group) slipped and fell going over some spiked railings. He was left crucified upside down like St Peter and cackling hilariously, with a spike through his calf. I think he was then rescued by Bob, one of the porters, who arranged to send him to Addenbrookes Hospital after sobering up fast.

Right: *Asparagus Ball posters.*

Below: *Austin 7 being hoisted onto the roof of the 'Bursar's Folly', South Court 1956.*

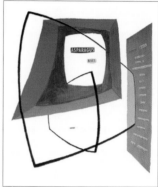

REVD J. F PETTY (1956)

I wrote many songs for cabaret at the Asparagus Balls. In this the actual nightmare words in Gilbert and Sullivan's *Iolanthe* were adapted to the Cambridge and Trinity Hall genre. The Dean was Bob Runcie and the Chaplain Tony Tremlett.

The Nightmare Song

It started and finished with Gilbert's words, but the actual nightmare itself suffered a take-over bid from an impertinent undergraduate.

When you're lying awake, with a dismal headache…
… you'd very much better be waking.

For you dream you are crossing a duck pond and tossing
About in a punt from The Mill,
And down in the water, you see the Head Porter,
Who's looking most frightfully ill.
So you get him a doctor, who's really a proctor

And fines you one pound, six and eight,
For dining in Hall wearing no clothes at all
On top of being five minutes late.
But this you won't pay, so you bid him 'Good day'
And you run down the stairs at a pace
With the intimate knowledge that half of the College
Has seen you and joined in the chase.
You're pursued by your tutor, perched on a green scooter
And only just miss being caught;
It's really quite frisky; he runs it on whisky,
Now petrol is ten pounds a quart.
In frightful despair, you leap in the air
And land on top of a 'bus;
You're surrounded again by rather smooth men,
Munching buttered green sticks of asparagus.

And into this scene emerges the Dean
In a shirt which he got from Bahamas;
It has one or two patches and nastily clashes
With the Chaplain's smooth pink silk pyjamas.
Along comes the Bursar with slide rule and curser
Attempting to balance accounts.
He's a bad engineer and the bills you still fear
Will be made out for quite wrong amounts;

UNIVERSITY LODGING HOUSE ACCOUNT

Particulars of permitted charges are printed on the back of
Lodging House Licences

HOUSE *97. Mawson Road*

Lent Term, 19 *55*

MR *J. Russell*

COLLEGE *Trinity Hall*

DUE TO *Mrs F. Smith*

	£	s.	d.
1. *Assessed rent of rooms	*18*	*15*	*—*
2. Hire of plate, glass, crockery			
3. Hire of linen *Bread*		*4*	*2*
4. Hire of piano *Extras*		*5*	*7½*
5. Hot baths			
6. Cooking lodger's own food			
7. Meals supplied *Milk*		*16*	*11*
8. Coals and wood			
Electric current (a) for lighting			
(b) for other purposes *Radio*	*17*	*0*	
eplacement of electric globes, etc.		*5*	
s for lighting			
for fires (according to meter)	*3*	*2*	*5*
ing boots and shoes			
& bicycle			
£	*24*	*6*	*1½*

March 11 1955

With Thanks

The Lodger has a right to occupy the rooms for ten weeks during Term time for the assessed rent.

*Mr J.C. Russell has ...
tutorial have to hold a
party in his lodgings (7 Nov
Term) for about 25 pe...
on Nov 5 for 7.45 —*

Shaun Wylie

Oct 29, 1954

University of Cambridge

PROCTOR'S NOTICE

... requests Mr *J.C. Russell*

... College to call on him at *1.45 p.m*

... Hall

... 16th November (on finding flat on Thursday 18th November)

Motor Control Office
Pumpole
(Nr Magdalen Bridge)

College

15.11.54

*Lodging account, tutorial letter and more
bad behaviour from John Russell, 1956.*

STEPHEN PÁLFFY (1957)

*Stephen Pálffy spent almost a year in Hungarian
prisons, in fear of execution at the hands of the
Communists after his aristocratic background and
foreign connections led to his arrest for spying whilst
serving in the Air Force. He was released by insurgents
in the winter of 1956 and fled on foot, with his mother,
to Vienna and then to London.*

Not long after – all of this happened in the space of a fortnight, between the 10th of December and Christmas – I received a letter inviting me to call on the Senior Tutor of Trinity Hall, Cambridge, the late Charles Crawley. On the appointed day I duly arrived in his rooms and, after brief initial pleasantries, he asked me how I was related to '*the* General Pálffy'. Lost as to whom he might mean, I replied that over the centuries there had been many soldiers in the family, and quite a few had made it to General, but I did not have a clue beyond this. Only after he had shown me a passage in a book taken from his shelves did I realise that he meant my great-grandfather Maurice (who had played a prominent, if not entirely laudable, role in Hungary in the 1850s).

That settled, we talked some more about history in general and family connections, until Charles Crawley told me that just then he could not find my papers, but had arranged with his wife that I was to join them for lunch. So we walked across the Backs to Madingley Road, Mrs Crawley received me kindly, and I enjoyed a relaxed family lunch with them (the Christmas Vacation having begun, all the young Crawleys, roughly my age, were at home too). Music, and its condition in Hungary was, as I recall, a topic of the conversation.

After coffee had been served Charles Crawley looked at his watch and, rising, said that he had to leave if he was not to be late for a College meeting. 'That's it!' I thought, 'But at least I've had a

*But as someone was saying, you still must be playing
This childish game 'hide and seek',
And, though you are puffed, you're really quite chuffed,
As the bulldog's turned into a peke.
And though it's still snowing, five days you've been rowing,
And have now bumped at least fifty-seven;
But it's really not fair, 'cos they're more than eight there;
When you count them you find they're eleven.
The right number for cricket, you dance down the wicket
In style that's really past caring;
You need just one run to achieve your first ton
When you wake with a manner despairing.*

*You're a regular wreck with a crick in your neck...
... and the night has been long ditto, ditto my song
and thank goodness they're both of them over!*

Malcolm Innes playing the bagpipes, flanked by Jim Taylor and Giles Dereham, 1960. From the album of Robert Hunt-Grubbe.

long before a compulsory retiring age was introduced), was, as was his wont, apparently half-dozing near the end of the table. However, when they got to my name he perked up, although generally given to being stone-deaf, and spoke: 'Pálffy? Pálffy, did you say? Went shooting with a Pálffy once – 1910, was it? Or 1911? Can't remember. Excellent shot, though. Must have this one!' So, rather than stick a pin in the list of candidates, the Fellows agreed to my admission, subject to a satisfactory interview with the Senior Tutor.

TONY PALMER (1960)

I had hoped it would be the best of times; in many ways it turned out to be the worst of times. A little lad from Lowestoft Grammar school, I had no idea for instance about 'eating in hall' – as far as I recall I had never eaten with anyone except my god-parents, who had brought me up. I didn't possess a tie, and was too poor to own a suit. I had never even shared a room with anyone except my younger brother. The year I 'came up' (the social implications of that still thunder across the years), the intake was about a hundred, of which no more than a handful were from other than a public school. Thus, the entire language and manners and rules which I was expected to understand and conform to were mysterious, even alien. I was made to feel isolated, unwanted and definitely unwashed. And when the student in the next room to me committed suicide towards the end of my first term, I was not surprised. The image of his coffin being taken down the staircase haunts me to this very day. It is a scene which has appeared in one form or another in many of my films.

Far from being helped, it seemed to me then that the College authorities ignored those who simply did not fit in, especially when it was discovered that I had no interest in rowing or rugger. By chance, I met a fellow grammar school lad (Trevor Nunn, Downing) who galvanised a hitherto little-realised interest in the theatre. Eventually I rose, by default I still believe, to become President of the Marlowe Society in which I had some local success and which, in its turn, persuaded me that the BBC held the key to

pleasant lunch.' However, to my surprise he added that, since Full Term started on the 14th of January I had best come up on the 12th, to stay with them until further arrangements had been made. And thus did I come to be *in statu pupillari* at Trinity Hall, Cambridge, by the Lent Term of 1957 – as far as I then knew.

For – as I learnt a few years later from Bob Runcie, at the time Dean of the College and subsequently Archbishop of Canterbury – the foregoing had had a prelude a week or so earlier. The Fellows had met to pick a Hungarian refugee to admit and support (all colleges were at the time taking in and supporting one or two Hungarian refugees). As the names of candidates were being read out Louis Clarke, one of the oldest Fellows of the College (elected my future. This is not a place I would recommend even to my worst enemy now, but at the time, the mid-1960s, it seemed a place of opportunity. However, it took three attempts to secure an interview at the University Appointments Board to enquire how I might join. I was told of a scheme called the 'General Traineeship', the purpose of which was to 'train' the future management of the BBC. 'Alas,' he said, 'we (I never discovered to whom the 'we' referred) don't think you are suitable material, so we cannot recommend you.' All I want is the forms to fill in, I told him, probably belligerently. 'Alas,' he said, 'we've run out' – clearly a lie. Of course, I then got the forms direct from the BBC. I did apply, and was one of seven chosen from over four thousand applicants.

I was 'saved', if that's the right word, by a bizarre series of coincidences. At the 'University's Fair', at which all freshmen and women are harangued into joining every conceivable club/political party/ego-soothing 'leisure pursuit', I was intrigued by the ten reasons given on a roneoed pamphlet for joining the Conservative Association, this notwithstanding an early visit to the Union where I had been sickened by the vulgar bombast of a man calling himself the President, one Leon Brittan. Item 10 on the pamphlet concerned the difficulties between town and gown, and advised that all good Conservatives should do their bit to smooth over potential ill-feelings. It said (and I have it still): 'Take out the girl from Woolworth's'. So I did, a blonde, buffoned bombshell called Christine, whose taffeta dresses would have made her the star of *Come Dancing*. I stayed loyal to her during all my years as an undergraduate.

I did find one senior friend in the College, the then Master, the distinguished constitutional lawyer, Sir Ivor Jennings. For reasons which I never figured out, except possibly that he too had been to a grammar school, he took to me. Perhaps he took to Christine, and it became a condition of my being invited to any College function that I brought her. For this I have cause to be grateful to the Conservatives.

And Christine it was who insisted that I take her to the première of a film about a new 'group' called The Beatles. At the time, my

only knowledge of music was Beethoven's Fifth, although I was not sure what the 'Fifth' referred to. I went to the press conference before the première at the old Regal Cinema representing *Varsity*. After the usual asinine questions and during the ensuing mêlée, I was accosted by one of the group's guitarists who asked what I did. A student, I replied. Of what, he asked? Moral sciences. Understandably he thought this hilarious. Would I show him round the University that afternoon, he said. No, I replied, he/we would be mobbed. Very well, he would come in disguise. And when I met him later he was sporting a long beard and dirty mackintosh. I took him to the Wren Library, King's chapel and so on; mercifully he had abandoned his 'disguise'. In fact, no one troubled us. Call me when you come to London, he said on parting. I did, three years later. We

TRINITY HALL, CAMBRIDGE

The following are the main rules to be observed:

1. Students must wear a gown after dusk, and when calling on any University or College official, and also at Lectures, at dinner in Hall and at Chapel services.

2. Smoking is not permitted when a gown is being worn.

3. A Student may not come up after, or more than four days before, the first day of Full Term without his Tutor's permission. He must, on arrival, whenever he goes away for one or more nights and when he goes down at the end of each term, sign the book provided at the Porter's Lodge.

4. Anyone wishing to be absent from Cambridge must apply to his Tutor for an *absit* (for the day) or *exeat* (for one or more nights).

5. A Student must not be out after midnight (11 p.m. outside Full Term, and in the Long Vacation Term), unless he has a Late Leave from his Tutor.

6. Undergraduates may not sign off Hall more than twice a week.

7. A Student may not give or join in giving in College without his Tutor's permission, or in lodgings without the permission of his Tutor and of the Junior Proctor, any party at which alcoholic drinks are consumed, and at which more than fifteen people are present.

8. A Student may not give a dinner for more than six either in or out of College without the permission of his Tutor.

9. A Student may not run up a private bill at the Kitchens exceeding £20 without the written permission of his Tutor.

[P.T.O.

10. Students may not entertain ladies, other than their relatives, in College before midday; nor may they allow any lady to remain in College after 11.0 p.m. A Tutor may, without giving reasons, require a student not to entertain any lady.

11. A Student may not keep or play a musical instrument of any kind (including wireless) in College without his Tutor's permission. Playing is not allowed before 1 p.m., between 5.0 p.m. and 7.30 p.m., or after 10.0 p.m., except that those authorised by the Music Club to use the piano in I.1 may do so up to 5.30 p.m. if the room is available. On Saturdays playing is allowed between 1.0 p.m. and 11.30 p.m. and on Sundays up to 11.30 p.m. This permission may be withdrawn if it is inconsiderately used.

12. No one is allowed to use or keep a motor vehicle without the permission of his Tutor and of the University Proctors. Save for exceptional reasons, Proctors' permission is not given to men under the age of 22 and Tutor's permission is not given to members of this College during their first two years.

13. All bicycles must have painted on the rear mudguard the College letter (H) and the number assigned to each man by the College. Bicycles must not be left in the courts or passages.

14. Walking across the grass in the Courts is not permitted, except in front of the Latham Buildings during the Easter Term.

15. No dog or other animal may be brought into College.

October 1958

has become the cornerstone of all that I have managed to achieve since. And such friendship is priceless and irreplaceable.

I once worked as a bus conductor. My driver, an asthmatic, disillusioned, book-devourer from a council estate off the Hills Road, referring to my student life which he regarded with envy, told me: 'Never forget. This is not a rehearsal for life. This is life itself'. I never forgot, but it was not something I was taught at Trinity Hall. Perhaps I should have been.

met, despite his being by then world famous, and John Lennon became one of my best friends, and greatly influenced the films I subsequently began to make.

So what is the moral of this tale? In retrospect it would appear that the College prepared me for nothing. It did what it interpreted as its duty but neglected what for me were in retrospect more fundamental needs. Jennings suggested that I attend whatever lectures I wanted, not necessarily associated with moral sciences. I did, and heard among many others Frank Leavis on the English novel and Jack Plumb on eighteenth-century British history. Of course, the times they were a changin'. The year before me had done National Service. The acceptance of non-public-school students has, I am told, affected the social mores of College life, although I am appalled by the apparent timidity of the present lot. And whether the inclusion of women students has enlightened the sex life of the inmates, I doubt.

Despite refusing to turn up for any graduation ceremony, I hold no bitterness towards the College. Being there has not damaged my career. It was irrelevant. Much later, I was offered an honour by the Queen. I could not resist replying: which Empire do you have in mind? It seemed equally irrelevant. The years at Trinity Hall were, for me, wasted years – except for one thing. The friendships I made then have stayed with me throughout, and the loyalty that resulted

Tony Palmer read moral sciences at Trinity Hall between 1960 and 1964. Since then he has worked as a television and film director, making films about popular and classical musicians. He holds twelve Gold Medals at the New York Film & Television Festival, and is the only person to have won the Italia Prize three times.

MAGNUS LINKLATER (1961)

I went up to Trinity Hall on the rebound. As an Etonian with an unusual collection of A levels (two) I was told I had a guaranteed place at Trinity. But after five years of Eton gossip, the thought of another three talking about declining grouse numbers and sexual conquests in the conservatory was too much to bear. Trinity Hall was the antithesis – small, perfectly formed, with a reputation for law, rowing, and a very low Etonian count.

I had little idea what to expect from university. It was, I knew, a place where one matured, though from what and into what was unclear. This was 1961, too late for post-war politics, too early for the 1960s revolution. I cannot remember a political thought crossing my mind at the time. I am amazed, looking back, to realise that this was the year the Berlin Wall went up, and Soviet and US tanks faced each other, gun barrel to gun barrel, across the German border.

But there, within the College itself, was an alternative world. It revolved, for me, around close-knit friendships, and a make-

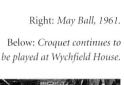

Right: *May Ball, 1961.*

Below: *Croquet continues to be played at Wychfield House.*

believe life, which centred, in my first year, on the Firbank Society, founded in memory of that most atypical Hall man, the novelist Ronald Firbank. His protagonists were a group of self-conscious, and, I think, self-parodying aesthetes, led by David Watkin and Alastair Langlands. They had set up house at Wychfield, where they held tea-parties with wafer-thin cucumber sandwiches, and played croquet on the lawn, wearing blazers and straw hats, swapping quotations from *The Prancing Nigger* or *The Flower Beneath the Foot.* I was entranced. I remember taking part in an entire reading of *The Artificial Princess,* uttering lines like: 'Flushed to the colour of a Malmaison, she was looking conspicuous in silver tissue and diamonds…' or 'She paused, and, picking up the rare first edition of *Unlikely Conversations,* flung it out into the night.'

The Preston Society was another way of introducing a little drama into our lives. I remember our production of *One Way Pendulum* by N.F. Simpson, and playing Snug the Joiner in a memorable outdoor performance of *A Midsummer Night's Dream* in May Week of 1962, directed by Lawrence Gordon-Clark, with Watkin resplendent as the Duke of Athens, making his entrance to a Britten crescendo, Tony Palmer as an outrageous Bottom, and Phil Steadman as Snout. We put on a smoking concert and thought we were every bit as good as the Footlights. We clearly had pretensions.

I still have a letter from Eugene Ionesco giving us permission to perform his play *Le Roi se Meurt* – but only in French.

The plan was to form another group which would move to Wychfield the following year. We made elaborate plans to bring ourselves to the attention of the Master and Fellows. We even threw a sherry party. Alas, our plot was rumbled, and we were despatched to Bateman Street, where real life intervened in the form of the Cuban missile crisis. I can even recall the day, 24 October 1962, when 'the world sat with its heart in its mouth,' waiting for Armageddon. I was with my great friend, and later room-mate, Michael Peppiatt, and we walked up Regent Street, instinctively looking up at the sky to see if the famous missiles were heading our way. It did not change us overnight into political animals, but it may have given an added intensity to our conversations. 'The fascination of a decision seems to me not to lie in the course decided but in the convolutions of the will that precede it…' begins a letter from Michael. I fear my reply may have been along similar lines. We were movie addicts, dissecting Godard, Truffaut and Antonioni for lunch, dinner and tea. We thought we were stylists – I bought a bottle-green corduroy jacket made in Paris, which I reckoned was the *dernier cri.* A year later, we were all together, eating in hall, when we heard the news of Kennedy's assassination. I remember the news coming down the table like wind through corn, and the deathly silence that followed it.

The frozen Cam, January 1963.

So what had all this to do with Trinity Hall? Everything. Within its walls, we formed some of the closest friendships I can remember, all of which depended on belonging to a place which was happy to indulge our pretensions. Yet all of them faded once we left. We drifted apart, almost as though the College itself had been the only glue that held us together. I had planned to go to Spain with Michael and find work there, but the spirit failed me. He went. I didn't. Somehow the fantasy could not be sustained beyond those three golden years. Real life beckoned instead.

Magnus Linklater read modern languages at Trinity Hall. He joined the Daily Express *in Manchester in 1965 and has since been managing editor of* The Observer *and editor of* The Scotsman. *He has written numerous books and is also a broadcaster and columnist for* The Times *and* Scotland on Sunday.

DAVID BELL (1965)

The Hall was a hard place to feel anonymous; but our freshers picture makes us seem rather conformist and I think we were. Some were still wearing ties or sports coats three years later. No one seemed to mind wearing gowns for hall. There were drugs – LSD was what terrified our parents – but not as many as *Varsity's* lurid stories about drug-making in the labs suggested. We drank quite a

lot, but not perhaps with quite the single-mindedness of later generations. The gates closed at midnight, but there were always other ways in. Girls were conspicuous mostly by their absence.

But there were some strains. Public school boys like me simply exchanged one boarding environment for another. Some of us had barely ever met anyone who had not been to a private school. Grammar school boys not only had to get used to being away from home, often for the first time, but also had to put up with bouts of unthinking and very unattractive arrogance. I remember thinking that it was like oil and water – we would never mix. I was wrong. We did mix eventually, but for some there would always be a certain wariness.

There was also a clear divide between 'scientists and engineers' and the rest. The A level system had done its worst – its ruthless emphasis on early specialisation more or less guaranteed ignorance on both sides. This is still one of my great regrets – it was where the oil and the water really did not mix. I read *The Double Helix* by Watson and Crick, which was published in my second year, and I dimly realised that theirs was one of the seminal discoveries of the century. But it was never the topic of conversation that it could have been.

Harold Wilson had not been Prime Minister long when we went up. His 'white heat of technology' sounded plausible. No one

worried about getting a job. I took seriously his exhortation that we should go 'into industry' and went on several career visits, each more dispiriting than the last. Journalism, rather a tradition in the College, was much more exciting and proved for me to be a permanent infection. Few of us were very radical. The *Daily Telegraph* was the most popular paper in the JCR.

The Vietnam war was in full swing, but Trinity Hall – as far as I remember – was not in the vanguard of Cambridge opposition to it. But America did dominate the news, week after week. I still remember exactly where I was (in Front Court) when we heard that Robert Kennedy had been shot. Civil rights, anti-war protests, flower power, Johnson and MacNamara were constant topics of conversation. The Senate House was occupied, the Garden House hotel 'stormed', but we were mostly bystanders. And everything took place against the background of the most fantastic music. We listened reverentially to new Beatles LPs, to the Rolling Stones and to so many more groups from both sides of the Atlantic. Satire, also almost a Cambridge invention, was hugely popular in the College and the University as a whole. And we seemed to have more than our share of people in the ADC or the hugely talented Footlights.

No one ever admitted to doing much actual work unless they were an engineer or a scientist or a lawyer. My week was half *Varsity* and half the weekly essay with the essay taking second place most of the time. The weekly supervisions were sometimes challenging, sometimes enervating. One man made up for yet another missed essay by sending his supervisor six red roses – and it worked. I was rather proud not to know people who went to many lectures, so I still don't know what we missed. But we did work hard before the exams and the College was in sombre mood each summer term until the end of May.

Of course we thought we were enormously mature. And we were quietly self satisfied about being part of an elite. I cringe now at what the College staff must have thought of us and still admire the way in which most of them knew how to put us in our places with just the right amount of disdain. In fact, the College servants,

as they were then always known, *were* the College. They were the continuity, they knew the traditions, they spotted the depressed and the despairing. They were the people we sought out first when we came back after graduation.

Looking back, I owe the College much more than I thought I did at the time. I have friends who are still friends. My tutor, Jonathan Steinberg, encouraged me to go to graduate school in America and in so doing changed my life. He was a great teacher and gave me a love for the United States which still endures. I was lucky to become editor of *Varsity* and luckier still that Trinity Hall seemed to be a college that understood the lure of journalism. The College was small, but it encouraged tolerance. We learned how to disagree fiercely, but stay friends and how to swallow Pimms, especially on the Latham Lawn on a hot June day.

David Bell read history at Trinity Hall and economics and social policy as a postgraduate at the University of Pennsylvania. He began his career in journalism on the Oxford Mail and Times *in 1970. In 1972 he joined the* Financial Times, *where he is now chairman.*

JON STERN (1965) AND MIKE WILLIAMS (1966)

The late 1960s, particularly 1968–69, are remembered as a time of radicalism, particularly student radicalism. Paris May 1968-style street barricades may not have come to Cambridge but, in 1965, a Vietnam protest banner was hung between the pinnacles of King's College chapel and a succession of protests culminated in the January 1969 sit-in at the Old Schools Council Room. At one level Trinity Hall was almost unaffected by these events; but, at another level the changes reflected and promoted by 1960s radicalism were to change it forever – and for the better.

The late 1960s were a wonderful time to be at university. It was a period of huge optimism and hope underpinned by a long period of steady economic growth, low inflation and, most importantly, low unemployment. Finding a job was not a major concern for Cambridge graduates. There was also a cultural renaissance, particularly in popular music, and a revolution in personal and sexual attitudes. In the meantime we could grow beards and long hair, swear more freely, rail against intolerance and racism, and laugh at our grey elders.

But, the worm was in the bud. On the left, there was increasing disillusion with the Labour Government of Harold Wilson and the war in Vietnam became a critical symbolic issue. British economic problems with growth and the balance of payments, the belated 1967 devaluation and other issues were harbingers of the economic problems to come in the 1970s. Across British universities, including Cambridge, the cry was for more 'participation'. At one level this was a plea for more consultation and the opportunity to give a view, but at another, it was a demand for students to be treated as adults and much more like equals. After all, before 1970, people under 21 did not have the vote or other important legal rights.

So how did all this affect Trinity Hall at the time? At the time, not much. Probably around 10 per cent of students had some kind of affiliation with leftish student bodies, but the number of activists was much less. In Dusty Hughes, later to be a leading light on the London avant-garde theatre scene, we had our own representative

of the counter-culture, but he was an exception. In general, Trinity Hall was something of an oasis of calm.

There was much that would have been recognisable to students of a decade earlier. We still had gate hours, although they were increasingly flexible, and no visitors after the evening deadline. Gowns were worn in hall, although the definition of collar and tie was increasingly stretched. Elections to the JCR committee focused on personalities not politics, with the committee's main task being to run the JCR bar – itself something of a shift in attitudes as its closing time seemed to get dangerously close to its opening time.

It was not that there was great hostility towards leftists – the worst that we can remember was one of us being told that 'you sound like Trotsky as well as looking like him'. But, in Trinity Hall, the Vietnam war, the British government's problems and demands for greater participation were not the major concerns that they were in King's and other colleges, and political debate was correspondingly muted. The 1969 sit-in was largely ignored except by a few active participants even when those present voted to tear down all college gates – the most visible symbol of Cambridge student oppression. That idea was dropped when it was realised that college porters might get hurt defending college property. Benevolent paternalism appeared still dominant in Trinity Hall so that both political and artistic activists spent their energies on University or Faculty rather than College concerns.

But, things were changing. In retrospect, at Trinity Hall and elsewhere, perhaps the most important development was the arrival of a new generation of dons. At the University level, liberals like Eric Ashby pushed for new ways and were aware of the need for change – as well as the potential for co-opting moderate student activists in this process as a way of frightening conservative opponents of change and heading off the radicals. At College level, there must have been the same debate over the need to move away from the benevolent paternalist model and to recognise that students had to be treated more as adults with clear rights, particularly over disciplinary offences and processes.

It was the issue of the admission of women that showed the way things would go. In 1969, a meeting of the JCR was convened to promote the admission of women. After all, Trinity Hall had changed its statutes in 1967 to permit the admission of women and King's, Clare and Churchill had announced that they would soon go mixed. The JCR meeting was well-attended – and overwhelmingly hostile to the admission of women students. It was loudly proclaimed that 'civilisation as we know it would collapse with women coming into breakfast'. A few College Fellows attended (including Graham Howes), looking increasingly unhappy at the tone of the meeting but, very wisely, keeping a resolute silence. The meeting concluded by setting up a committee involving JCR representation to establish the practical implications of what would be needed if women were to be admitted – at the time, probably an attempt to kick the issue into the long grass.

This, though, was far from the end of the issue and when women were admitted, civilisation as we know it did not collapse at breakfast or any other time; indeed, it was distinctly improved. That would not have happened without the social pressures and legal changes produced by the 1960s, not least the Sex Discrimination Act.

On this, as with the move to the treatment of students as adults with rights, Trinity Hall in the 1970s did adopt many of the changes advocated by the student movement of the 1960s. It did so in its own time and in its own way, but it did make these changes, even if the protests of 1968–69 seemed to touch only fleetingly the tenor of the Hall at the time.

It was a great time to be a student and at Trinity Hall, not least because of these battles. Oases of calm can also be places of fun.

Jon Stern read history and economics at Trinity Hall 1965–69. He joined HM Treasury's economics group in 1970 and now works at the London Business School and as an economic consultant to governments, regulatory agencies and the World Bank; Mike Williams read economics at Trinity Hall, working for much of his career in HM Treasury. From 1998–2003 he was (the first) CEO of the UK Debt Management Office, managing the government's debt and cash needs; and now works as a consultant to other governments.

How civilization survived

11

THE ADMISSION OF WOMEN

SANDRA RABAN

In January 1976 the first women, two Fellows, were admitted to the College, followed in the autumn by the first woman graduate student. At the end of the same Michaelmas Term, the first undergraduates were selected for admission in October 1977. Women had arrived, or had they? When one looks at the staff, the pace of change was a good deal more stately. There had, of course, been bedmakers, a housekeeper and secretarial staff for many years. It was not until the 1990s, however, that the College acquired its first woman butler and bar manager, while we have had to wait until 2003 for the first woman porter.

As one of those two original Fellows and the first to become a Fellow Emerita on retirement, I witnessed at first hand most of these developments, and this explains why I have been asked to write about them.

Trinity Hall in the 1970s liked to think of itself as unpretentious and cautiously progressive. The admission of women typified this. It was not the first college to take the plunge, but it was at the forefront of the second wave. To some extent the timing was dictated by the Colleges' Committee (a committee for all Heads of Houses), which controlled the pace of change in order to protect the women's colleges. As it happened, when the College's statutes were revised in the late 1960s, care had been taken to remove the definition of person as 'male person', so there was in fact no longer any statutory obstacle to the admission of women. In a very Trinity Hall way, the clinching argument for this had been to save the expense of changing the statutes in future, which indeed it did. When the time came, it is

thought that Trinity Hall was the only college to escape this preliminary chore. Convenient though it may have proved, however, the change left the College in the curious position whereby it was legally empowered to admit women, but members of the Governing Body had reached a gentlemen's agreement that this would not be done without a formal decision requiring the same two-thirds majority required for a change in the statutes.

In the mid-1970s this procedure was set in motion. The debate and vote were orchestrated by Ernest Frankl, then Senior Tutor and consummate collegiate politician. Reportedly he achieved the necessary support by means of consultation so relentless that no-one was left with anything further to say. A Committee on Co-residence was established and, in the late summer of 1974, its report was discussed at extra meetings of the Governing Body. Every Fellow was invited to set forth his opinion in a five-minute speech. There is no written record of the proceedings, but rumour had it that one sticking point was anxiety as to whether such a small college would be able to perform to a high level on the sports field with even fewer male players to chose from. Institutional self-interest proved a powerful counterweight. With limited places in Cambridge open to women, there was a pool of talent waiting to be tapped by colleges quick off the mark. Many Fellows, of course, simply felt that it was the right thing to do. Because of the anomalous constitutional position, the vote was carefully taken at a gathering which was not a formal meeting of the Governing Body. This means that no agenda or minute survives among the Governing Body papers. The first evidence that something had happened is the record of the meeting

Freshers photograph, 1977, showing the high proportion
of women in the first mixed intake of undergraduates.

held on 17 November 1975, when the election of two women Staff
Fellows was agreed. *Varsity* which, at the time, was much concerned
with the funding of the central Students' Union (CUSU), announced
the JCR's decision to make its contribution at the same time as the
Governing Body's decision to admit women, under the sublime
headline 'Tits May At Last Pay'.

The decision having been taken, it was implemented with
remarkable skill. The election of women Fellows before
approaching schools to ask them to send their girls reflects credit
on the College. Kareen Thorne was elected to represent the
Sciences, while I represented the Arts. I have a vivid recollection of
my own interview in a darkened Senior Tutor's room, confronted
by a group of Fellows who looked like something out of Van Gogh's
Potato Eaters. No doubt it was the effect of the heavy panelling and
lighting so dreadful that one could barely see to read, as I
discovered when I came to inherit the room nearly twenty years
later. I remember too the consternation of the Committee when
one of their number asked a question which, even then, was
politically incorrect. Clearly my somewhat frivolous response
struck the right note. In the best Trinity Hall tradition, I received

no formal notification of my subsequent election, although I do
still have Ernest Frankl's handwritten note inviting me for
interview. How different from today's carefully documented
appointments!

Once admitted, at the same time as the new Master, Morris
Sugden, we were made to feel very welcome – for about ten days.
After this we were treated just like anyone else. The only teasing I
can recall was from the Head Porter, who called us 'fellowettes' with
a provocative twinkle in his eye. At the end of that Michaelmas
Term, we were included in Professor Austin's magnificent Eden
Oration, which he declaimed in Latin and Greek from memory,
according to tradition. The rubric to the printed text noted, in the
manner of a nineteeth-century scholarly edition:

'Upon Drs Raban & Thorne myn poem bistoweth laud ppetuall'

A later generation of feminists might claim, with some
justification, that we established ourselves as 'good chaps' and were
accepted on that basis. It took rather longer for the Governing
Body to acknowledge that women academics might face special
problems and therefore need special support. Babies continue to be
something of a stumbling block, although even here the hard edge

of resistance to anything resembling positive discrimination has softened as younger Fellows bring different notions of what is appropriate. Notwithstanding the occasional wrangle (lines for netball on the new and expensive tennis court come to mind), a strong and genuine commitment to women was evident from the beginning. Only gossip enabled us to identify who had voted against the change and even those few recanted in generous tribute in later years.

It fell to the first women Fellows to advise on steps to be taken to prepare for the initial intake of women undergraduates. This was good fun as we knocked at random on the doors of young men and invited ourselves in to look around. In the event, a few full-length mirrors were deemed sufficient to make the premises acceptable for female occupation. At the time, everything was studiedly low key. When asked why women freshers were never allocated ground-floor rooms, for example, Mr Frankl would blandly reply that it was to prevent them having to make coffee for the whole staircase.

To read the *Trinity Hall Newsletter* for these years, it is hard to detect any change in the rhythm of events. The issue for April 1978 observed that: 'The absorption of women into the College has gone very smoothly. Their academic results are yet to come; but women candidates won half of the fifty-two open awards last December (five more than the previous year's record). They have also gained two half blues (for swimming and chess), while the Ladies eight scored three bumps in the Lents.' Thereafter women were rarely singled out, although for some years, the Tutorial Office insisted on pink labels for the women's files and blue labels for the men's, and the names of women were prefixed by 'Miss'. Academically, the first year set the tone for the future. In the 1980s the College climbed to the head of the Tripos league table. In 1980, it came fifth, the highest ever. In the following year, it came top, and there it remained for several years. At the same time, the 1982 *Newsletter* reported that the College had come Head of the River in the Lents for the first time since 1948. In October 1986, the Penguins made their first appearance 'to promote and gain recognition for ladies'

Sara Rhodes, Cambridge's first woman butler, was appointed in 1997.

sport in the College.' All the fears about the loss of sporting prowess were proving groundless.

Women constituted approximately a third of the 1977 undergraduate intake, a highly satisfactory outcome at the time. Precise figures are hard to come by because women were not recorded separately in the statistics, but since that first year, numbers have grown. At the beginning of the current academic year, they made up 46 per cent of the undergraduates and 45 per cent of the graduates. Soon, it is to be hoped that they will reflect the balance between men and women in society at large, although the small number of women coming forward in subjects such as the physical sciences and computer science remains an impediment.

Women students quickly became an integral part of the College and have distinguished themselves by their achievements in every aspect of University life. Within College, they were soon elected to a wide range of offices. Indeed, they have been some of the most effective presidents of the MCR and JCR, one persuading the Bursar to write off the entire JCR debt, and another winning the representation of junior members at Governing Body meetings long after this was a fashionable student cause. More unusually, an early graduate student featured as playmate of the month in *Playboy*, while Trinity Hall provided the hardy streaker who gambolled across the pitch at the Varsity Match in December 1997. An Old Member rang the Tutorial Office demanding to know whether she was 'one of ours'. Having cautiously admitted that this was indeed the case, he confided, 'To tell you the truth, I was rather proud'.

Everything had gone very successfully, triumphantly even, though I suspect that junior members sometimes found it tougher than the Fellows appreciated. Despite a certain amount of heavy-handed male humour, relations were generally excellent. On one occasion when things undoubtedly went too far, a deputation of women came to plead that 'they were good boys really', a claim borne out by the fact that the perpetrators had innocently signed their names to the offending material. Trinity Hall has always enjoyed a strong collegiate spirit and the advent of women seemed to bring an added dimension of mutual supportiveness. This made the tutors' life a good deal easier. The recently lowered age of majority to eighteen was an added boon, since there was no longer any question of having to police students' personal lives *in loco parentis*.

A more difficult issue, which touched Trinity Hall, although it essentially concerned the wider University, was the underperformance of women in Tripos, a problem first raised in *Varsity* in the early 1990s. Despite much agonising throughout the University, convincing explanations were hard to come by. The one thing on which all were agreed was that it was no longer an issue of overt discrimination. A particularly interesting insight emerged from a questionnaire conducted within the College in 1995–96 by the then JCR Women's Officer, Emma Bell. Tellingly, in a year when the proportion of Firsts gained by men and women was very similar (20 per cent and 18.6 per cent respectively), 13 per cent of men but no women had anticipated one. Among the finalists, Trinity Hall women had come top of the Philosophy Tripos, third in the

Above: *Sandra Raban, Fellow Emerita.*

Left: *Hall women have already made their mark in many spheres of life. Suzanne Pegg flies the flag at Twickenham in 1997.*

Economics Tripos and both women classicists had gained starred Firsts. Truly an exceptional year, yet in a host of different ways, the findings of the questionnaire suggested that women felt unsure of themselves. Seemingly Cambridge remained in some ways a macho environment. Women were more often disconcerted by the 'sink or swim' attitude still prevalent in some disciplines. Happily any feelings of being an adjunct to an essentially male institution are diminishing with academic success and increasing numbers of women role-models from the Vice-Chancellor down. When I recently asked a woman student whether she ever felt uncomfortable in Cambridge, she did not understand the force of the question.

As a senior member, I too found that I needed to be more assertive in what remained a largely male Fellowship (a revelation that my colleagues will no doubt receive with incredulity!). The number of women increased more slowly in the Fellowship than among junior members. The first woman Research Fellow was elected in 1979 and for some years Research Fellows were the only, intermittent, additions to the two women Staff Fellows. Today there are nine women and thirty-four men in the Governing Body, showing that there is still some way to go. However, the rate of change has accelerated markedly in recent years and, in the meantime, women have served as Bursar, Senior Tutor and Admissions Tutor. We have also elected our first woman Professorial Fellow. It is only a matter of time before a woman is elected Master. Although the admission of women seemed a giant step into the unknown in 1976, it is now hard to remember what all the fuss was about.

Sandra Raban is a historian of the Middle Ages. She read history at Girton and became a Research Fellow at Lucy Cavendish, following her PhD. She came to the Hall as one of the first two women Fellows in 1976 and has since served as Director of Studies, Archivist, Admissions Tutor and Senior Tutor, as well as sitting on a number of committees, including the University Council and the Local Examinations Syndicate.

Joanna Wade and Martin Williams (1977)

Joanna: 'I am the first woman undergraduate to open this fridge', 'I am the first woman undergraduate to read a lesson in chapel', 'I am the first woman undergraduate to lose a library book'. I was very proud of these pioneer activities but this was an easy place to be a pioneer. The profuse, informal but skilfully planted flowerbeds which were a major reason for my wanting to go to Trinity Hall proved to be an accurate representation of the indulgent and almost casual way in which Fellows (generic term) and staff welcomed the first women in.

For example, the fact that the gender mix was pretty much 50/50 in our year and that staircases were mixed from the start meant that any mystique evaporated quickly as we jointly and equally failed to wash the bath or respect the fact that the gas ring in the kitchen was intended for boiling an egg and not for cooking dinner for fifteen. My friend Martin, who arrived with me onto N staircase, was probably more uninhibited when it came to cooking than most women. I remember our bedder Stella moaning to me that the fridge on his floor was so full of bones oozing blood that it was like a graveyard. Whereas I would have used an Oxo cube, he was planning to make stock from source. I was also perplexed to hear that some men at Trinity Hall were ironing their socks because that was what their mothers did. I rather scorned this slavish adherence to what they believed to be normal and their lack of, well, pioneer spirit.

I am told that I used to say that I did not feel like a guinea pig, nor like a gerbil. I cannot remember saying this and I suppose I was trying to be clever, but across 25 years I think I was saying that I felt secure. Whilst initially alarmed by the boorishness of the men who had plastered a pink *papier maché* tit over the College crest in the Hall, I soon decided that there was nothing wrong with them that a good dose of feminist drama could not fix. So I spent the rest of the next three years appearing in and directing plays such as 'Wife Fronts,' 'Brute Farce' and 'The Mummy's Curse'. The football team obligingly stayed around in the JCR afterwards to discuss their prejudices and be cured.

Joanna Wade rowing at bow in the Ladies' Second May Boat, 1981. Sue Williams is rowing at stroke, cox is Karen Howie and nos 2 and 3 are Rosie Beaufoy and Bridget Finch. They were the fastest second boat in the Fairbairns of 1980 winning their oars.

Martin: Of course, male or female, we were the people least likely to notice any change in Trinity Hall. I had come from a single-sex boarding school, but had applied to an attractive, small, mixed college in the centre of Cambridge. That was exactly what I found. Trinity Hall was full of new experiences, but one of the few continuities, the few certainties that stayed constant from the moment I arrived, was that it was mixed. With the serene indifference of the first-year undergraduate to what had occurred in the dark days before I arrived, I simply took this as the natural order of things.

No doubt this was helped by everyone around the Hall seeming so cheerful about it. It was common gossip that our year had seen very strong competition for places, and that we were not merely a mixed intake, but an academically able one. Jonathan Steinberg assured me, Joanna and our historian colleagues that we were a very, very interesting collection of people. Acquaintances at single-sex colleges were intrigued, envious, and generous with party invitations to get to know us. The Hall football eleven helpfully reached the Cuppers final in our first term, demonstrating that sporting traditions would continue. Even the Head Porter, Ken Golding, a forbidding figure on first acquaintance, closeted in the Porters' Lodge back room, grew steadily more avuncular and would occasionally comment that things seemed less rowdy. If there were traumas about the end of a six-hundred-year tradition, they did not loom large amid general self-congratulation at the march of progress.

Occasionally I was reminded that some in the College had indeed had seen their lives change. The Porters' Lodge remarked on the transformation in the morning habits of Stan, an elderly bedder on P staircase. 'It used to be, "I'll have another cup of tea, Ron," and he'd be nattering away half the morning. Now Stan can't wait to get out of here and into those bedrooms. Must be the first time in twenty years he's had so many pretty girls smiling at him.' Stan's female colleagues may have been less charmed by the smiles of the pretty girls, but even here there were compensations. Stella made it clear to me that female undergraduates tended to be tidier, and to provide a more congenial audience for gossip about who was doing what, and with whom. Joanna, in the room below me, was fortunately a fairly early riser, and a good listener. And for her to be there felt completely natural and right.

Joanna: In no sense did I feel oppressed or marginalised by my experiences at Trinity Hall and instead I felt special, part of a new generation which was making changes in Cambridge – then forward into the World. That most of us have not in fact changed the world has been apparent from the College reunions which Martin and I go to with glee every time they are announced, but so what? Trinity Hall was a place where many of us made lifelong partnerships and friendships. I am proud to be godmother to Martin's daughter. The idea that it might be a strange new thing for me to be going to College with her father must be puzzling to her. I hope she finds the chance to be a pioneer at some point in her life and that it proves to be the positive experience that it was for us.

Joanna Wade was in the first intake of women in 1977. She is a solicitor and partner at Palmer Wade specialising in discrimination and employment law. She is also a part-time employment tribunal chair. She was awarded an MBE for her work on sex discrimination and employment issues in 2002; Martin Williams read history at Trinity Hall, coming up in 1977. He has been a civil servant since 1982, and is now at the Department for Education and Skills. He plays trombone in the South London Jazz Orchestra.

JILL MEAGER (1977)

I think my tutors were pretty tough on me, perhaps because they hadn't dealt with women before and didn't realise a different approach might be needed. I certainly felt disliked and rather stupid – not what I had expected and not good for confidence.

I was very involved in University theatre so spent a lot of time outside College, giving me a different perspective on the immaculate and pervasive self-confidence of the public school male I encountered at the Hall. Coming from the state sector, I found this bewildering and rarely ate in hall or went to the bar.

By my second year, I felt quite alienated by the whole process and at the same time, I received a very good offer of work from a London theatre which seemed more in tune with the way I wanted my life and career to go. Although I had decided to leave, I wish, nonetheless, that there had been a climate in which I could have voiced my worries sooner and received some encouragement to stay.

I think I was a casualty of the changeover from single sex to mixed when the importance of pastoral care in such a high-pressure environment was underestimated.

CAROLINE NEWTON (1977)

When it came to the Boat Club, there was some reserve, if not hostility. Having rowed and coxed at Oxford, I spoke to the Captain of Boats, who was not optimistic there would be anything for me to do. However, he put me to coxing the 2nd Fairbairn Boat. The first time I went to the Boathouse, the boatman was horrified at a woman taking out one of his boats. Despite my experience (or maybe because of it) he would only let me take out a clinker boat. But relations did improve when I managed several outings without any damage to his precious boat.

The chapel choir was not for me, as I can't sing. I think the choir had been importing girls from Homerton to provide some sopranos, but this began to change once there were female undergraduates in College. Chapel breakfasts were a delight – bacon sandwiches in B1

The wedding of Caroline Newton to Stephen Lynas in 1979, the first Trinity Hall couple to marry in chapel.

after the service, and some convivial conversation. It was there that I met my husband-to-be, and I suspect that we were the first Hall students to marry, which we did in College in October 1979.

BRIDGET WHEELER (1977)

What I remember is that the first year was pretty well half and half male/female (which differed as I recall from other newly co-ed colleges where the males continued to outnumber the females for a while.) And most of the girls were blonde. Another thing was the

'One of the claims to fame of my era is that the cox of the third Lent boat in 1978 was Mrs Vicki Englund. She was a law graduate over for one year from the USA. The year she left Cambridge she featured as the centre pages of Playboy *magazine (Sept 1979) with the pictures taken around Cambridge. Although the Boat Club did not make it to the centre pages, recruiting oarsmen was easier the following year!'*

Peter Needham – Captain of Boats, 1979

kindly paternal idea of positioning the girls at the top of staircases (for safety, I suppose – although after the first year that all changed as the ballot swung into practice). And the rather strange idea that with the advent of women, the College should purchase some clothes horses and distribute them one to a room. I never quite worked out what they were for.

The year as a whole was a pretty tremendous one – producing an assortment of QCs, political journalists, actors, etc. And the welcome we received from the existing students was impressive, especially as they may have been unaware when applying to the College that female intake was planned during their time there. So egalitarian was it, in fact, that the sports association – the Crescent Club – pretty well alone amongst the colleges at the time extended its membership to women. This, in a small college where membership rules were restrictive, was generous.

We were a sporty lot. My neighbour, Lis Aitchison, arrived as a (dare I say it) rather plump natural sciences scholar from Cheltenham Ladies College – within a term she was running the ladies boat club, and by the end of her time at the College had rowed bow in the blue boat. Jan Legrand – now a leading lawyer at DLA, swam for the University, and I managed to win the first blue awarded to a woman at the Hall in athletics and captained the University – more than twenty years on, my record for the 200m still stands.

Left: *The chapel, with* The Salutation *by Tommaso Manzuoli lent by the Fitzwilliam Museum.*

Far right: *Monumental brass set in the floor of the College ante-chapel commemorating Walter Hewke, Master 1512–17.*

Matters of the spirit

12

CHAPEL AND FAITH

Everyone called the evening service on Sundays by the name Flemingsong. This was a hybrid between Evensong and the name of the Dean and Chaplain, Launcelot Fleming. And it was a hybrid in liturgy; it was the evensong of the Anglican prayer book minus one lesson and one canticle and a creed. This was because the service had to be slightly shorter to fit between two halls on Sunday night (for in those days the undergraduates had to dine five nights a week or at least to pay for five dinners a week whether or not they ate them). Launcelot was not an Old Testament sort of patriarch and did not think the recitation of creeds in worship helped average young men in their religion and was convinced that an excess of length in prayers was counterproductive. Every Sunday night between the two halls the chapel was crammed.

One reason for this was the lovable personality of Launcelot. A second broader reason was the date. We were reacting against the Second World War. That did not mean that we were pacifists; a majority of the College had fought Germans or Japanese or Italians. They were older and more experienced than undergraduates before the war. What concerned them was international morality and its foundations: How had Hitler happened? What was the moral basis of a civilized society? This meant

that many of them minded what happened in our chapel, and how its ideals might help.

The Control Commission in Germany sent to Cambridge young Nazis with the notion that it might give them better ideals or at least ideas. We were sent one; smartly dressed, presentable, finding an English college odd, even archaic though he was too courteous to do more than look surprised. We persuaded him to come to chapel. By a calamity, but by pure accident, the hymn for that evening was *Glorious things of thee are spoken* by the ex-pirate John Newton. The tune for that hymn is Josef Haydn's tune for the Holy Roman Emperor of 1797, which was used as the setting for the national anthem, *Deutschland Deutschland uber alles*. It was, thus, banned after the war from being sung in occupied Germany. Our guest did not open his mouth as we sang the hymn with Haydn's tune but on his face was a passionate mixture of resentment with puzzlement. I had a nagging fear that he thought this to be fixed on purpose. That was the only occasion when I was embarrassed by anything that occurred in the chapel of Trinity Hall.

We were not aesthetic. This did not mean that the Fellows were unaware of possessing a beautiful chapel or that they did not care about it. When during the earlier eighteenth century the chapel was given most of its present ornamentation, the big

Ordained in 1933, Launcelot Fleming was given leave of absence the following year to join the British Graham Land Expedition, the last amateur polar expedition; run on a shoe-string and taking enormous risks, it nonetheless discovered more scientific data than many.

painting behind the altar, which by size (about 12 ft by 8 ft) and position dominated the décor, was *The Presentation in the Temple*, painted by Sella and given to the College by Dr Chetwode; a harmless picture of no artistic merit. It happened that one of our Fellows, Louis Clarke, was Director of the Fitzwilliam Museum; and walking in the cellars where the public is not allowed to penetrate, observed a picture of much the same size but of better quality as art and stronger as devotion: *The Salutation* by Tommaso Manzuoli, painted at Florence about 1576 for a nobleman's chapel in the church of S. Pier Maggiore. It was too big for the museum to wish to hang it in a public gallery, so the syndicate agreed to offer it to us on permanent loan. That meant altering the surrounding woodwork about which there was hesitation, partly on grounds of its expense. But it was done and the chapel décor was given a strength which before it had lacked.

The Master, Daddy Dean, and his wife Irene cared about the chapel. He hardly ever said anything to chaplains but he was usually at Flemingsong. In one way that concerned religion the Fellows needed to press him. He found it hard to think that a Roman Catholic ought to be a Fellow of the College. The University Printer was then a Trinity Hall man, Brooke Crutchley, a humane outward-looking Roman Catholic. The Fellows in the Arts subjects felt him to be distinguished in the University and that it was wrong not to make him one of the Fellowship. They met the argument that Fellows ought to be teachers of a subject; but they were not sure that this was the real objection. However, gradually they got their way and Brooke was elected, to the great benefit of the College.

In the late summer of 1949 we suffered something of a disaster when Launcelot was offered the see of Portsmouth. So Trinity Hall needed a chaplain. We threw a spider's web towards a delightful Oxford man but could not catch him. We tried a former rowing blue who fitted the riverine side of our pastoral ministry but he was tempted elsewhere. Then we heard of one Tony Tremlett, just back from serving in South America. He was a King's College man, one of the disciples of that fine Dean of King's Milner-White. He

suffered from two minuses – he knew nothing about rowing and his academic record was not thought to be eminent, particularly by our young and able classics Fellow. But he had a distinguished record as a chaplain in the Guards during the war. From King's College and from the Army and from the South American bishop everyone agreed that he was an exceptional pastor. There was a little wonder whether one who had enjoyed Milner-White, expert in beautiful liturgy, would be happy with Flemingsong. But he came, and most of us never regretted it. Most dons had the realistic view that good pastors do not need to know much about anything.

He took up the Launcelot tradition. His door was open, his sherry flowing, his hospitality warm, his humour fun. The Boat Club valued his constant attendance at their watery endeavours. He had a shrewd and wise judgement of character. One of the most remarkable parts of this was his placing the vocation to orders before good men. Out of these interviews came valuable recruits to the service of the church; and even apart from this there were those who felt grateful for a more profound moral or social insight.

Launcelot's favourite preacher in the chapel was Charles Raven of Christ's. Launcelot was a sort of disciple; for he also was both a scientist and a man of deep religious feelings and he shared Raven's approach to Christian truth. Raven retired and, in the same year that Tremlett came to the Hall, Michael Ramsey was elected to be Raven's successor. Ramsey's mind was different from Raven's. It was much more Catholic, his devotion more mystical, he cared about that tradition in the Church of England. Tony revered Ramsey. That through Trinity Hall they should get to know each other was a happy coincidence of timing, for later, when Ramsey was Archbishop of Canterbury, he took Tony to be his chief pastoral assistant in that diocese. When Tony left for a wider sphere, the College and chapel were in the era of Robert Runcie.

Owen Chadwick read classics, history and theology at St John's, where he captained the University Rugby Club in 1938. He was elected to the Fellowship at the Hall in 1947 and became Dean in 1949. He left the Hall to become Master of Selwyn College in 1956 but was elected an Honorary Fellow at the Hall in 1958. Since then he has been Dixie Professor of Ecclesiastical History, Regius Professor of Modern History and Vice-Chancellor from 1969 to 1971. He was Chancellor of UEA from 1985–94.

Launcelot Fleming: An Appreciation
Giles Hunt (1948)

The decision to let Launcelot spend what turned out to be three years as chaplain and geologist in Antarctica was percipient. Owen Chadwick has described how 'the chapel was crammed' in the years after a war which had made people think about 'morality and its foundations' and receptive to what the chapel had to offer. But even before the war, when Launcelot returned to Trinity Hall in 1937 as Dean and Chaplain, its chapel gained the reputation of being the best-attended in Cambridge. This was largely because, during the Antarctic years, he had to preach in a base hut before a small, invariable congregation of intelligent men well able to pick any

holes in the sermon they discussed afterwards and, even more testing, had to live cheek-by-jowl with companions who could always see how far he practised what he preached.

Launcelot did not have the gift of the gab; but as Daddy Dean wrote when putting Launcelot's name forward for a bishopric, 'the boys love [his sermons] and listen to him with a close attention, perhaps because they are so fond of him.' They knew that if he said anything he believed it, and it was a reasonable belief. Nor was he some ivory-tower academic; although he didn't talk about the dangers and hardships of the sledge journey that made the last major terrestrial discovery (King George VI Sound), or of his experiences as chaplain of a battleship in the Mediterranean during the war, these experiences had left their mark – and incidentally probably contributed to his delicious sense of humour.

Because Launcelot went on to be a bishop, it is often forgotten that he was a notable geologist. In 1939 he was the leading authority on glaciology (admittedly in what was then a very thin field), and was made head of the Scott Polar Research Institute at the age of forty. Part of his success at the Hall was that when science was thought to disprove religion, here was a scientist who was a Christian. (Nor, during his time at the Hall, should his support for the Boat Club and skill as a coach be overlooked!)

A later Dean, Robert Runcie summed it all up. 'If you put him in a room full of students… each of them would tell you they'd had a memorable personal conversation with Launcelot. Yet there will be little evidence that he ever finished a sentence. It was simply his friendship and his ability to listen – they were truly charismatic.' To which I would add, having been his bishop's chaplain, that Launcelot was the least pompous clergyman I have ever met.

Giles Hunt was at Trinity Hall when Launcelot Fleming was Dean, and later served him as bishop's chaplain in Portsmouth and Norwich. His Launcelot Fleming, A Portrait *with an introduction by Owen Chadwick, is available from Trinity Hall.*

The Boer War Memorial in the College chapel.

DAVID SHEPPARD (1949)

When I was Bishop of Woolwich, I was invited to preach in the Hall chapel. In welcoming me at the start of the service, the Dean described a conversation which took place over a meal in hall not long before. One said 'If it wasn't for the Cambridge Inter-Collegiate Christian Union (CICCU), David Sheppard wouldn't be where he is now.' 'Yes,' retorted his friend, 'In Trafalgar Square with the longhaired lefties.'

Both parts of that conversation were true. The CICCU Mission of 1949 brought the beginning of days for a lively and personal faith for me, and I remain thankful for it. I was given an encouraging welcome in the small CICCU Group in the Hall, led by Keith Weston. And over the twenty years that I served in Inner City London – and later twenty-two years in Liverpool – I came to believe that Christians needed to fight for justice and better opportunities.

There were other Christian influences that I received in the Hall. Going up for a scholarship exam in 1946, I joined that long line of Hall men who played squash with Launcelot Fleming, then the Dean. When I was a curate, Launcelot invited me to come and

stay with him, now Bishop of Portsmouth. I wrote back, 'Dear Bishop…' He replied 'My *Christian* name is Launcelot, and I like people to call me that.'

By the time I had served my two years of National Service, and arrived as a freshman, Owen Chadwick was Dean. Over the years, he gave me great encouragement. After my first year, cricket interrupted my studies, as I was picked for the England team that toured Australia in 1950–51, being away from September to April. Would the College grant me an aegrotat if I went? No, I must take my Part I exams in the summer, but they wouldn't send me down if I failed. I scrambled a 2ii and, after seven terms and Part II exams, needed to 'keep residence' for two terms. One member of staff told me that the Master would sign my Certificate of Diligent Study with his eyes shut. Another said that it wouldn't be an automatic matter. In the event, I wrote several big essays for Owen Chadwick, and learned a great deal from those supervisions. His encouragement over the years was an important influence in emboldening me to write books about the mission of the church in urban areas.

Cricket played a major part in my Cambridge years. It was always difficult to keep up with studies, when committed to intensive net practice in April and then matches against the counties six days a week. There was a gap of three matches to accommodate exams! Most of us were two years older than university cricketers are today, having served our National Service, and had already been blooded in some first-class cricket. The team I captained in 1952 included six current or future Test players – Peter May, John Warr, Cuan McCarthy, Gerry Alexander, Ramon Subba Row – another Hall man – and myself. We held our own with the county sides – particularly at Fenner's where a true wicket gave a firm base for young players to build confidence.

David Sheppard left Trinity Hall in 1953, having captained the University XI. He went on to play at both county and international level before devoting himself to inner-city ministries in London and on Merseyside. He was Bishop of Liverpool from 1975–97 and was created a life peer in 1998. He was elected an Honorary Fellow at the Hall in 1983.

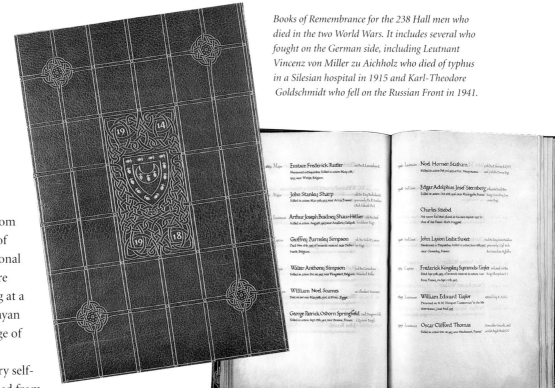

MARK TULLY (1956)

There were many of us for whom Cambridge was the first taste of freedom. I had led an institutional life for sixteen long years before coming up to the Hall, starting at a boarding school in the Himalayan hill station Darjeeling at the age of five, and only escaping from a discipline imposed on me to try self-discipline when I was demobbed from the Army. Perhaps then it's not surprising that I didn't do very well at self-discipline as an undergraduate. Knowing of the time I spent in Morley's Wine Bar in the Market Place and the Blue Boar opposite Trinity, remembering his pastoral visit to me when I was in Addenbrooke's Hospital recovering from my failure to negotiate the spikes on top of the Trinity Hall wall, being aware of my supervisors' adverse reports on my academic progress, my tutor, Bob Runcie, sent me a sharp note at the end of my first year. He informed me by post that I had somehow managed a 2ii and wrote, 'This shows you must have some brains. Why not try using them?'

That was the only time I knew Bob Runcie to be severe or sarcastic about one of his less satisfactory students. Boarding school and the Army had not suited me nor had I suited them. At my public school I was one of a very select band who was never given any position of authority. For some reason I have never been able to understand the War Office Selection Board ignored my school record and did promote me to a position of authority, the very limited authority of a second lieutenant. That did not cure my rebelliousness, or as the Army put it, bolshiness. When the adjutant ordered the junior officers to write an essay about the future of the Army I expounded the theory that the distinctions between officers and other ranks should be abolished. The adjutant did not think that was amusing. Inevitably when I came up to the Hall I saw tutors as representatives of authority, to be rebelled against. But it was very difficult to rebel against someone as caring as my tutor. So during my second year I did try using my brain and managed a 2i.

What was to become much more important in my later life than exam results was the role that Bob Runcie, the Chaplain Tony Tremlett, and the College chapel played in my second year. The only part of my public school life which had left a lasting impression on me was chapel, and when I sat for my entrance exam I had intended to read theology with the hope of being ordained. The Army had left me unsure about my vocation so I decided to read history Part I. But I had still attended chapel regularly during my first year and also went to hear the redoubtable socialist vicar of Great St Mary's, Mervyn Stockwood, preach. So Bob Runcie did not give up on me. At the start of my second year he persuaded me to allow the Chaplain to take me under his wing. Somehow Tony Tremlett persuaded me that my fondness for beer, and my rebellious nature, were not the grave sins I imagined, but a natural reaction to a restricted upbringing, and so I changed from history to theology for my third year. At the end of that year I went on to Lincoln Theological College. There, however, my resistance to institutional living revived and after two terms the Bishop told me he thought I was more in place in the pub than the pulpit.

SUNDAYS			SUNDAY EVENING SERVICES	
HOLY COMMUNION	9.30 a.m.		3 October	*Trinity XVII* (Freshmen's Service)
There is breakfast in the Dean's rooms after the Sunday Communion Service. All those who attend the Service are welcome. There is also lunch in Dr Eden's room.				THE DEAN
			10 October	*Trinity XVIII*
EVENSONG AND SERMON	6.0 p.m.			THE RT REVD D. S. SHEPPARD
				The Bishop of Woolwich
WEEKDAYS			17 October	*Trinity XIX*
HOLY COMMUNION				THE RT REVD A. P. TREMLETT
Tuesdays	8.0 a.m.			The Bishop of Dover
Thursdays and Holy Days	6.05 p.m.		24 October	*Trinity XX*
MATTINS (not Saturdays)	8.30 a.m.			THE RT REVD J. H. L. PHILLIPS
				The Bishop of Portsmouth
EVENSONG (not Thursdays, Saturdays			31 October	*Trinity XXI*
or Holy Days)	7.05 p.m.			THE RT REVD A. K. HAMILTON
COMPLINE on Fridays	10.30 p.m.			The Bishop of Jarrow
			7 November	*Trinity XXII*
HOLY DAYS:				THE RT REVD R. A. K. RUNCIE
S. LUKE	18 October			The Bishop of St Albans
SS. SIMON AND JUDE	28 October		14 November	*Trinity XXIII* (Remembrance
ALL SAINTS' DAY	1 November			Sunday)
ALL SOULS' DAY	2 November			THE RT REVD F. T. HORAN
S. ANDREW	30 November			The Bishop of Tewkesbury
			21 November	*Sunday Next Before Advent*
The Dean (16) and the Assistant Chaplain (9 1 and 41 Fulbrooke Road) are glad to see members of the College at any time.				THE RT REVD R. A. S. MARTINEAU
				The Bishop of Huntingdon
			28 November	*Advent Sunday*
				CAROL SERVICE

TRINITY HALL CHAPEL

MICHAELMAS TERM 1971

Bob Runcie had sponsored me for Lincoln and had every right to be disappointed in me but he never made me feel I had let him down. He took my marriage service, helped me to find my first job, and remained in touch until he died. My credit in the Delhi office of the BBC soared when my secretary announced that the Archbishop of Canterbury was on the telephone. The Archbishop had rung to persuade me to take the job of BBC Religious Correspondent which was vacant. I didn't listen to him, but when I eventually left the Delhi office and started to present *Something Understood*, the early Sunday morning programme on Radio 4, he readily agreed to be interviewed.

In a life which Christians would certainly not regard as orthodox, the influence of Bob Runcie, Tony Tremlett and College chapel has never left me. They have bequeathed me a love of the Anglican church, its liturgy and its ritual, a faith which never quite goes away, and an interest in theology which, in some strange way, is much stronger now than when I was a student. Two lessons in particular I learnt from Bob Runcie. He admitted to doubt and he pursued the middle way. During the controversy over the ordination of women the press, which only sees things in black and white, accused the Archbishop of 'nailing his colours to the fence'. But, as Bob Runcie once said to me, 'it needs more courage to pursue the middle way than it does to take sides. My job was to keep the church together not to drive it apart.' Thanks in no small measure to Bob Runcie's inspiration I no longer seek for certainty, and I believe that life should be travelled along the middle way.

After graduating from Trinity Hall in 1959, Mark Tully joined the BBC in 1964, where he was Chief of Bureau in Delhi from 1972–93. He then spent a year as South Asia Correspondent before going freelance. He was awarded a KBE in 2002.

CHAPEL TODAY
JEREMY MORRIS, DEAN

Where *is* the chapel? That question, heard frequently from visitors and sometimes even from students, would be inconceivable at many of our neighbouring colleges. We have no mighty specimen of Perpendicular architecture to rank with King's or Trinity, or anything to match the Baroque splendour of Clare, or the Gothick scale of St John's. The modesty of the Hall's chapel ensures that it remains truly hidden to many. Hidden, but not without interest and beauty of its own. It is indeed small, tucked away in a corner of Front Court, with scarcely any distinguishing external features, and – of all things! – student rooms above it. Yet it is one of the oldest of the college chapels, and one that gives more clues than most to the size and layout of the medieval foundation, for it is still, in outline and in basic structure, the original fourteenth-century building, never extended or demolished to be rebuilt in a more grandiose fashion.

Over the last hundred years or so, the relationship of the chapel to the College at large has changed substantially. Compulsory chapel disappeared with the tacit acknowledgement that not all members of the College would be professing Christians, or at least members of the same church. It has long ceased to be true that worship in chapel would gather together the whole of the College community, like a school assembly. Now, we simply could not accommodate more than a fraction of the much-expanded College there anyway. The chapel community remains a substantial and significant part of the College, but a minority even so. The worship of God inescapably is the centre of the chapel's weekly routine of services. But the chapel retains something of a College-wide role, nevertheless. Major public events in the life of the College are still marked there – the commemoration of benefactors, the admission of new Fellows and Scholars, a carol service for College staff, the Eden Oration, amongst others. In chapel we can also celebrate publicly changes in the lives of College members – baptisms, weddings. Or celebrate and regret those who have gone – funerals, memorial services. In this way, even for the many who do not wish to attend regular services, still the chapel may be a place from time to time for public as well as personal reflection or serious sentiment.

How, then, has the 'hidden chapel' changed in the course of the twentieth century? The physical changes – usually the most obvious of all – have been little. Major changes in the appearance of the chapel happened in the sixteenth century, when much of the medieval decoration and imagery was removed after the Reformation; in the early eighteenth century, when Nathanael Lloyd completely overhauled its external as well as internal appearance, producing its Baroque finish; and in the middle of the nineteenth century, when the old treasury was demolished to extend the chapel some eight feet eastwards. By 1900, the chapel would have looked much as it does today. In the early 1920s, the organ gallery was created and the first organ installed. In Launcelot Fleming's day, the pressure of growing College numbers led to the provision of extra seating in the collapsible benches still in use. But it was done so carefully and sensitively that scarcely anyone thinks it might be quite recent. Owen Chadwick describes the installation of Tommaso Manzuoli's painting of the visit of Mary to her cousin Elizabeth. It suits the chapel interior perfectly, an adornment and focus without being overpowering. With the admission of women in the 1970s, the College could have a mixed choir formed largely from its own students. Choral evensong, choir tours, occasional concerts, have all become over the years a feature of what is, for a small College, a lively musical life.

The aspect of change that most members of College recall, thinking of the chapel, is the succession of people who have served it, and in particular the deans and chaplains. The office of dean was created in 1887 or 1888, in order to concentrate collegiate, clerical responsibilities in the hands of one person, after the general connection between ordination and the holding of a Fellowship had been severed. The Hall's deans have usually been scholars (theologians and historians particularly) as well as clergymen, combining teaching and research with pastoral responsibilities and a host of other, varying tasks. But there have been more unusual figures, and two of them went on to high office in the church. Launcelot Fleming was one, Bishop of Portsmouth and then of Norwich. The other was Robert Runcie, Dean from 1956 to 1960, later Archbishop of Canterbury. In the ante-chapel, two stained glass roundels by John Hayward to celebrate Archbishop Runcie's association with College and his elevation to the see of Canterbury were installed in 1980.

But the greatest changes to affect the College chapel, and the Christian life of the College in the twentieth century, have been imperceptible. The steep decline in church-going in Britain that began in the 1960s has inevitably influenced the way the chapel is seen by many students. Chapel attendances have held up very well, and yet what attendance at chapel signifies has become more sharply defined in comparison with the seeming indifference of students more generally. The rise of ethnic and religious pluralism in Britain since the war has also had an impact. The presence in College in much greater numbers than ever before of Jews, Muslims,

Left: *The Runcie windows, designed by John Hayward to celebrate the elevation of Robert Runcie to Archbishop of Canterbury, were installed in the ante-chapel in 1980.*

Hindus, Buddhists and others has meant the end of what was, basically, a Christian monoculture. Tact and openness – always a mark of good pastoral work – are more important than ever before.

Jeremy Morris is Dean of Trinity Hall, and Director of Studies in Theology. He read modern history at Oxford, and trained for the Anglican ministry at Westcott House, Cambridge. He specializes in modern British church history, and modern Anglican theology.

Jenny Tomlinson (1979)

When people write about Trinity Hall, there are often references to the sense of community and the mutual support offered there. These are terms that can be used too readily, in a way that is misleading or meaningless, but for me they were realities in my undergraduate days, from 1979–82. As I look back, I realise how relevant the experience of living in that fairly heterogeneous Cambridge community has proved to be to my subsequent life and work.

After reading history, I stumbled into health service management, and spent six very fulfilling years working in hospitals large and small. The sense of being part of a community with its own life and ethos was strong regardless of the size of the institution. In fact, the three years that I had spent in an intense community which was the primary focus of its members' lives had

been very useful preparation. I have to admit to being one of those strange people who actually enjoys communal breakfast, and being in an institution, albeit of a different kind, was familiar. I knew from experience how the growth and success of strong group identities – whether boaties, thespians or musicians – contributed to the well-being of the whole enterprise, rather than threatening it. Even a relatively small community like Trinity Hall could accommodate and indeed appreciate its larger-than-life characters. The individual was not subsumed into the greater mass.

In the NHS of twenty years ago the dignity of the patient was less the subject of documentation and laid-down standards than today, but still of central concern to most staff. Again, and somewhat surprisingly, I see that there was a connection with the culture which certainly prevailed at that time in Trinity Hall. The much-vaunted friendliness of the College ran deep, and created an underground stream of compassion, kindness and selfless practical help which bubbled quickly to the surface in time of need. The pursuit of excellence, in its academic and other forms might not at first sight appear a likely environment for such qualities to flourish, but I saw them all in action, quietly enabling students to cope with ill health or other difficulties.

The Falklands war coincided with my last term in Cambridge. It was striking to be in a place with so many young men at a time when others of the same generation were experiencing something

quite foreign. I remember thinking how different the place would have been during the First and Second World Wars.

There was something new about the atmosphere in College, in any case. The endless discussions about the rights and wrongs of the situation sometimes put a strain on relationships. There was a slightly sombre quality to life in the early weeks of term, and some students made a point of being in the JCR for the television news. A community which had never seemed to me to be very politically active responded to a tragic and unexpected turn of events.

I left the health service to return to Cambridge, this time to train for ordination in the Church of England. Little had I suspected how formative the time spent in the Christian community within Trinity Hall was to prove. Over the last twelve years of ministry I have learned much more about communities, which has deepened my appreciation of what I encountered at College. Shared life and experience bond the most unlikely people together. And whilst every college, hospital and church needs its star performers, those who form the chorus make just as vital a contribution.

Jenny Tomlinson read history from 1979–82, then spent six years in hospital management. She trained for the Anglican ministry at Ridley Hall and was ordained in 1991. She was among the first women to be priested in April 1994 and is now an assistant parish priest in Chelmsford diocese and a part-time chaplain for Thurrock Primary Care Trust.

The words of Mercury and the songs of Apollo 13

MUSIC, DRAMA AND POETRY

EDWARD GREENFIELD (1949)

In the years immediately after the war Trinity Hall was not a college one associated with cultural life in Cambridge. I would go to friends in Jesus or Cats to enjoy music-making or undergraduate dramatics. There was also King's to go to for Evensong. Then in my third year one big development at the Hall was the arrival of a grand piano set in noble isolation in a very bare room in the South Court. We would put down our names on a list for an hour's practice, just as you would book a squash court. Unremarkable as that development might seem today, it could well have been a key factor in what has proved a transformation of the College and its cultural life over the half century since then.

I also remember that in that same room (or possibly another empty one) they would have at the end of each term an exhibition of framed prints which we could choose for beautifying our rooms the following term. The great majority of us in those years were 'doubled-up' with each set shared between two of us, which made it preferable to go along with one's room-mate before making a choice. Luckily I had no trouble on that score.

I remember my choice for one term was a semi-primitive by Christopher Wood, an artist I had never come across before. His vigorous painting of *Mousehole Harbour* in Cornwall, complete with trawler bouncing in the waves, was such a success with me, conveying the saltiest atmosphere, that promptly after graduating I bought a copy myself, which I still treasure. Having that painting for a term certainly added to my appreciation of twentieth-century art, and I am sure that many other borrowers had similar experiences.

Another vivid memory of those years was of a Sunday afternoon tea-party at the Crawleys' home. Rather to my surprise I quickly found myself in animated discussion with Charles's wife, Kitty. Like me she was a devotee of William Walton's *Façade Entertainment* with its Edith Sitwell poems, and we both lamented that at that point it was impossible to track down all of the 21 poems in the regular *Entertainment*, when Dame Edith had excluded half a dozen or more from her published collections. Kitty and I, investigators both, eagerly exchanged our discoveries of missing texts, both then and later, until within a year or so the full set was finally published along with the music, and we exchanged messages of triumph. I was sad not to see her again.

For some years after graduation I had little contact with the College, but I was delighted (having become a music critic on *The Guardian*) to find that Alexander (Sandy) Goehr, on his appointment as the new University Professor of Music, had settled for Trinity Hall as his home college, becoming one of the Fellows. By that time I had got to know him. Indeed one of my very first music reviews some years earlier for the then *Manchester Guardian* was of a Piano Sonata by Goehr, which he wrote while still a student in Manchester, one of the Manchester New Music Group along with John Ogdon, Harrison Birtwistle, and Peter Maxwell Davies.

It must have been about the same period that the chapel choir was founded. Not that I registered that development at all until very recently when the choir was celebrating its 25th anniversary, and I was asked to speak at the celebratory dinner. That followed on their excellent performance in chapel, when the choir of

Previous page: *The Music Room.*

Right: *The College choir in the chapel.*

present members was augmented by an impressive number of former choristers.

The success of the choir is the more remarkable when the chapel is so small, and I imagine that its foundation went along with the foundation of the College's Music Society, another organisation almost inconceivable in my day. I was delighted to find what a flourishing society it is when – with women undergraduates among the prime movers – I made another visit to the College to talk at an annual dinner. I confess I was also open-mouthed on that occasion at being put up in the most luxurious guest-suite imaginable, so different from the Spartan box at Balliol, Oxford, where 48 hours previously I had spent a painfully sleepless night.

Now, when along with all the developments I have mentioned the College – uniquely in Cambridge, so I have been told – has its own theatre on the spot, I am more than ever proud of being a Hall man, one who far from deploring what has happened over the years ('Not like it was in my time, old man!') actually welcomes the changes alongside all the traditions we cherish.

Edward Greenfield read law at Trinity Hall, graduating in 1952. For forty years he was on the staff of The Guardian, *succeeding Sir Neville Cardus as chief music critic in 1975. He still contributes to the record column he founded in 1954.*

Frank Conley in the Trinity Hall University Challenge *team, 1965. They eventually lost to Pembroke College, Oxford.*

FRANK CONLEY (1964)

Music was certainly thriving in Cambridge in the 1960s. Many undergraduate musicians were to become well-known names: David Atherton, Andrew Davis, David Munrow and Anthony Pay, to name only a few. Trinity Hall could not claim such eminence, but it was still an exciting time. I arrived in 1964, and knew I would be at home when I saw the grand piano in the Music Room, and learned that there were designated music hours. At the same time a new organ scholar, Alistair Jones, had been appointed. He had studied at the Royal Academy of Music, and expected to carry on in Cambridge with the sort of events he had organised in London. Donald Burrows and I were signed up as sub-organists over dinner on the first evening, and before long there was a sizeable body of singers and instrumentalists willing to form a chapel choir and to play a variety of instruments.

It is probably best to draw a veil over the chapel organ at that time, arguably the worst in Cambridge, tonally undistinguished and mechanically unreliable. At one point we could play tunes on the ciphers, and it memorably misbehaved during a commemorative service, prompting a complaint from the Bursar.

Fortunately we could use the fine new instrument at St Edward's Church, for practice as well as recitals. The church was also the venue for what became annual choral performances. Since the College was still all-male, wives and girlfriends were persuaded to sing. We performed Fauré's *Requiem* with organ in 1965, Mozart's with orchestra in 1966, and in 1967 Bach's *St John Passion*, drawing on resources from the whole University and providing an unforgettable experience for all who took part.

Not all the music-making was that solemn. There were informal recitals by College members in the Music Room, now the Robin Hayes Room, with too many fine performances to list, though I well remember a riotous account of Elgar's *Pomp and Circumstance* for piano duet. There were more formal recitals in the newly-built Combination Room, sometimes involving young professionals and musicians from other colleges, and May Week recitals in the JCR (now the Graham Storey Room).

The final event of the year was always the May Week concert in Hall. The one in 1965 stands out: a largely sight-read canter through a Stanford choral ballad was followed by Haydn's/ Leopold Mozart's *Toy Symphony* with members of the Fellowship including the Dean and the Chaplain showing an exceptional range of ability on toy instruments such as rattle and cuckoo. In 1969, after I had gone down, Donald Burrows assembled an orchestra to play Wagner's *Ride of the Valkyries*, showing how far College music had come in those few years. When I read accounts of College music and the chapel choir in the annual *Newsletter* I feel very proud to have been involved in these early stages. Put another way, if today's College musicians feel overworked, it is quite probably our fault!

Frank Conley read history and political science at Trinity Hall. He then became a teacher, first in Tunbridge Wells and, until 2002, at the Harvey Grammar School in Folkestone. He has written numerous articles about the reed organ and its composers and is a contributor to The New Grove Dictionary of Music and Musicians.

PETER FREEMAN (1959)

Arriving in Cambridge as a member of the National Youth Orchestra I already knew a number of musicians in the University, and was quickly swept up into a dizzying round of rehearsals and concerts. Performing the Verdi *Requiem* and *The Dream of Gerontius* in King's Chapel were spiritual and emotional experiences unlikely to be found elsewhere (I still play the recording of the latter made by our Chaplain, Martin Chadwick). Other highlights of my musical life include playing from the top of St John's Chapel on Ascension Day; playing in the Inter-Varsity Jazz Competition with the University Big Band, which led to regular Saturday night engagements with the Ken Stevens Big Band at the Rex Ballroom and sitting in with Johnny Dankworth's Band when he played at a Ball in the Corn Exchange. I taught exceptionally musical boys at King's College Choir School to play brass instruments; and made early music with David Munrow (later to found the Early Music Consort). I had the interesting experience of being conducted at CUMS by Benjamin Britten and meeting Aaron Copland when he came over for the Opera Group's English première of his opera *The Tender Land*. I was given the enormous privilege of playing the Haydn Trumpet Concerto for CUMS under David Willcocks; when I warned the College that I would need to make a lot of noise in preparing for this they showed remarkably good sense by putting me at the top of O staircase so that the only people disturbed by my incessant practice were Trinity College undergraduates on the other side of Garret Hostel Lane. I met my wife-to-be when she sang in a concert I was playing in at Homerton – in those days there were so few women around one had to seize every opportunity that presented itself.

Sadly, there was little opportunity to make music in the Hall. I helped to arrange a May Week Concert in the JCR: all but two of the performers had to be imported. I arranged the music for the May Week production of *Henry IV, Part I*. However, what I remember most vividly was the May Week production of *Julius Caesar* on the terrace overlooking the river. I was persuaded to

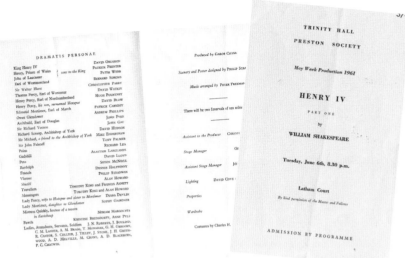

Left: Henry IV, Part I, *1961.*

Bottom: *Carsten Lund at work on the new organ for the College chapel.*

dress up as a Roman soldier in order to march out carrying a long fanfare trumpet, stand on the brick wall, and play a few notes to announce the start of the proceedings. I then had to march away with as much dignity and haste as possible in order to scrub off whatever body make-up was likely to be exposed, change into my dinner jacket and rush over to King's to play in the first half of their May Week Concert. I then had to sprint back to the Hall, get back into Roman uniform and full make-up in order to play another fanfare to announce the end of the interval and immediately dash off as before to play in the second half of the concert at King's.

If I had put as much effort into working for my English degree as I expended in making music I might have achieved more than a 2ii, but I would not have had nearly as much fun.

After leaving Trinity Hall, Peter Freeman became an English teacher in Manchester and then Maidstone. After four years as Deputy Head at Simon Langton Boys' Grammar School, Canterbury, he became Head of Carre's Grammar School, Sleaford, in 1983. He retired in 1998.

A NEW CHAPEL ORGAN FOR THE HALL
DAVID SANGER

The present organ was built by a local builder, William Johnson, whose best organ is that in St Catharine's College, Cambridge. The organ built by him for Trinity Hall in 1981 is sadly not of that standard, and has caused a lot of trouble in recent years. Fresher organ scholars quickly notice that the keys have been cut haphazardly, and are very uncomfortable to play; the stop knobs are noisy in operation, and difficult to manage. Worse still, inside the organ chamber there is evidence of poor quality action parts – it looks like a toy mechanism! Perhaps the College council at the

time were strapped for cash, and thought that a cheap organ would serve the College sufficiently well. It is easy to look back with hindsight!

As Consultant to the Organ Project I saw no earthly point in trying to restore this organ. It would have to have been completely rebuilt to reach any sort of sensible playing standard, but it would still sound thin in tone and rough in its voicing. It is for this reason that I recommended that the College should consider a completely new organ from one of the world's top builders.

I was determined that the future organ should be built of the finest quality materials throughout, to ensure perfect playing order for decades to come. It should be designed for easy maintenance, stable tuning, aesthetic appearance and have an appropriate quality of tone for accompanying the chapel services.

Choral accompaniment is its most important function, but solo organ voluntaries are also catered for in the design. The Organ Scholars, of which there are usually two, need a sensitive and responsible tracker action on which to practise, if their playing skills are going to improve. The instrument should be an

Alexander Goehr studied music at the Royal Manchester College of Music and the Paris Conservatoire, and is associated with the group of composers who emerged in the 1950s from Manchester. After teaching in the United States, he became West Riding Professor of Music at Leeds University. In 1976 he was elected to a Professorial Fellowship at Trinity Hall. He retired in 1999 and is an emeritus Professor and Fellow. His compositions include chamber music, symphonies, a ballet and several operas and choral pieces, of which Kantan *and* Damask Drum *(1999) was performed at the ADC in 2002.*

inspiration to those who take their playing seriously. Working together with the Organ Builder I will endeavour to achieve a suitable sound, rich in colour, but gentle and warm in effect, which would enhance the beautiful historic chapel, and serve the worship as perfectly as possible. I will look for quality, and not necessarily quantity, durability and reliability in operation, and a pleasing visual aspect from the chapel floor.

The possibility of placing the organ further forward on the gallery has been investigated. Indeed, the gallery panelling will be replaced with a balustrade to allow greater egress of tone. The work to build a new organ went out to tender, and Carsten Lund of Denmark, who proposed a twenty-stop organ in a simple casework, won the contract. The hammered front pipes will give an unusual effect, almost one of rustic charm, while the overall look of the instrument from downstairs will be contemporary – not outspoken contemporary – but modest and appropriate.

The College is indebted to a former student at the College, for generously donating the necessary funds to purchase this organ. There is no doubt in my mind that the new organ for Trinity Hall chapel will set a new standard in organ building in the UK, and, from the experience I have of Carsten's other instruments, will encourage young organists in Cambridge and those who visit the various courses on offer to them to great heights in their playing skills.

David Sanger studied at the Royal Academy of Music and was Professor of Organ there for many years. He is a renowned international concert organist and teaches organ at both Oxford and Cambridge. He has acted as a consultant to the Trinity Hall Organ Project.

DOUGLAS HAYWARD (1947)

I had been involved with puppets for some years before coming up to the Hall in 1947, having given my first show when fourteen and, during the war years, had been in some demand to perform in aid of Holidays at Home, Warships Weeks, Wings for Victory, Salute the Soldier, and similar events. I had not, however, anticipated that experience having much relevance to my time at Cambridge. But, in the way things happen in a small college like the Hall, word got round through friends of friends and when the support of the College was sought to raise funds for one of the children's charities I was contacted by the coordinator. The upshot was the most original series of shows I have ever been involved with: quarter-hour marionette performances from the back of a lorry parked, presumably with police approval, outside the Senate House, near the top of Senate House Passage. The programme was a selection of variety turns, the finale for each featuring Christopher Robin kneeling by his bed 'saying his prayers', which seemed appropriate to the cause we were collecting for. Between times, I took a puppet around various cafés and coffeehouses – the KP, the Whim, etc. – performing on a table top to publicise the next show. I have no idea how much we collected but it was an interesting day.

Love's Labour's Lost, directed by Nicholas Hytner, the Fellows' Garden, 1975.

A HOTLINE TO SHAKESPEARE
NICHOLAS HYTNER (1974)

'The words of Mercury are harsh after the songs of Apollo. You that way, we this way.'

The last speech of *Love's Labour's Lost* is probably its most famous, but it didn't suit whatever it was I thought I was doing to the play during May Week 1975 in the Fellows' Garden, so I cut it. I genuinely can't remember why. There was, I think, some elaborately staged musical farewell for the four couples whose betrothals are cut short by news of the King of France's death, and I suppose I couldn't work out what the hell Mercury and Apollo had to do with it.

On the opening night, which I thought had gone pretty well (undergraduate directors never lacking self-confidence, an attribute which dribbles remorselessly away during a life in the theatre), I got stuck behind a very old man shuffling down the steps of the rickety stadium seating. He was mumbling something over and over, and he seemed distressed. 'The words of Mercury,' he was saying, 'are harsh after the songs of Apollo. You that way, we this way.' I was within an inch of tapping him on the shoulder and telling him to get over it, when I recognised him. It was I.A. Richards, the founding father of modern literary criticism, and I'd pissed him off. The inventor of close reading thought I was a fool and a vandal, and he was telling anyone who'd listen.

But the point is I didn't care. I do now, but then I was impervious. It was impossible for me to imagine *Love's Labour's Lost* being done better than it was done there, on the lawn beneath the willow tree. No matter that it was interrupted constantly by the sound of punts lurching up the river carrying the sloshed survivors of the afternoon's parties. Nor that it was completely obliterated one night by some glam rock wannabes warming up for the Clare May Ball. It was, or so I thought, unimprovable.

Love's Labour's Lost was produced jointly by the Preston Society and the ADC. I was not, I confess, a very active member of the Preston Society; but I was a hyperactive member of the ADC. I was less a Hall person than a theatre person, though I realise now that the Hall's tolerance of the stage-struck was a central feature of my academic career. So tolerant were they that I was able to deliver to the ADC for its May Week production one of the most coveted of all Cambridge's outdoor arenas. To the Preston Society, I brought the budgetary might of the ADC.

The show was lavishly costumed and full of the kind of stuff I'd seen the RSC do with the Shakespeare comedies. It was set in the long hot summer of 1914, which I thought was a stroke of genius: the play as an anthem for a doomed generation. It was an idea so obvious that I've seen it done three times since, and I almost certainly ripped it off from some previous production that I'd read about. Undergraduate theatre is long on ambition and short on originality, but it has always been a seedbed for professional directors, most of us still ambitious and still thrashing around for new ideas.

But it is the blissful self-confidence that I remember most fondly. The show was probably as terrible as I.A. Richards thought it was, but as daylight gave way every night to precariously slung floodlights, it was possible to imagine that we were breathing the

Far left: *A Hall student production of* Grease, *1992.*

Left: Kantan & Damask Drum, *by Alexander Goehr, the ADC, 2002. Theatrical direction and set design were by Sarah Chew.*

very essence of romantic comedy. Cocooned by the darkness and buoyed up the audience's unshakeable determination to enjoy itself, a determination that rose as the temperature fell, we thought we had a hotline to Shakespeare.

Nicholas Hytner read English at Trinity Hall before embarking on a career as a film and theatre director. He joined the Manchester Royal Exchange as an Associate Director in 1985 and has since directed many plays, operas and films. He is now Director of the National Theatre.

SARAH CHEW (1995)

College gave me many things to be grateful for, but if I have to thank Trinity Hall particularly for one really huge thing in my undergraduate drama activities, it was letting me direct *Ghetto* by Joshua Sobol. This massive documentary play had 30 actors, an onstage band, specially made film sequences, a live hanging – astonishing, really, that the Preston Society didn't decide we'd end up bankrupt or imprisoned for manslaughter. Even more astonishing was the fact that it opened the week before I sat my finals, and nobody stopped me.

But that's what I remember as being so special about theatre in Trinity Hall. It's a small college and the Preston Society's budgets were modest, but it supported big ideas, wacky ideas, any ideas that were presented with passion. By choosing projects more for the enthusiasm of their creators than for any more material guarantee of success, the Society ended up with an astonishingly varied programme, of which many repertory Artistic Directors might be advised to take note.

The three plays of 1996–7 would be an example. There was a beautiful dance production of Sam Shephard's rarely performed verse play *Savage / Love.* This meditation on desire, choreographed by Hannah Bruce (who now has a significant career in dance, and recently won a bursary from Chisenhale Dance Project) transformed the lecture theatre, through Nancy Peskett's design of empty picture frames floating in space, into a room no longer the home of College Bops and the occasional fire drill, but a delicate, evocative space for the contemplation of our most fragile emotions. The same space, a term before, housed the anything-but-contemplative Fresher's Pantomime: funny, filthy, and a vital initiation rite into College life as well as a theatrical venture. That

147

summer, Latham Lawn and the river were home to Eliott Shrimpton's cross-dressed *Midsummer Night's Dream*, which, with its 1980s-inspired costumes and interesting approaches to gender politics, certainly made me see the play anew. It bewildered two blokes on the other side of the river, making their way between Suicide Sunday parties: the sight of Rhona Clelland dressed as Margaret Thatcher delivering 'I know a bank whereon the wild thyme grows' through a loudhailer on a punt might have served to curtail their subsequent drinking…. And I don't remember her being too happy when they tried to join in.

It wasn't just the productions which were such an invaluable start to a theatre career, or the classes the Society also organised – although many were brilliant, and two in particular, one on Shakespearean verse-speaking and one on Feldenkrais movement technique, still find their way into my own rehearsals – but the sense, from College in general as well as the Preston Society, that drama wasn't just a hobby, it was something that mattered.

Once I co-directed a production of *Measure for Measure*: we had lost our original performance venue at the eleventh hour and were threatened with disbandment on the grounds of homelessness. A Preston Society delegation made a last-minute dash to the Senior Tutor, Master and English Fellow, which resulted in our miraculously being allowed to use the dining hall. I held my breath and repeated the mantra 'Listed building. Listed building' as we dragged in a lighting rig and a shocking-pink set I'd only just finished painting, and which dripped ominously. It was a generous gesture; and if Drs Raban, Lennard and Lyons had second thoughts when they saw the hall graced, for probably the first time in its illustrious history, with assorted transvestites and dominatrixes in full bondage gear (it was a punk interpretation…), their first-night smiles didn't show it. I should have learned my lesson about recently painted scenery. In my third year, my 'college daughter' directed the Fresher's Pantomime; as a responsible College parent, I couldn't refuse her request that I do her scenery. We tacked bed-sheets to her wall, upon which I proceeded to paint the scenes she

wanted. They looked quite nice – as did the walls, which, when we took the sheets down, had identical images on them, soaked through the fabric to the wallpaper beneath…. At least directing the panto seemed less stressful to my 'daughter' when confronted with our need to repaint the walls of her room without the bedders or porters noticing. I like to think I taught her resourcefulness – but suspect she didn't see it quite the same way.

I reckon the 1990s was a good vintage for Trinity Hall's thesps. I was too late to see the early work of playwright Chris Goode, but see it now at various theatres, including the Camden People's Theatre, where he's making a big impact as Artistic Director. I also missed out on Belfast-based director David Grant, previously of the Lyric Theatre and now Head of Drama at Queen's University, but am making up for it by working with him on a couple of plays later in the year. From the years I was around I can count two directors, a good handful of actors including a Perrier award winner and a *Manchester Evening Standard* award winner, a choreographer, a designer – and many others who, despite their inexplicable decision to pursue another career which might actually earn them a living, remember their undergraduate theatre experiences with affection. Making a career in theatre means enduring poverty, rejection and tremendous competition; to survive takes faith, vision, and more grit than I would ever have imagined as an undergraduate. The generous but artistically and intellectually demanding environment of Trinity Hall provided a good training for me; from the impressive roster of Trinity Hall alumni who have made it in the profession, I imagine many would say the same.

I had wanted to direct *Ghetto* because its original British production, in 1988 at the National Theatre, was one of the plays that made me want to be a director; by a curious coincidence it was directed by Nicholas Hytner (see above). The play's author, Joshua Sobol, saw my production when he was here as a Visiting Fellow, and thanks to our subsequent working relationship I am now directing the UK premiere of the play's sequel, *Adam*. There is, in fact, a third connected play, which has never been performed in

Britain: I wonder if it will be premiered by another former Trinity Haller, in another fifteen years…?

Sarah Chew came up to Trinity Hall to read English in 1995. After graduating she was involved in setting up the Municipal Opera House in Saigon before joining the National Theatre's Emerging Directors Programme in 2002. She is now a freelance theatre and opera director, running an international theatre company, Critical Mass.

Rachel Weisz (1988)

I remember being in the lunch queue at Trinity Hall during my first term when David Farr asked me if I would be interested in auditioning for Ophelia in his production of *Hamlet*. David was in my year also studying English. He had unruly, black hair, which he constantly fiddled with, and the biggest, brightest green eyes you have ever seen. I liked him immediately. He also looked about fourteen, so I politely declined, assuming his production would be earnest and juvenile. I went to see it a few weeks later. It is the best production of *Hamlet* I have seen, before or since. Ben Miller played Hamlet and made sense of every word. It was like witnessing a very gifted stand-up comedian confess his battles with depression, loss, women, angst, paranoia, and love. David and Ben went on to win prizes at the National Student Drama Festival for *Hamlet* and David now runs the Bristol Old Vic.

Very chastened by my arrogance, I asked David if he wanted to form a theatre company with me. He agreed and we asked Rose Garnett, who was next door at King's and who was (and is) my best friend, to be the producer, and Sacha Hails to be the other actor. We had ideas of writing our own material and of making the pieces very physical.

The first piece was called *The Song of Songs*. We performed it in the Trinity Hall lecture theatre, where sometimes people would wander in from the bar, mid-performance, to find themselves on the stage. We felt this only made things more exciting. Sacha and I were the two creatures who fall in love with one another but cannot kiss. The relationship turns cruel. We drew heavily on French clowning techniques and mixed these with sharp, funny, fast dialogue. Drama meets performance art.

The company was called Talking Tongues. We wanted to take the show to the Edinburgh Festival so we needed funds. The Trinity Hall Preston Society gave us our first cheque and we opened a bank account. We were full of passion and ideas; and we were entrepreneurs; enough money had to be raised to cover theatre hire, travel, and accommodation. By going to all the different colleges we raised enough. We returned to the Festival for the next two years. Sacha and I devised and performed around six plays together. At the end we didn't have anything written down: the text was in our heads. David typed them out for me much later as a birthday present. He had heard them so many times, he could remember every word.

It is not a great read: the plays were about energy and performance. Often very absurd, cruel, with a style that one critic called 'fraught naturalism', and always very physical, perhaps violent. We were always (proudly) covered in bruises. It is a time that I remember vividly, never again would our work be so bold and free and (sometimes literally) dangerous. In one piece, *Slight Possession*, we would hurl each other from a step ladder, which was our third character, while the audience gasped. We performed this in many different spaces, all we needed was two floral dresses and the ladder.

I don't think we realised at the time how unusual our experience would be. How the big bad world would threaten our creative idyll, and such optimism and collaborative passion would be hard to match.

Such is undergraduate life.

Rachel Weisz read English at Trinity Hall and was a frequent performer at the Edinburgh Festival in student productions. In 1992 she became a professional actress and has established an international reputation in films such as The Mummy, Enemy at the Gates *and* Runaway Jury.

Of Poetry and Poets
Stephen Romer (1975)

When I came up to Cambridge in 1975, my head was full, not of Shelley, but I suppose his modern equivalents, the Liverpudlian lyricist Brian Patten – the most romantic of the Mersey Sound group, I always thought – and of Thom Gunn, who had quit these shores for the sunlight and sexual freedom of California. A strange pairing, in retrospect, but such are the random and passionate attachments of late adolescence. As it was, my first visit to the Cambridge Poetry Society, held in those days in a set of elegant rooms in Green Street, proved a mortifying experience. The assembled tyros were handed copies of two poems, unsigned. To my delight, I knew one of them to be by Patten. The other seemed a rather chilly piece to me. We were then asked to divide into two groups, according to which poem we preferred. I think there were only two of us in the Patten camp, and it was a little like facing a critical firing squad, aligned along the other wall.

Out of some bloody-mindedness of my own, or a sense that this was a very Cambridge rite of passage, or baptism by fire, which had to be gone through, I returned for fresh humiliation the next week. The numbers were considerably reduced, and to my greater chagrin, it seemed that nearly all the women had voted with their feet and stayed away. Their instincts were probably right; the Poetry Workshop was a fairly unforgiving and untender milieu in those days, but we were lucky that one highly intelligent young woman, with cropped hair and a lean intensity, returned from time to time to attack what she deemed our unreconstructed phallocentric poetics. I think of her now as an intrepid vanguard of attitudes that are currently the critical orthodoxy. Those weekly meetings, in which texts were circulated and discussed, taught us a great deal, I think, and helped deflate pretentiousness. I shall never forget when one member of the group, a genial elderly retired barrister (for the workshop was open to the public) deemed one of my poems 'clever, of course, as usual, yes; and absolutely hollow!'

By my third year I was vice-president of the society, or whatever the title was, and meetings were held in my rooms in Trinity Hall, in N5 to be precise, with a gorgeous view over the lawn to the river. I think I affected a Meerschaum pipe, back then, and wore a repellent black chiffon cravat-like thing which I never took off; it seemed the thing, it seemed dandified and Baudelairean, for by then I was starting to read the French. One bonus of my position was that of choosing and hosting the visiting poets. This provided thrilling insight into 'the poet in the flesh'. George Barker, the wild boy of 1930s Soho Bohemia, came and drank so much that the kindly barman at the Hall stopped counting at one point, thus preventing the CPS from being drunk into irremediable debt. His contemporary, David Gascoyne, also made the trip with his wife Judy; a tall, saintly figure, he was just then entering his 'second life', after years of confinement and alienation. Andrew Motion, then a young lecturer at Hull, came bearing news of Philip Larkin.

At the Hall itself, my tutors were Peter Holland, Graham Storey and Christopher Gillie. All of them, in their different ways, looked benignly on my creative attempts, though in those days it was very much an extra-curricular activity, and in no way a substitute for the weekly essay and supervision. In the University at large, the legendary figure for aspiring poets had his dwelling next door to the Hall, in Caius. J.H. Prynne's lectures on 'Poetry and Language', with their flourishes and arcana, held us spellbound, just as his own work did. Impenetrable, or at least syntactically resistant to 'meaning', his infrequent pamphlets were a kind of benchmark for us; and it seemed right that something none of us could understand, but which seemed very clever indeed, was being concocted over the road. Now his epigones and admirers hold sway in Cambridge poetry, his true influence can be more accurately gauged, and I understand more clearly the intellectual positioning of such poetics; but as undergraduates we were more impressed by Prynne's physical presence, the immutable black suit, white shirt and bold orange tie. With his locks curling over his collar, and his immensely high forehead, he seemed the image of the poet, as imagined by Edgar Allan Poe.

Another figure in black haunted me in my second year, when I shared some dank digs in Castle Street with friends. It would appear from time to time on the top of Castle Hill, which I could see from my window. Black-hatted. Reading too much mediaeval allegory, I became convinced that Death himself was surveying me. It wasn't until a year later that the real identity of the mysterious figure became known to me. It was none other than the poet Michael Hofmann, who was my close contemporary at Cambridge. He was far too much of a loner then, and too deferent, to attend the Workshop, but he did leave some poems under my chair in N5, after his first, tentative visit. Michael had a kind of angelic, hovering quality about him then. I discovered his sheaf, read them, and announced that I had discovered a genius. However that may be, he was writing poems of ironic sophistication that were streets ahead of most of us. One of them I recall was entitled *Solemn Young Poem*, while the rest of us were perpetrating 'solemn young poems', but without knowing it. That was the beginning of a long friendship, one of several gained at Cambridge.

Other memories crowd back, other friends, but space does not permit. And finally it is the poets I *read* at Cambridge that live within me now, poets like Coleridge and Hopkins whose words combine organically with memories of ecstasy – the word is not too strong. I recall completing my Part I dissertation on Coleridge's conversation poems, and emerging like a mole from a room in the Wychfield site; it was early spring, and walking down the Huntingdon Road in a gusting wind, my face was brushed by blossoms, and then the burning sensation of snow. To forget Cambridge, as Hopkins said of *his* university, would be to 'undo the buttons of my very being'. The poem below is really about him.

This Poem for Burning

'I founded my house on meaning, the extreme
that knelt in yellow to the west, or spoke
from a simple twist of light, an arrow
pointing upward on my wall. How I lay
in wait for it, for what it told, and why

the window set it there! To steal a glance
I broke a penance of the eyes. Visible grace
Flying in the air, the daily floodings in
And ebbings out of light were signs to be read
Richly into, for I knew him by these things.
A residue of dry secrets. Those corrupt
Picturings on the prie-dieu. Schoolmen and dust.
There is nothing to see, touch, taste, smell, hear.
I am a bell they left in disrepair
Without a tongue. Looking back is my sin.
I have a narrow bed to meet despair,
Pen and paper to and blood to dare to tell
Of a thing that I know. His indifference
Is a stern mercy. The sleep of the just
Is not different from the sleep of the lost.'

Stephen Romer read English at Trinity Hall (1975–78). He has published three collections of poetry, Idols, Plato's Ladder *and* Tribute *(OUP/Carcanet) and an anthology* Twentieth-Century French Poems *(Faber). He has taught at universities in France and the United States.*

A World Elsewhere
Katrina Porteous (1979)

Long before I came up to Trinity Hall to read history in 1979, I knew that poetry was the important thing. I chose the College partly on aesthetic grounds: I liked the gardens. My three years there were mostly very happy, always intense, and not always easy: one long collision of different selves and different worlds. Poetry and academia do not sit comfortably together, but it was more than that. It was a question of where I belonged.

I grew up in County Durham, near Consett ironworks. Although my parents were professionals and I attended an independent school, the prevailing culture was separated from Cambridge by more than miles. The differences could be classified as 'working class' and 'professional', 'North' and 'South'; but I prefer 'old world' and 'new'.

Katrina Porteous.

By 1979 the College was entirely mixed. I had no siblings, my school was single-sex, and I had scarcely spoken to a boy since the age of eleven. I did not feel particularly odd in this respect, though. My year seemed divided between worlds of innocence and knowing. There was more to this than shyness. When my first-term supervisor criticised an essay for its 'nineteenth-century clichés', I thought he had seen my soul. Going home in the vacations, I felt that I was stepping back in time, into a different moral universe. Where I came from, I knew no one whose parents were divorced; unmarried sex was a shameful, secret thing; and marriage generally meant keeping house and serving your husband. But there were women at Trinity Hall who seemed free of this weight – socially confident women, lovely seals at ease in the water, while I floundered about on dry land.

Intellectually, I found it much easier to adapt. What was harder in this case was returning home. Everything they teach you at Cambridge – questioning, precision, intellectual acuity and confidence – is misconstrued in the old world, where 'clever' may be a pejorative term, confidence read as condescension, and an argumentative woman is even worse than one who is too pretty. So much about College life was a masculine dialectic, intellectual cut-and-thrust. In the old world, a woman is not supposed to answer back.

Re-reading my diaries, I'm amazed by how frequently I fell in love: about once every nine or ten days, but sometimes several times in a week, or an evening. The intensity is staggering. Where did I find that energy? Of course, this was not sensual love, but intellectual; a passion for ideas, which fastened itself upon one person after another. For three years I was in a state of perpetual intellectual excitement.

All the time, I was trying to write, but found the life of the mind insufficiently balanced. I felt as if my head was cut off from my body. Poetry is a physical art, dependent on the senses for its imagery, rhythms and music. I missed the richness of Northern dialects and the familiar landscapes of the North East, from which I had so longed to escape. Years later, as an unhappy graduate student, I wrote the poem *Factory Girl* in the UL, expressing my frustration with academic research.

Conversations with my tutor, Jonathan Steinberg, who valued poetry, and with poets in the wider University, especially Geoffrey Hill, gave me permission to take my writing as seriously as I did, and to concern myself with unfashionable matters of rhyme and form. Counterbalancing this was the University Poetry Society, which was hijacked by revolutionary Marxist-anarchists. A typical workshop involved a naked poet tearing up newspapers, while playing Wagner recordings at ear-splitting volume and spraying the audience with deodorant.

The College provided a safe base for such excursions: my abiding memory is of its cosiness – for better and for worse. Approachable parental figures abounded; not only academics, but Mrs Jeffs in the office, Mrs Hinton in the library, and Frank, the Polish porter. The security of College, and the villagey nature of the staircases, or even ghastly, freezing Bateman Street, made intellectual adventures possible; and this combination provided a sense of belonging that was stronger than home.

One Saturday afternoon in my first year, I visited a friend in Cherry Hinton, a Poetry Society anarchist on the fringe of the University. An older, non-University neighbour dropped by, distressed that his girlfriend had gone missing on her release from Holloway. We got the whole story: drugs, prostitution, alcoholism, stabbing and suicide attempts. When I arrived back at Trinity Hall, my student friends, who had spent the afternoon by the river watching the Bumps, were toasting crumpets round the fire. In that instant, I felt everything that was best, worst, most privileged and precious about College life: the comforting, nursery atmosphere, which for a moment protected us from the precariousness of the world beyond.

Factory Girl
Five nights a week I work as a factory girl.
My job's in Necklaces. Cartons of colourful beads
Run down the line and I thread them. The Sorter leads,
Popping them into their boxes – a difficult task,
For sometimes the green look blue, the blue look black,
And many fit all six boxes equally well;
But the Sorter has to be certain they don't get mixed.
Everything's made to fit. The order's fixed,
See, by the day, and we stick to it, or else
There's plenty others wanting jobs…

                    My shift's eleven
At night till the early morning bell drills seven
Into my dreaming. Then I go home to bed.
I don't know whether it's dark or light out there.
In here it's always the same, summer or winter.

With all of our necklaces made to the book, as we thread
In the given order (green today, then red;
Tomorrow, red then green), to me they appear
So much the same; like the nights, the bus-ride here,
The sequence of stop after stop, long as the Tyne,
Counting the lights in the water, the broken line
Down where the shipyards were that went redundant.

I think of the oddest things to unsettle the pace:
Sometimes of Dad. I try to remember his face
And the stories my Mother told me: ('You should've seen
How he looked in his uniform, Hin, when he went to the War!
I don't think I'd ever loved him so much before.'
'What a knees-up we had when the fighting was over! At last
We were done with the sirens, the blackouts and rations.
        God willing,
He'd still have his job at Swan Hunters.' But that was gone.
'When he heard, he looked like a factory shutting down,
The lights going out in the workshops, one by one…').

Well, I string this together. I try to make sense of the past.
But pieces are all I have. I can't force them to mean
Anything much. I just see what I want to. It seems
A haphazard collection of memories, turned in the telling
This way or that by a whim, as an order's cast;
O, nothing seems to make logical sense any more.
I go home, and I dream of necklaces snapping, beads spilling
Into their moving millions, over the floor.

From The Lost Music, *(Bloodaxe Books, 1996)*

Katrina Porteous is an award-winning poet who lives on the Northumberland coast. Her work is frequently broadcast on BBC radio and is published by Bloodaxe.

Power and money

RUNNING THE COLLEGE

COLLEGE GOVERNANCE
PETER CLARKE

Having served as Master of Trinity Hall for four years, I sometimes joke that this is almost as long as Churchill's wartime premiership – long enough to make a difference, if not to world history then at least to our own 'poore society', to use the haunting phrase of one of my predecessors, Dr Eden. Yet four years is a very short part of the period since our foundation in 1350 – only 0.6 per cent. If I talk about how the College has been governed through the ages, you must take 99.4 per cent of it on trust and only on the remainder do I speak with any real authority.

Authority is something that Masters really did have at one time. Remember that, until the nineteenth century, Fellows were often young men waiting for preferment in either the church or – especially in Trinity Hall – in the law. The Master was obviously set above them as a more senior figure in every way. He alone could marry, he and his family could reside in the Master's Lodge supported by a bevy of servants. The Heads of House between them virtually ran the University.

The Mastership was usually held until death, which helped make for long tenure. In all, eleven Masters have served for more than twenty-five years, the last of them Professor Henry Dean (1929–54), still remembered by generations of alumni as 'Daddy Dean'. He died in 1961, still clinging to his professorship in the University under the old statutes which did not prescribe retirement, though the College already stipulated an age limit of 75 (now lowered to 70). Dean, moreover, served his turn as Vice-Chancellor, in the days

before that became a full-time office. It is already impossible to think that one person could do all of this, let alone for so long.

Yet the College statutes, though amended, have not changed out of recognition. Rather, we try to work within them to maintain the historic constitutional checks and balances of a self-governing community while adapting to the professional demands of the twenty-first century. It is still the case that, like a medieval corporation or the Trinity itself, the foundation consists of three parts: Master, Fellows and Scholars. This can be seen at meetings of the Governing Body. The Master presides, all the Fellows are expected to attend and these days we have student representatives from the JCR and the MCR (though they withdraw when reserved

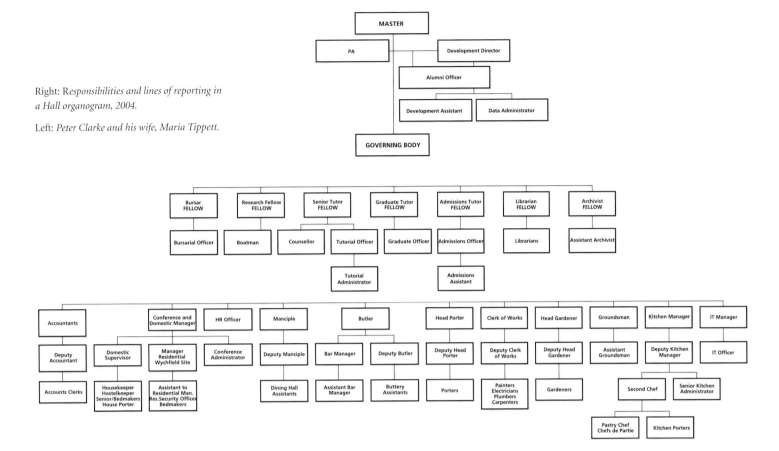

Right: *Responsibilities and lines of reporting in a Hall organogram, 2004.*

Left: *Peter Clarke and his wife, Maria Tippett.*

business is discussed). We still meet wearing gowns; there is a certain formality to the proceedings; members are addressed by the names of their College offices or by their academic titles – we have not followed the cabinet in using first names only (though of course we do so in ordinary conversation). A sense of history and respect for tradition in all this? Certainly. An outdated and inefficient rigmarole, stultified by the dead hand of the past? I think not.

We get through a lot of business in this way and with a high degree of consensus in reaching decisions. The Master is not a CEO, with a structure of top-down line management. Most recent Masters have kept their professorships in the University. This keeps us in touch with the wider academic world beyond the walls of Trinity Hall. It also means that, like most of the Fellows, we have to juggle responsibilities in both a University department and in the College.

In College this is possible nowadays because of the professional support from our staff. Former Masters as recent as Sir Morris Sugden, who tragically died in office in 1984, managed without a full-time secretary, just dictating letters through the Tutorial Office. Today, inescapably, a new approach is necessary in running the College, watching over our finances and keeping in touch with

alumni. Thus we have created a suite of offices adjoining the Master's study, accommodating not only the Master's PA but also the associated activities of the Alumni Officer and the indispensable work of the Development Office, with four full-time posts filled by busy and able members of staff.

I see the essential task of a Master as that of winning consent for the decisions that are necessary to move the College forward. Some of this involves one-on-one meetings with key figures, especially regular meetings with College officers such as the Bursar and Senior Tutor. Sometimes, too, prompt fire-fighting is needed before an issue flares up. Good contacts with the presidents of the JCR and MCR are necessary. Entertainment and other social functions, in the Lodge or elsewhere, help sustain face-to-face relationships with not only Fellows but students and staff too. That makes several hundred people altogether whom I meet as Master one way or another, even if only for a few words as I am crossing the courts; and that takes no account of our thousands of alumni. Yes, I do wish I could remember everyone's name!

A lot of donkey-work on College business is done in committees: eighteen of them with regular scheduled meetings throughout the year. Student representatives play a big part on some of these (Finance, Education Policy, Library and Archives, Information Technology, for instance) and members of staff on others (especially the Health and Safety, Staff/Fellows Liaison, and Kitchen Committees). One of my favourites is the Gardens Committee, where our expert Head Gardener will explain his ideas to invariably appreciative Fellows and students.

Most of these committees are chaired by the Master – two or three most weeks – but the Vice-Master plays an important role in chairing others, like High Table, Graduate Students and the Alumni Liaison Committee, at which the Master usually sits in too (to his own benefit). Then there is the Investments Committee, involving not only the Fellows on the Finance Committee but also our much-valued external advisers, responsible for a portfolio that has, in recent years, produced results that have exceeded all benchmarks and reinforced the College's assets. Judging by results like these, Trinity Hall must be getting something right!

We do so by involving key members of the College community in the decision-making process. By the time that issues come to the Governing Body, with snags ironed out and objections taken into account, arguments for sound proposals are already well on the way to being won. So at the Governing Body itself – it only meets twice a term, and rarely for more than an hour and a half – most items on the agenda are 'starred' and the recommendations go through on the nod, unless particular Fellows ask for them to be reopened. We try to reserve our time for the big or awkward issues where opinion needs to be sounded and potential conflicts resolved. It is thus possible to change and to reform where necessary within a structure that Daddy Dean, and even Dr Eden, would still recognise.

Professor Peter Clarke studied history at St John's College where he was a Fellow from 1980–2000, when he became Master of Trinity Hall. He retired in 2004 and is succeeded by Professor Martin Daunton of Churchill College.

Masters in the Victorian Age
Thomas Thornely

… A Master's position was then a much easier one than at the present day, when 'Black Care' sits as readily behind him as behind any of his subordinates, and can give as good a reason for being there in the one case as in the other. Little more was expected of him than to preside, with becoming dignity, at meetings of the Governing Body, and on other formal occasions: to show some interest in University matters, and to be prepared to take his turn as Vice-Chancellor, if fate so willed.

If, as sometimes happened, he chafed at inactivity, and wished to take part in ordinary College affairs, he was free to do so, but these rare intrusions bore a close resemblance to those occasional descents from Olympus which were the cause of so much embarrassment to the ancient Greeks. If, on the other hand, he preferred to sit aloof among the clouds, and devote himself to lonely study, tempered only by a stately interchange of civilities with his peers, he was as much entitled to do so as was Bishop Watson, in an earlier day, to live the life of a cultured squire at Windermere, and leave his Welsh diocese and his Cambridge professorship to take care of themselves.

Dr Geldart, the Master of Trinity Hall when I first joined it as an undergraduate, belonged to this ancient order to things, and interpreted his duties in accordance with its spirit…. We caught an occasional glimpse of him as he was being led or pushed by his wife, with seeming reluctance, into his seat in chapel. Beyond this we saw nothing of him, and were only dimly conscious that something which had no meaning for us was lurking in the background of our College life….

Henry Latham may almost be regarded as a second founder of Trinity Hall. Though one of the most ancient, it was one of the smallest of the Colleges in point of numbers when he entered upon his tutorship, and it had grown to be among the first three or four when he succeeded Sir Henry Maine as Master. A stately row of buildings, bearing his name, was added at his sole expense, and his life and fortune were freely devoted to its welfare….

The port table in the Senior Combination Room.

His influence over undergraduates, many of whom were of a class not easily brought under control, was due to the deep interest he was known to take in all that concerned their well-being. He knew his way to a young man's heart as few have known it. In him they were conscious of having a friend to whom they could always turn in time of trouble without fear of unprofitable scolding, and with the certainty of a sympathetic hearing and treatment.

He would gently expose their folly, seek and generally find a way out of their difficulty, and then dismiss them with a pat on the head or cheek, telling them not to be 'great silly boys' another time, but to come round to his house in a day or two and be introduced to his ravens and the other pets with which he loved to surround himself. If at times he erred a little on the side of leniency, his trust was seldom abused, and there must have been many who were kept from serious offence by their knowledge that it would give pain to 'Old Ben'….

When in a playful or mischievous mood, he would boldly cast aside all regard for truth or probability, and try how much he could coax his hearer into believing.

I overheard him once explaining in French to a Balkan prince, who was honouring us with his company, that the little

contraption, which carried our bottles from one end of the Combination Room table to the other, had given Stephenson his first notion of a railway. The prince was duly impressed, but the rest of the company had some difficulty in keeping their countenances.

From Cambridge Memories, *(Hamish Hamilton, 1936). Thomas Thornely was a Fellow under three different Masters.*

Henry Dean's style
Brooke Crutchley

In the portrait of him by Oswald Birley which hangs in the dining hall the autocrat is apparent, and also the hint of mischief which was never far below the surface. It might have been expected that he would be painted by Gerald Kelly, a Hall man (which Birley was not) and distinguished Academician – he was President in 1949–51. But they were both men of strong personalities and, after a sitting given up wholly to the taking of photographs, Dean never went back for a second.

Dean made most of the decisions for the College and his technique for defeating any move which he did not favour was to find ways of deferring discussion until the danger was past. He had the chef and the butler in his pocket. Theoretically there was a wine committee but it was for him as chairman to summon it and he preferred to go his own way. Similarly with food, he settled the menus for feasts and guest nights – for the latter invariably spatchcock preceded by Cornish craw and, to make sure that the craw was fresh and had not been hanging around in some station luggage office over a weekend, guest nights must be in the last half of the week.

The College statutes, dating from 1352, had become encrusted with amendments and Sir Ivor Jennings, an eminent constitutional lawyer who became Master in succession to Dean in 1954, favoured a complete revision. One of the new statutes prescribed that the Vice-Master should be elected by the Fellows and should serve for a period of four years; previously he had been appointed by the Master on a

John and Danielle Lyons.

yearly basis. No specific duties were laid down, except for standing in for the Master in his absence, but it was generally felt among the Fellows that two matters needed immediate attention, the long-term policy of the College and the organisation of its business. Because it was thought that my experience of the outside world would be useful, I was cajoled into accepting the post. Two of the most thoughtful members of the Fellowship, E.K. Frankl and J.C. Laidlaw, joined me in a deliberately small committee and we proceeded to ask ourselves, and others, what the purpose of a traditional Cambridge college was in the mid-twentieth century. This seemed to be a necessary preliminary to tackling the questions of future policy and the administrative organisation needed to pursue it.

Brooke Crutchley was University Printer from 1946–74. He was elected to the Fellowship at Trinity Hall in 1951 and was Vice-Master from 1966–1970. He died in 2003. This is taken from a memoir deposited in the College archive.

SIR JOHN LYONS: AN APPRECIATION
PETER HUTCHINSON

John was born in 1932, had a distinguished career at Christ's (finding time to gain a blue) and, after short spells lecturing in London and back in Cambridge, he obtained his first chair (Edinburgh) at the remarkably young age of 32. A chair at Sussex was to follow, and finally (again, surprisingly young) the Mastership of the Hall in 1984. His knighthood in 1987 was awarded for services to linguistics, and his list of publications is long and diverse. More important than all these achievements, however, was his marriage in 1959 to Danielle, a partnership which was to prove of immense importance to the Hall.

John and Danielle applied themselves wholeheartedly to ensuring that the College was a harmonious institution. John, in particular, could never walk through Front Court without stopping to chat to a student, a Fellow, or a member of staff, while he delighted in welcoming alumni at reunions, gatherings and

commemorations. Danielle proved a role-model for the growing population of women, not only running an aerobics class, but even taking to the river in one of the women's boats. Yet this was a period in which the Hall also came top of the academic tables, was Head of the River, and consistently raised more money for charity than any other college. Towards the end of John's Mastership a fund-raising campaign transformed the library, the endowment, and especially funds for student support. The period 1984–2000 was, then, of crucial importance in the College's existence – to which a very large number of alumni can happily testify.

HOW MUCH DOES TRINITY HALL HAVE?
JOHN PEGLER, BURSAR

I am sure many of our alumni wonder why Trinity Hall seems to have a major fund-raising campaign every few years and never seems to have enough money. The perception is that Cambridge colleges are wealthy organisations. In which case, why do they keep going round with the begging bowl? But the image of all the colleges having large sums of money at their disposal is as inaccurate as the popular view that Cambridge is full of students from wealthy backgrounds leading privileged lives as portrayed in *Brideshead Revisited*. Most readers will know that to be far from the truth.

But just how rich is Trinity Hall? Up to the nineteenth century, the College had significant land holdings, mainly agricultural and around Cambridge. These properties were then adequate to provide the income necessary to maintain the buildings and to support the day-to-day operations of the Hall. In the early twentieth century,

Right: The Milton South site and (far right) *Wychfield.*

because it was felt that securities would generate more income, many of these properties were sold and the proceeds were invested in trustee securities, so that the College could do more than barely survive on the relatively meagre income from rents. But we still had significant properties in Cambridge, in particular Bateman Street and Norwich Street were largely owned by Trinity Hall.

In the 1950s there was a change to the College's statutes and, for the first time, investments could be in equities, which were better able to keep up with inflation. As a result, in the 1960s most of the Bateman Street and Norwich Street properties were sold or leased. This was about the time that there was a significant growth in the numbers of Fellows and undergraduates, with corresponding strains on the College's resources and an ever-greater pressure to maximise the income from investments. For example, money was needed to fund a number of alterations to the historic city centre buildings and for the development of student accommodation on the Wychfield site, which had been bought in 1911 and turned into a sports facility in the 1920s and 1930s.

Today, the College's income-generating assets fall into three categories: property worth approximately £6 million, equities worth £40 million, and cash of £15 million. These figures are constantly changing; for example, cash holdings are temporarily high in anticipation of major capital expenditure in the near future (see below). Between them, these assets provide a return of about £4 million a year, some of which is ploughed back into investments so that, taking the long view, their values and therefore the income they generate keep pace with inflation. As a rule-of-thumb, after this plough-back, £1 million generates £40,000 income and the College draws about £2½ million a year income from its investments for spending on operations. Some of the property investments are held more for their potential to increase their value significantly than for the income they generate now. In this way the Hall aims to ensure that future generations have the benefit of windfalls similar to the one from which the College is currently benefiting as a result of the premiums for commercial leases for developments at Milton South,

an area of land adjacent to the Science Park. Windfall is, perhaps, an unfair term for the proceeds from Milton South: my predecessors were canny in their husbandry of Trinity Hall's land holdings and realised that this land had great potential that, in collaboration with Trinity College, we are now realising. The majority of the proceeds from Milton South have been earmarked for Strategic Plan initiatives, but some has been added to the general funds to finance operations, of which I shall say more later.

As well as income from the investments, Trinity Hall receives fees paid by students or their local authorities, charges to members of the College (Fellows as well as students) for accommodation and catering, and sundry other sources, giving additional income of approximately £3¼ million a year. Although conference income is a useful part of many colleges' income, at Trinity Hall it is relatively insignificant, mainly because we do not have *en suite* bedrooms and there is a shortage of conference facilities on our compact city centre site. This means that we cannot compete with some other colleges that are not similarly hamstrung. But these characteristics are the same phenomena that give the Hall its unique character that so many alumni have enjoyed, and therefore it would be somewhat churlish to complain too loudly about the lack of large amounts of conference income.

Maybe this is the point to divert onto an explanation of how financial management operates in Trinity Hall, now and in the past. The Bursar is the Fellow who is responsible for the 'support' activities such as maintenance, catering, domestic services, the

Mountainous Landscape *by John Bellany, RA, a former Fellow Commoner. This painting hangs in the parlour of the SCR whilst his controversial portrait of John Lyons hangs in the Dining Hall.*

gardens and sports facilities, the porters, information technology, human resources, conference business and financial management. In the 1920s, the Bursar was the Hon. I.M. Campbell, a Scottish laird and part-time lecturer in Estate Management. He was succeeded from 1930 to 1952 by Cecil Turner, another part-time Bursar who specialised in Roman and criminal law. In response to the growing complexity of the job, Trinity Hall's first full-time Bursar, Brigadier Francis Curtis, was appointed in 1952, and ever since then the College has had a full-time Bursar, who was for a period supplemented by a Domus Bursar to look after the day-to-day operations of the College. Today we are relatively unusual in having reverted to just one Bursar. There has been a growing trend among Cambridge colleges to move away from recruiting Bursars from the armed forces and these days many Bursars have a background in one of the professions such as accountancy, investment management or construction.

On the financial side, the Bursar is supported by the Accounts Office, previously called the Bursary but whose name has been changed to reflect the more modern and professional image we wish to project. The Accountants (previously called Chief Clerks) head a small team that is responsible for collecting income, paying bills, cash management and preparing the accounts.

In 1976, Trinity Hall established thirteen committees, one of which, the Finance Committee, is responsible on behalf of the Governing Body for having an overview of the Bursar's management of the College's finances. The Committee meets ten times a year. It is chaired by the Master and comprises seven

Fellows (some appointed *ex officio*, others *ad hominem*) and the Presidents and Treasurers of both the MCR and JCR. In addition, when it meets to discuss investment business, it is advised by a team of four external experts in equity and property investments. These advisors help us to maximise our income while staying within an acceptable level of risk bearing in mind that investments can go down as well as up in value. As with other committees, the decisions of the Finance Committee have to be ratified by the Governing Body, which comprises all the Fellows of Trinity Hall. The process is that all committees' minutes are distributed to all Fellows before each of the nine meetings a year. As can be imagined, the number of committee papers can be considerable, and so the College adopts a streamlining system, known as 'starring', to restrict (but not to stifle) debate of uncontroversial items at Governing Body. This is probably not the place to go into details of the starring system, nor the division between 'unreserved' and 'reserved' items on committee and Governing Body agendas except to say that the latter are the sensitive items that are debated *in camera* without staff or students being present.

But back to finance. The obvious question is where does all the College's income go? In 2003/2004, Trinity Hall had approximately 360 undergraduates, 180 graduate students and 50 Fellows. 450 of the students and 13 of the Fellows lived in College-owned accommodation, which makes the College equivalent to a very large hotel that clearly takes a lot of money to run, employing roughly 100 staff supplemented by a number of casual workers who principally work in the dining hall. Approximately £2 million is spent each year on salaries and associated costs. Although one of the obvious charms of the Hall is its old buildings, these are very expensive to maintain, a problem shared by all the historic colleges to a greater or lesser extent. In addition to the Maintenance Department salaries, a further £½ million pounds is spent annually on routine maintenance materials, services and contractors. Then there is the £¼ million pounds set aside for financial support of students and the £¼ million pounds of catering costs. The balance of our income is consumed by such things as the Master's and Fellows' stipends (although most Fellows are primarily employed by the University and receive very little pay from the College), heating and lighting, insurance, laundry and cleaning materials, stationery, IT costs, purchase of books for the library, etc. Trinity Hall is a complex organisation with a multitude of activities, all of which cost money.

As well as the routine maintenance, there is a never-ending succession of major work on the fabric of the College, either to improve facilities or to repair the more serious ravages of time. The College prudently makes provision each year for the transfer of some of its income to a fund for major works. But these transfers are only sufficient for major repairs. New buildings and major improvements to the existing property require additional funding. £14½ million of the capital generated by the lease premiums at Milton South have been earmarked for several building projects, including the demolition and reconstruction of the sports pavilion at Wychfield, the construction of new accommodation, also at Wychfield, and the improvement of the historic buildings in the centre of Cambridge. But even £14½ million are not enough to cover all the costs of these projects, and therefore the College will be seeking donations of between £4 million and £6 million. These donations would enable the College to equip and staff a new gym at the pavilion, to complete the accommodation project at Wychfield so that we can meet the expected growth in student numbers for a further five years and house a higher proportion of our graduates, and to ensure the central site can meet the demands that will be placed on it in the coming years.

In addition to the above capital projects, some of the proceeds from Milton South will be transferred to general capital, the income from which will be used to finance new operational activities such as additional teaching Fellows employed by the College, increasing the levels of financial support for undergraduate and graduate students, and employing additional staff to meet the ever more regulated world in which we operate and the expectations that services will be to the highest standards.

The College has set aside £5½ million for these initiatives, but we calculate an additional £1½ million will be needed from fund-raising to allow the Hall to achieve all the ambitions stated in the current strategic plan.

In the past, fund-raising for operational activities has been on the basis that we have sought sufficient capital to fund the activities in perpetuity. But the College realises that our generous benefactors have also recently felt the cold draught of declining values of equities. We also recognise that we are living in a world that seems to be changing at an ever-increasing rate, and therefore the activities that we want to fund today may be irrelevant in the future. Consequently, we are changing tack in certain instances and asking our benefactors to make donations that will fund the proposal for maybe twenty years if we spend the capital as well as the income. The advantage of this approach is that £1 million will enable us to spend £75,000 a year over twenty years, compared with the £40,000 a year quoted previously if the capital has to be retained in perpetuity. The downside is, of course, that in twenty years' time we may need to go back to a new generation of alumni and other benefactors to ask for more money to continue to fund the activity if it is still appropriate to the College.

To summarise, Trinity Hall is not rich; it manages its investments carefully and with professional advice; the costs of running such a complicated organisation are high; and the College will almost certainly need to keep coming back to its alumni for more money in order to fund the improvements that are necessary for us to continue to be an effective college that we can all be proud of. What is it that they say? If you don't move forward, you die. And I'm sure that's the last thing that we all want of Trinity Hall.

John Pegler is a Chartered Civil Engineer and a Chartered Accountant. He spent nearly twenty years in the public sector designing and supervising the construction of roads, bridges and buildings. He then re-trained as an accountant. He worked at the National Portrait Gallery before joining Trinity Hall in 2001 as Bursar.

Changing roles and relationships

COLLEGE STAFF

ALBERT SLOOTS
PASTRY COOK 1939–1940, KITCHEN MANAGER 1946–80

When the war started I was working at a small hotel at the back of the Ritz. The day the war started the West End of London literally died…. That left me out of a job. I came up for an interview at Trinity Hall, and was so taken with the place. Cambridge itself was charming, even though there was a war on. The undergraduates were still coming up in those days, and the Kitchens were absolutely magnificent. They were spotless. The copper pots, there are still a few in the College now, were nickel-lined and they were absolutely like burnished gold…. It was absolutely beautiful. It was a lovely place. The money was a bit low…. I was offered £3 a week, but I needed a job.

One got one's food. On top of that, because things were rationed at that time, you also got a weekend joint given to you from the College to take home. The Kitchen staff and the cooks all sat down properly at a table with the chef at the top, which was the old style of these things…. The lower staff, that is the kitchen porters, and the apprentice boys, they fed in another room outside. You had to give your ration book to the College, because they needed them and undergraduates had to do the same.

We had an old-fashioned oven at the other end of the Kitchen, one which you fired and took out; an old baker's oven. I had to make things in my department and cook them down the other end of the Kitchen. There was an old Fellow named Revd Angus, and I had to cook for him every morning for breakfast two wholemeal rolls. And this oven, to heat it, took about three hundredweight of coal. It was used afterwards in the day, but it had to be heated early

because he wanted his breakfast by eight o'clock with these rolls. Freshly baked, two wholemeal rolls every morning….

At that time there was a manageress in the Kitchen Office, who really had a lady's life. The one before her, who I didn't know, was Mrs Leggett and she had such a status in the place that she had her own waiter, her own crockery and her own wine in the cellar. As time moves on, of course, things change, and the next one, Miss Wain, didn't have quite the same things.

[There was no union] for catering workers. Having worked in the College any small length of time and shown that you were worth working in the College, they cared for you. I don't say they did anything especially for you, but they cared for you, you belonged. In those days if you were ill there was no pay. The College didn't pay you. When someone was genuinely ill, Trinity Hall sent them from the Kitchen to their home a pint of consommé, and a baked custard, every day, to help them get better.

[Before the war] if someone broke a plate in the Kitchen – which nowadays they break by the dozen and generally burst into laughter over – they would have to take it to the manageress. She had a bell. You rang the bell and there were two lights. You pressed the bell and one said 'wait' and one said 'come in', and if it said 'wait', you had to wait until it changed to green, almost like today's traffic lights, and she would look at your record, and if you had broken one already in that term, you would have to pay for it….

A gyp in those days [before 1939] was a very honourable and honoured member of the staff. They mostly worked with their wives. the man and wife worked on the staircase…. The wife was the

162

bedmaker and her job was to make the beds, generally clean the rooms and so on, and the gyp was literally the man's personal servant who would take the man his morning tea. He would take him his shaving water because there was no hot water on the staircase in those days…. He would do almost everything for that man on the staircase except clean his shoes. There was a shoe man, a bootman, and he was employed to clean the shoes. This was until about the 1950s. There was also employed a bicycle man for undergraduates' bicycles, up to about the early 1950s. A man employed just to look after the undergraduates' bikes, clean them, mend the punctures, but of course the undergraduates were much more moneyed people….

The people in lodgings used to order meals from the College to go to their lodgings. First of all, we had a box-tricycle in the College, which was there for a long time after the war. The College gyps, besides the College staircase they worked on, each had a staircase or a street for which they were responsible for delivering orders. They had a large wooden tray, about four inch deep, iron bound and about 2ft 6ins by 2ft as an idea of the size. They varied in size actually, and they had a green baize, like the baize you might have on a billiard table. These were used in colleges a lot until very recent times, to keep food warm. Suppose we take as an example of a man living at the top of Jesus Lane and he wanted to give a dinner party for four. So he would order his dinner: soup, meat, sweet, savoury, coffee, liqueurs, etc. The kitchen clerk would take his order and compile an order for the necessary accoutrements, the crockery, the cutlery, the glasses, the linen. Of course, it was all linen, not paper, in those days, and this he would give to the pantryman in the Kitchen. The pantryman would take one of these big wooden trays and he would line up that order on it. Now the gyp concerned would collect that and take it on his head, walking, to the top of Jesus Lane…. Then he may well have to take wines to match up, so he would take those on his head and then, at the time the meal was wanted, he would take the meal in containers, there were various types of containers, as well as dishes, and he would take that on his head, generally in one go. You could get a lot on these trays you see…. It could happen that there were three orders on that

night and he would have to do that three times in different parts of Jesus Lane because that would have been his street. Of course, next morning he would go and collect…. It continued a little in the early part of the war but very, very few orders [were] given after the war….

Around that time the Master of the College was Professor Dean. Prior to the war the Master's Lodge took all that building of which the Master's Lodge is now part of. It took all the building and they had up to the war fifteen servants in the Master's Lodge. The College revolved round him. He knew everything that went on in the College. He had two pet hates. One was undergraduates' bicycles, which he would not have anywhere except in racks. There were racks in those days. Any bicycles he saw around the College he would tell the gardener to throw into the river, which indeed he did. Another thing he could not stand was a cat and if he saw a cat around, he would tell the gardener to shoot it, which indeed he did.

Interviewed by Martin Harris, 1981

DON TARRANT
VARIOUSLY IN THE BUTTERY AND KITCHEN, THEN A GYP, 1925–55
COLLEGE BUTLER 1955–73

[The job] was advertised in the paper and I applied for it. I was fifteen years old. About fourteen boys applied for it. The wages were very poor in colleges. I started at 7s a week, of which they stopped a 1s 1d. I started work in the Buttery. We used to start at between 7.15 and 7.30 in the morning. And the bedmakers used to come from the staircases to collect the butter and the milk, which were in big urns. And we used to dish out pint containers. The butter was always ¼ lb pats, and they used to take it back a pound at a time. The bread was also dished out from there.

We didn't have any half days, except one Sunday in six, despite the fact that you worked 60 hours a week. The hours were long and they didn't improve before the war at all. In spite of all this, you were happy; you made your own fun. There was always the chance to have a joke. Round the back where the bins were kept, the lids of them were suspended on a rope and we used to go round there and beat the lids with sticks and sing at the tops of our voices – operatic stuff. We were stopped by Mr Potts because of the noise we used to make. That used to be our entertainment….

Breakfast and lunch were very good meals, a key consideration for anyone working in a college. I remember one man, he used to keep his family on the bits he was allowed to take home. In those days, food was plentiful and of course there are so many things that when they have been cooked can't be cooked up again. All these sort of things he used to take home for his kids…. In the afternoons the joints of meat were put to hang and the fat used to drip into the tray and the dripping was sold by the cooks. It was considered to be one of their perks. And they used to sell it to the staff at 6d a pound, which was really good stuff, and in consequence they sold a great deal of it.

The undergrads in those days were a different lot. They were very good to the staff. You could always tell an undergrad in those days because so many of them wore plus fours, and the quality of their clothes…. One thing they didn't like was anyone who was scruffy. Undergrads from Eton would set about other undergrads and throw them in the river because they were scruffy.

When I was [a] University constable, if you picked anyone up in the street, the next day you had to deliver a note to their rooms calling them to see the Proctor, and they always treated it as a big laugh. But after the war they used to think we were dirty because we were constables. But these older boys used to have fun out of us. They used to come up to you in the street and deliberately bait you. Most of them were good athletes; they could run. We had to be good athletes too. I had some real good fun chasing undergrads. One night on Parker's Piece, a young undergrad was cuddling a young girl and I approached. He saw me and ran off. I chased him and caught him. Went across flower beds and everything. That young man offered me £100 to let him go. And he was only going to be fined 6s 8d. I didn't take it.

Interviewed by Joanne Eccleshall, 1982

RUBY CHAPMAN
BEDMAKER 1945–80s

I used to get here at 6.00 with my husband, go home at 8.00 and see to the children, get them off to school. I used to bike back again… and stay till they finished. My husband was in Hall till gone 9.00. He was entitled to a breakfast, but he would never have it because he'd come to help me. We used to have to scrub the stone staircase on our hands and knees in those days, which took me and him ten days to scrub. I've seen such a lot of changes, and I think it's better for the College. They've got central heating. We've all got a Hoover which we didn't have. In those days we had carpet sweepers. And there was no carpets all over, and some of the carpets had holes in, and most of the edges were polished. Mr Hall of Burleigh Street used to come and sweep all the chimneys, during the vacation, the whole staircase. All the carpets [were] rolled back, all the furniture covered up. Gosh, we used to work like the dickens when he came. We had to work all the vacation. Sometimes we had a day or two off because they only used to be done once a year. There used to be soot everywhere. I used to wear a scarf over my head, you know, like nurses have, to keep my hair clean because you got so dirty.

[Undergraduates] Well, they used to have their shoes cleaned. They used to be put out overnight and a man named Peter Fuller, who lived by the old hospital, he used to do Trinity Hall, Clare College and Trinity and they used to pay him so much a term for cleaning their shoes…. A lot of them in those days were moneyed people. I had, I think it was nine [students] all told, and I used sometimes to get a pound off each one, but only at Christmas. That odd pound, nine pound to me, was a lot of money then. And of course Fred used to get paid for top table, but would always leave his, if he could, till the end of term, when he used to buy things for the children: 8s 11d a pair of shoes…. They say the good old days, but we did have to struggle to keep right. They were hard days. It's no good saying….

Interviewed by Jonathan Steinberg, 1984

Ged Pilsworth, Clerk of Works since 1970.

GED PILSWORTH
CLERK OF WORKS 1970–

One of the jobs I was most proud of would have been the Master's Lodge. After Professor Deer retired and Lady Sugden came in, we refurbished the Lodge, knocked walls down, altered bathrooms and all sorts of things because it was in a bit of state…. So this is where the refurbishment of the Lodge started, which is a very interesting job. And I've also done it twice. Actually, the second time was quite interesting also for Lady Lyons who had all new floors put down… and that was a very interesting job.

In 1970, most areas of the College were sets and in 1972, I believe it was, we started on N staircase, taking the sets away and turning them into bed-sitters, which was a massive programme to get done in twelve weeks. We did achieve it, as far as the living accommodation goes, and the rest of the staircase was finished actually in term time. But most staircases in 1972 were sets and no central heating. They had night storage heating and we also had a programme in 1973 of putting central heating everywhere in the College, which we did.

Now we're in 2002, we do need more planning permission. Back from the 1970s up to the mid-1990s we more or less had a free hand with the building inspectors and planners. We got away with a lot and they knew it. The planners knew what was happening. Providing the standard of work was OK, they didn't object, but I think from the mid-1990s they began to pull the colleges over the coals over doing these jobs, so now we just ask and normally everything's OK and above board. That's all internal. If you come on the external of the College then you have to go for planning permission and it's all checked by building inspectors.

The only disaster I've known of is when we had a terrible storm, I believe it was in 1987, when it actually snowed in June. We had a thunderstorm and it caught the chimney stack on the end of Q staircase. And that is the only building disaster that I've seen in the College. When they decided to put up the new building in Cherry Tree Court, there was a mains sewer connection just inside the old

Andrew Ives (1964) took this photograph of the Chaplain, Revd Paul de N. Lucas, 'after a good dinner' and during renovations to the Master's Lodge, 1966.

entrance to that parking area, before the new building was put up, and a gang of Irishmen who were piling the system – piling round the outside of the area to take the new building – they were told about this. Anyway, it seemed to be ignored by somebody either through Coulsons or through the people who were doing the piling, and they busted through the main connection which went from the manhole just inside the gate. They were pouring concrete in by the lorry loads and they couldn't understand where it was going. Of course, it was blocking up the main sewer which ran down Garret Hostel Lane. It was blocked from there approximately 28 feet. A nine inch sewer pipe was blocked solid with concrete, which took an awful long time to get down to, which was about 21 feet down and replace pipes…. We weren't popular. To get in and out of the College, we had to come from Queens' Road down Garret Hostel Lane and over the bridge… for about three months.

Interviewed by Sandra Raban, 2002

Outstanding Chefs
Roy Calne, High Table Steward

When I was elected to the Fellowship in 1965 the Kitchen provided excellent food with a rather limited conventional menu. The Fellowship was small and for many years there was very little contact between the consumers and the Kitchen. The new and younger Fellows at that time felt that the Kitchen staff were well-trained and had adequate funds for the raw materials, but since they were unaware of the reception of their efforts, they lacked stimulation and criticism. I was appointed to the new honorary post of High Table Steward with a responsibility to be the go-between the Fellowship and the Kitchen to provide feedback in both directions. I still hold this post in my Honorary Fellowship status and I had the privilege of working with three outstanding chefs: Mr Sloots who had been with the College before the war and, on being demobbed, re-joined and retired in 1980; Mr Wright, with a French mother and a Cornish father, had had a hard training in the Negresco hotel, Nice, where his

uncle, their chef, was a strict disciplinarian and chased his nephew around the kitchen with his cooking knife when he felt his trainee's efforts could be better. Mr Wright was with us for fourteen years until 1995 when our current chef, Nigel Fletcher, was appointed. He trained at Trinity Hall and had worked closely with Mr Wright.

The High Table food at Trinity Hall has gone from strength to strength and has become increasingly imaginative. The Kitchen is prepared to travel the world with dishes from all countries and the chefs seem to be extraordinarily clever at obtaining the ingredients, even for the most exotic recipes. My role as 'feedback' has been as a friend to the chef, supporting him in any way I can, particularly when he is short of staff, and ensuring that his budget marches with the index of inflation.

I have a deep admiration for the Kitchen. Those who are unfamiliar with its workings do not realise that every day deadlines have to be met to provide appetising dishes on the table at the right time so that the consumers are not disappointed and hungry. On top of the High Table commitments, the Kitchen provides food for the undergraduates, graduates, numerous conferences that come to College and special occasions such as private dinners, feasts and May Balls. The Kitchen can only work if all the staff respect and obey the chef and dovetail their efforts so as to co-operate with colleagues and take great care with hot dishes, ovens, hobs, sharp knives and mechanical instruments, any of which is a potential hazard that can rapidly result in disastrous injury or fire. The whole set-up reminds me very much of a busy operating theatre, where, without discipline, chaos ensues and the patient's life is in danger.

We instituted a system of Kitchen Office lunches where the chef, the Wine Steward, the Bursar and one or two of the Fellows in rotation are invited to eat with the chef, discuss what they like and don't like, perhaps bring in special recipes that they cherish and which they hope will provide dishes in College similar to those cooked lovingly by their mothers. Fellows sometimes bring in special produce and in my travels I have brought back spices for South East Asian dishes.

Mr Sloots and Mr Wright *by Professor Sir Roy Calne.*

The proof of the pudding is in the eating and word has got around that an invitation to High Table at Trinity Hall, besides the usual expectations of collegiate company and conversation, will be a gastronomic treat and it is seldom that they are disappointed, yet our staff and food budget do not differ from most other colleges. It just shows what a dedicated chef and his team can do. I have always encouraged simple dishes with fresh, non-convenience products and without too many tastes mingling in one dish. From Mr Sloots we have inherited traditional Trinity Hall recipes going back to the time of the Mastership of Professor Dean. One of his favourites, cheese fondue, was a speciality that we still enjoy. Mr Wright gave us many French dishes and also outstanding Cornish pasties, which he explains were long and rigid so that they could be handed down from miner to miner in the tin mines of Cornwall. He was also a master of soups and I tried to persuade him to write a book on the subject but he never got around to it, sadly for those who enjoyed them, and would have liked the secrets to be passed on.

Mr Fletcher has brought the lessons of the past to the present with exciting innovations of his own. He has the added burden of producing vegetarian menus as there are now a significant number of Fellows with vegetarian wishes, varying from the extreme vegan to the 'piscatarian'. This all adds greatly to the work of the Kitchen but they respond magnificently and the vegetarian cuisine matches the normal diet in quality.

I enjoy very much my contact with the Kitchen. I started off with no claims of being a food expert and still would not aspire to that description, but over the years much has rubbed off, thanks to the excellence of the Kitchen staff, and I have commemorated Mr Sloots and Mr Wright, who are both still in good health, with a painting and I hope to do the same for Mr Fletcher. Both Mr Sloots and Mr Wright are avid coffee drinkers. Neither eat very much, but maybe it is important to be hungry in order to appreciate the subtleties of good cooking.

T.W. DICKINSON, BURSAR'S CLERK
JOHN PHILIP JONES (1950)

Key to the whole operation was Mr Dickinson, who ran the College accounts in the large room on the ground floor of L staircase, and who produced our College bills in handwriting; one of the largest items was invariably the credit at the bottom of the bills for

Left: *Snowy Farr, Hall gardener, who raised over £60,000 for the blind and partially sighted and was awarded an MBE for his charity work.*

Below: *Alan Payne, Hall gardener, at the Cottenham Young Farmers' Show with a team of Suffolk Punches, 1979.*

'Returned Empties'. Another very important figure indeed was Mr Loveday, the Head Porter, who acted as regimental sergeant major to the undergraduates who were playing the role of unruly subalterns. The word *porter* has a clear enough meaning, but the only occasion I actually saw Mr Loveday carrying a suitcase was when Anthony Eden, an Honorary Fellow, visited the College. The undergraduates were more startled by the sight of the Head Porter carrying a bag than they were by the greetings from the Foreign Secretary in his best electioneering manner (although he could not on this occasion find babies to kiss).

ALAN PAYNE AND SNOWY FARR, HALL GARDENERS
ROSAMUNDE REICH (1978)

Many students of the late 1970s will remember Snowy, surely the Hall's most sartorially vivid gardener. Dressed in his assorted military uniform, he might be seen on weekdays striding across the

lawns behind a motor mower, but on Saturdays he was to be found at the corner of Petty Cury and Market Hill. Having carefully positioned his small tractor and trailer, he entertained passers-by, especially children, with his collection of mice, poultry and other animals. The collecting boxes attached to the trailer showed his support for Guide Dogs for the Blind, but I seem to remember Snowy insisted that he was collecting for Blind Dogs. Whatever the order of words, he colourfully and loyally gave the collected money to his chosen charity, and must have sent them a considerable amount over the years.

Although less flamboyant, Alan Payne, the College's gardener who lived in The Lodge at Wychfield, was a skilled and knowledgeable person. As a landscape architect taking the Graduate Diploma in Polar Studies at SPRI, I became used to the inevitable questions resulting from both my initial profession, and the course I was taking during my self-awarded sabbatical. Talking to Alan became part of Wychfield life, and during these conversations, various other aspects of his life emerged. Alan had left school as a young teenager, sometime in the 1930s, and started work as 'the boy' on one of the few remaining Cambridgeshire farms that was entirely powered by horses. He rose in the ranks, and was proud to describe himself as a horseman – not a man who rode, but one skilled in looking after and working with heavy horses. Alan had a pronounced limp, due to having been kicked by a horse when he was a young man. He admitted he had not sought medical advice early enough and was now living with the consequences. Nevertheless, within the farming community he was known as a highly proficient worker with horses, and in early spring of 1979 this led to the request for him to break-in two young Suffolk Punch mares. It entailed teaching them to wear harness, and learn how to pull, so that they could ultimately be used for ploughing.

Alan admitted his lameness was a drawback, because the two Punches were both lively and powerful. Their owner was willing to assist, but further help was required and I was tentatively asked if I could help. In the end, we devised a workable timetable for all parties. Alan would finish gardening at about 4pm, and have a quick cup of tea. I would be in my room on the top floor of Boulton House and would break off from my work, which at that stage had reached the writing up of my dissertation ('Tourism in the Antarctic – its present impact and future development'). We would then meet by Alan's Land Rover and drive to the horses' paddock which was off the far end of the Huntingdon Road, on land now covered by new University buildings. Then followed an energetic hour, catching and harnessing the mares, before taking them through their training. For me it was a marvellously refreshing break from my work, and often the occasion for hard physical work. Trying to persuade a young horse that commands to walk on meant going in a straight line at a steady pace was interesting!

As far as his gardening work was concerned, Alan carefully tended the asparagus beds, and gave advice about the herbaceous border outside the Old Library. Just before completing my course and leaving Cambridge I wrote a brief report about the trees at Wychfield, recommending new planting, especially near the Huntingdon Road boundary. The Fellows accepted my suggestions, and I believe Alan had to oversee their implementation. When passing the site now, nearly 25 years later, it is encouraging to see the maturing trees.

Rosamunde Codling (née Reich) came to Trinity Hall to take the Diploma in Polar Studies. She completed her PhD with the Open University, visiting the Antarctic Peninsula with FCO sponsorship. She has continued to work in landscape planning and polar research.

Ken Golding, Head Porter
Andrew Stilton (1975)

During my first year, Ken Golding, the Head Porter, always seemed rather stiff and unfriendly and a stickler for the rules. It was, therefore, with some caution that my friends and I chose for our second year to move into 51 Bateman Street, where Ken would be our landlord.

He greeted us with a rather convoluted explanation of how 'I tend to take a different view of things when I am wearing my Bateman Street hat from when I am wearing my porter's hat.' The gist of this was: Have a good time, enjoy yourselves but be discreet about it.

The accommodation in 51 Bateman Street was superb. My room looked out over the Botanical Gardens and was big enough for the College second cricket eleven (which I captained) to use for slip-catching practice after a few pints. And we got on extremely well with Ken.

He and Mrs G lived on the ground floor but had their bedroom in the basement: My friends and I often used to congregate in Brian Crowe's room on the ground floor and Ken always claimed that every night he would be woken by the crash on the ground-floor boards as I ran down the stairs three at a time and jumped the last couple on my way down for a late-night coffee with Brian.

Several years after I left, Mark Hughes and I drove up to Cambridge and, after an evening in the Baron of Beef, ended up sleeping on the floor of Clive Costaldo, who was living at 51 Bateman Street. For old times sake, I ran down the stairs and missed the last couple. Sure enough, this resulted in the immediate appearance of Ken in a dressing gown, who greeted me cheerily: 'I knew it was you. I would recognise that crashing anywhere.'

Gyps cricket match, 1902.

Bert Stearn, Tutor's Clerk
Joan Durrant

The College Office was run by Bert Stearn, a very cheery and affable man who was well loved by all the undergraduates. He knew everything that an undergraduate needed to know, and entered them for their public exams. His office always looked like the residue from a jumble sale. Paper lay everywhere in heaps and yet he always knew where to find everything you wanted. Mr Crawley used to send me over to file some of this paper when Bert was on holiday, much to his dismay – he said he couldn't find anything when he got back. I had had a job sorting it and separating the half-eaten sandwiches and apple cores from the paper, but we all loved him.

Joan Durrant came to the Hall as Charles Crawley's secretary in 1947 after being demobbed from the Royal Navy, where she served with Launcelot Fleming.

Ian Walker, Porter 2000–

Whoever described war as 'periods of inactivity interspersed with bursts of frantic action' must once have been a college porter. When the post (four sackfuls) has come late, your colleague calls in sick, a bar delivery has just arrived, the back gate needs opening to admit a skip wagon, the phone rings again, and two bare-foot, shivering undergrads appear in dressing gowns, having locked themselves out while showering – well, one can feel just a bit beleaguered. Normally, of course, that won't all occur at once; still, when it does, a porter may well suffer what a priest would call a 'crisis of faith', and begin to doubt their vocation: at least for the time it takes to sort things out.

Managing it all as smoothly as possible is what the Porters' Lodge aspires to: for the good of the students, Fellows, staff and even the tourists – provided it's not the Easter (exams) term, and porters haven't already had to chase strangers out of staircases or off the grass. Many visitors turn out to be looking for the Wren library. It is a continuing source of satisfaction politely to inform them of the Hall's two-hundred-year seniority over Trinity College before directing them 'next door'.

Fortunately, unlike our neighbours, we do not sport bowlers, yet many and various are the metaphorical hats worn daily in the Trinity Hall lodge. The keepers of the keys must, each one of them, be a combination of: safety officer; First Aider; fire warden; switchboard operator; hotel receptionist; revenue collector; mail sorter; message taker; upholder of tradition; lender of gowns; school prefect; frequent puller of party plugs; agony aunt; dispenser of common sense, tea, sympathy and sometimes paracetamol; assuager of fears and exam stress; friend to the fresher; giver of second chances; judicious blind-eye turner; scourge of the unmannerly; trumpeter of every example of excellence; recognizer of 650 or so names and faces; and fount of all knowledge… showing commendable modesty withal, of course.

The porter's job, once a certain confidence has been gained, is largely its own reward. It offers the satisfaction of working in unique surroundings and of seeing bright young people develop to realise their potential, have fun and do well.

Every now and then something quite exceptional happens to astound and delight the lodge. Many students work hard, but some play even harder. Imagine my surprise last summer, then, as I went about locking up and dousing lights at 2am to find probably the most renowned player of his year beavering away in the library attic a week or two before his finals. Both student and porter were taken aback but the student quickly recovered: 'For heaven's sake,' he said, 'don't tell anyone you've seen me here. It would ruin my credibility.' He ruined that himself soon after when he graduated with a First.

Ian Walker worked for twenty years as a journalist, mainly on the Surrey Advertiser *but also as a sub editor on the* Cambridge Evening News, *before opting for a quieter life as a porter at Trinity Hall in 2000.*

Battling thews and sinews

HALL SPORT

BRIDGET WHEELER (1977)

Trinity Hall students have exhibited enthusiasm for their sport, and varying degrees of success within the University and without it. Today's students participate in a wide range of sports and are competitive in various leagues set up within the University in most sports. Participation at University level continues to be impressive, with over a dozen different sports regularly represented. It was not always so. In the latter part of the nineteenth century, for example, rowing was such a dominant sport within the College that until 1892 the Hall had no field for cricket and football (although it had great players), whilst it remained a matter of considerable importance to ensure the presence of the first boat in the First Division (and up to seven other boats on the river). This may explain the outstanding success of the Hall at Henley in 1887 and on the water at the early Olympic Games, as the following articles describe.

It was, however, only a matter of time, with the acquisition of playing fields, before association football would become a similarly important sport, and one in which the Hall from time to time enjoyed considerable success, winning Cuppers on several occasions, and regularly providing players to the University squad. It was a similar story with rugby football, and over the years a number of successful individual sportspersons have enjoyed outstanding success in their own sports – for the College, University and often their country.

In common with other colleges, Trinity Hall sportspersons formed together to create a social arm for themselves in the form of the Crescent Club, whose origins are obscure, but which was already a lively association over a hundred years ago. In 1978 this forward-thinking association first elected women, although in 1986 the women formed their own black and white club, known as the Penguins. Both associations continue to thrive.

ROWING DYNASTIES

The Hall has spawned several dynasties of great oarsmen. Augustus Bayford rowed in the first ever Boat Race in 1829. His son, Robert, stroked the first Hall boat to go Head of the River in 1859, under the inspired coaching of Leslie Stephen. His son, also Robert, won a rowing blue in 1893 and grandson, Richard, was a freshman stroke for the Hall in 1922. Of four Landale brothers at the Hall, Percy rowed for the University three times in 1887, 1888 and 1889 and his brother Walter, twice in 1891 and 1892.

By far the longest-running and most successful dynasty of Hall oarsmen must be the Swann family. Sidney Swann has been described as 'the greatest all-round athlete of whom there is any memory at the Hall.' Highly competitive, he could never resist attempting to break a record, which led him to extraordinary feats in running, cycling, swimming and even sculling across the Channel at the age of 49. He also tried to fly a home-made aeroplane by starting the engine,

Left: *Sidney Swann, the legendary Hall athlete, in his home-made aeroplane.*

Left: *Sidney Swann, the legendary Hall athlete, in his home-made aeroplane.*

Below: *THBC at Henley, 1920.*

Middle: *Bevis Sanford and teammates in training for the Boat Race, 1940.*

Bottom: *Timothy Swann (left), then secretary of THBC and another member of the rowing dynasty, with Andy Moyes, Robin Woodhouse and Tony Bigland, 1950.*

putting it into gear and jumping on behind. It apparently did fly, if only for a very short way. However, it is as an oarsman that he is chiefly remembered at the Hall. He rowed for the Hall four times, twice while already a curate in Plymouth, getting one crew to come and train in Plymouth harbour to great effect since they went on to win the Grand Challenge Cup. He won three rowing blues between 1883 and 1885, winning the Stewards' and Visitors' Cups at Henley in a four which included fellow Hall man, Charles Bristowe.

Sidney's two sons, Sidney Ernest (Cygnet) and Alfred, both came up to the Hall. Cygnet had been a cross-country runner at school and thought perhaps he might do the same at Cambridge, writing to his parents that he had visited Fenner's on his first free afternoon. This elicited a terse telegram from his father, which read: 'AT THE HALL THEY ROW – FATHER.' This proved useful advice as Cygnet went on to row for the Hall, the University and the country, winning a gold medal in the British eight at the 1912 Olympics as well as the Colquhouns, the Visitors' and Wyfold Cups. While President of CUBC, he and his brother Alfred won the Silver Goblets at Henley. Both returned to the Hall after the First World War, Cygnet serving as coach and College chaplain from 1920 to 1922 and competing in the 1920 Olympics where he won a silver medal. The same year, Alf won the Colquhouns, became President of CUBC and gave THBC its hundredth seat in the Boat Race. He stayed on as a coach and, together with Cygnet, was instrumental in the revival in College rowing between the wars, recognising the importance particularly of the lower boats.

The Second World War saw a new generation of Swanns take over the THBC. Cygnet's son, R.D.S. (David) was Captain of THBC and rowed in a blue boat in 1941, although the Boat Race that year was

called off at the last moment by Oxford. Alf's son, J.T. (Timothy), though better known as a runner, also trained in a blue boat and edited the supplement to Henry Bond's *A History of the Trinity Hall Boat Club*.

Finally, with the advent of women at the Hall, the Swann family was not slow to provide an oarswoman: Lucy Byrne, David's niece and Timothy's cousin, won her oars rowing at bow in the very successful Ladies' First May Boat of 1980, which climbed ten places in the Mays over two years.

A Boat Club Saga
Julian Ebsworth (1960)

'Fix upon the mound of my grave the oar that in life I pulled among my comrades', Elpenor in Homer's *Odyssey*, Book XI, 77–8

Trinity Hall Boat Club's history on the river is a stunning tale for a small college, remarkable for how long its success has lasted. It is the stuff of a good novel, from which dreams are dreamed, and which has contributed to happy and heartwarming friendships lasting lifetimes.

Rowing began on a semi-organised basis during the Regency period at Eton, Westminster, and then at Oxford and later Cambridge colleges. Unlike the Thames, the Cam was a difficult river for sport, being part of a navigation canal for coal barges, wholly insalubrious, narrow, twisty, reedy with the nearest decent stretch between locks on Midsummer Common and at Chesterton. The Backs themselves have always been totally unsuitable. It is to 1827 that THBC traces back its debut, two years before the first Boat Race. This was also the year when both the CUBC was formed and bumping races began; indeed it was in Trinity Hall rooms on 9 December 1828 that a new set of rules for the racing were drawn up by CUBC.

Racing took place initially between named boats of four, six, eight or even ten oars, rather than between colleges. There is a record of a Trinity Hall boat mysteriously called *The Ghost*. Until the introduction of the outrigger, boats were large cutters, or gigs, broad of beam, very heavy, 40 foot long with huge rudders, costing with a set of oars around £80. (Exact replicas were made for the commemorative contest held before the 150th Boat Race on 28 March 2004.)

THBC's presence on the river (with only one boat) was fairly modest until the 1850s. Positions in the order were typically between tenth and twentieth. THBC began an inexorable rise towards the top in 1852, when it made eight bumps, remaining in the top half of Division 1 for very many years. A second boat also 'got on' for the first time that year. The rise coincided with the appointment in 1852 of Henry ('Ben') Latham as Tutor, later to become Master, and of Leslie Stephen as a Fellow, who was also a leading coach (he also composed a boating song for the bump suppers). THBC was quick to interest itself in Henley Royal Regatta

THBC race successes 1859–2004.

ON THE CAM		HENLEY ROYAL REGATTA							
Head of Lents	Head of Mays	Grand	Ladies	Thames	Stewards	Visitors	Wyfolds	Goblets	Diamonds
*									
	*								
	*								
			*						
					*	*			
	*	*							
	*	*	*	*	*	*			
	*					*			
*	*								
	*					*			
	*								
	*								
	*	*							
	*								
	*								
									*
							*		
							*		
			*				*		
			*						
						*			
	*		*						
	*								
						*	*		
								*	
								*	
							*		
								* (a)	
			*						
						*			
						*		*	
	*(b)								
	*								
						*			
*									
	*(c)								
						*			
						*			
* (M) * (W)									
* (M) * (W)									
* (M)									
* (M)	* (M)								
* (M)	* (M)								
	* (M)								
	* (M)								
* (W)									
* (W)									

(a) with 3rd Trinity

(b) Timed Race

(c) went Head on 1st night but bumped down on last night

which had begun in 1839. It made its first foray into the eights event, the Ladies' Plate, in 1855. The 1850s culminated with THBC taking its first Headship in 1859 (the last year in which first boats raced in the Lent term). Two more Headships followed in 1862 and in 1864.

Since 1864, THBC has enjoyed particularly purple patches in eights, although the overall level of achievement, with one or two

A Boat Club ledger from 1880.

temporary hiccoughs, has been high throughout all these years. If one includes successes at Henley, these periods are 1880–1912; 1935 to the mid-1950s; and more recently on the Cam 1982–3 and most of the 1990s. There have also been some occasional highlights in between. These periods have also been paralleled by equal success in other events on the Cam for which space does not allow more than a mention here – the University Fours, the Magdalene Pairs, the Colquhoun Sculls, the Lowe Double Sculls, the Foster Fairbairn Pairs and Junior Sculls and the Bushe-Fox Freshmen's Sculls.

THBC's first win at Henley was in 1880 in the Ladies' Plate. Both the Stewards' and the Visitors' – four-oared events – were won by the same crew in 1885, to be followed by a capture of the premier event, the Grand Challenge Cup, in 1886. As every THBC member knows, however, the most fabulous year of all was 1887 when the club won no less than five events at Henley – the Grand with the first eight, *both* the Ladies' *and* the Thames Cup with the second eight (!), and the Stewards' and Visitors' fours events with mostly members of the first eight. No other club has been able to remotely emulate this achievement, which is all the more remarkable for having been achieved with only 19 men (one of whom rowed having caught mumps). Telegrams from Henley back to the College reporting the wins still hang in the Bursar's Folly. The 1890s at Henley finished in fine style, with a further win in the Grand in 1895 and B.H. Howell's win in the Diamonds in 1898 (he went on to win the Wingfield Sculls, the top sculling event in the country, that year).

Returning to the Cam, THBC was Head of the Mays from 1886–88 and 1890–97, its longest sequence at the top, It also went Head of the Lents for the first time in 1890. The *annus mirabilis* of 1887 was further marked by having three boats in the Mays first division, at Head, sixth and eighth. The second eight was the

F. J. Furnivall (64 3/4), Sunday, 13 Octr, 1889.

Dr Frederick Furnivall, who studied mathematics at the Hall in 1842, was one of the more colourful characters of the Victorian age. An eminent philologist and early contributor to the Oxford English Dictionary*, he was the founder of the Early English Text Society. Strongly influenced by Christian Socialism, he also helped to found the Working Men's College in London. He became almost as famous for his foul-mouthed feud with the poet Swinburne as for his friendship with Kenneth Grahame, who immortalised him as the Water Rat in* The Wind in the Willows*. Whilst at the Hall he rowed in the first eight and had a passion for sculling. His enduring legacy at Cambridge, however, was as a boat designer. It was he who introduced the outrigger to the Cam, which represented a quantum leap in the early development of the modern racing eight and led to a surge in the popularity of rowing as a sport at Cambridge. He was elected an Honorary Fellow at the Hall in 1902. He was also in later life an ardent and somewhat scandalous advocate of rowing for women and would have been very proud of the success of the Hall ladies' boats.*

highest second boat for twelve years (in 1892 it rose to fourth position) and THBC was, with 1st Trinity BC, the only club to have three boats on the river for nearly 25 years. Moreover, nearly one-third of the CUBC Boat Race crews between 1885 and 1897 were from the College, in one year filling six seats in the boat.

During the first decade of the twentieth century, THBC never fell below third in the Mays; it went Head twice, in 1907 and 1908, also winning the Ladies' Plate again in 1907, the (four-oar) Wyfolds on three occasions and the Visitors' once more in 1910. THBC had three representatives in the Olympic Games in 1908. Rowing then came to a complete halt during World War I.

THBC's second successful period, from 1935 to the mid-1950s, was notable for nine more wins at Henley, including the Ladies' Plate in 1935 and in the pair-oar Silver Goblets plus a run of three wins in the Visitors' in 1947, 1951 and 1955. Small boat wins on the Cam were especially numerous, and rowing continued, albeit in a reduced form, throughout World War II. Peacetime brought THBC to the Head of the Mays in 1946, and for the second time to the Head of the Lents in 1948, a year in which the Fairbairn Cup was also won for the first time (also later in 1975).

Within very recent memory, THBC successes on the Cam have continued, despite academic pressures. The most striking has

Trinity Hall Boat Club Ball.

Savoy Hotel.

Monday, July 9th, 1923.

been the arrival of THBC women on the river. After a quite remarkable climb through the ranks of the Ladies' Divisions 2 and 1, the Ladies' Mays crew (in fours in the early years, in eights since 1990) went Head in 1982 and 1983; other fours events were also won at the time. Happy years for THBC, for the men also went Head in the Lents in these same two years. There was also much to celebrate in the 1990s – for the men, a four-year run as Head of the Mays from 1992–95 and one of three years of the Lents 1991–93 (their 'doubles' in 1992 and 1993 were the first since 1890); and for the women going Head of the Lents in 1996 and 1999 (rowed in eights since 1976).

A boat club would not be successful without an underlying efficient infrastructure. THBC can count itself particularly fortunate. Firstly, the boathouse is one of the largest on the Cam, and built one hundred years ago in 1905. It was updated with the help of a generous donation from the late M.J.H. Nightingale in the 1980s. It now, of course, incorporates facilities for women, and a proper workshop and weights room. Secondly, university rowing, because of the relatively transitory periods of participation by its members (compared with non-academic rowing clubs), is heavily dependent on boatmen, coaches, and old members, heavy or otherwise, to provide the continuity. In Percy Masters (1934–73) and Martin Fordham (1974 onwards), who together span no less than seventy years at THBC, the club has been blessed with essential boatbuilding skills, astute coaching abilities, and utter loyalty through the years. They are excellent examples of the special 'watermen' breed. Of coaches there have been legion, too many to mention individually here – from the Senior Common Room, churchmen, international oars and CUBC coaches to the willing and unsung helpers who come back from near and far, year after year, to share their experience and engender THBC's mixture of

The Lent Bumps, 1938.

enjoyment, fun and success. Since 1973 there has been a THBC Advisory Committee to determine strategy – and dance around the delicate topic of admission procedures. Thirdly, THBC's history is delightfully recorded in three sumptuous volumes – the former Master Dr Henry Bond's (covering 1827–1928), J.T. Swann's (1928–49) and D.I. Sparkes' (1949–87). Theirs together form one of the most telling chronologies of a club's history, spiced with some delightful vignettes of individuals who have been involved down the years. Last, but not least, finance: THBC was the fortunate recipient in the 1920s of part of the large residue of the estate of A.J. Gillott, who rowed in the 1887 3rd May boat, and there have been successful appeals in the last twenty years.

Just one reflection: For THBC, 2005 will mark not just the 150th anniversary of its first entry at Henley but also the fiftieth of its last win. Sadly, regular entries by THBC to the regatta have become a thing of the past, even in years when it has met with success on the Cam. Although the Henley Committee of Management has tried to grapple with the problem of college rowing, the last Cambridge college to win in eights was in 1967 and in fours 1974. THBC oarsmen are, of course, still to be found in CUBC crews. But *plus ça change, plus c'est la meme chose* for Dr Bond's history records the difficulties of the 1855 Ladies' Plate crew. And the Cam, even if it may be much more salubrious and less reedy now, remains as narrow and twisty as always. And, oh, those cold Siberian winds in the winter !

Julian Ebsworth read economics and law from 1960 to 1963. He worked in the Civil Service (DTI and Foreign Office) from 1965 to 2001, and in retirement is Honorary Secretary of London Rowing Club.

Patrick Macleod (1935)

In 1938, the Hall's rugger team was not strong and, predictably, was beaten in the first round of the Cuppers. Coincidentally, the Captain of the Boat Club was badly short of a crew for the fifth Lent boat.

Somewhat pompously the latter approached the rugger team captain and implied, in so many words, that if eight rugger stalwarts could be found to man the fifth Lent boat, it would probably only lose four places in the races. In this way, the fifth Lent boat would stay on the river and not have to start at the bottom of the division in 1939.

Naturally, everyone selected to crew the fifth Lent boat vowed that not only would a place not be lost, but that every effort would be made to better the boat's position on the river.

Ably coached by Bill Leishman, after three weeks training everyone was in tip-top form. Despite one of the crew 'catching a crab' on the third day, the fifth Lent boat made six bumps, over-bumping twice.

To the envy of many THBC members, the fifth Lent boat crew had won their oars after rowing for only four weeks. It was a great consolation for eight of the rugger team's otherwise dispirited members and an enormous surprise for the THBC Captain.

Standley Bushell (1943)

Sometimes there were two, perhaps three, boats on the river. There was always a rugger boat in the Mays. We managed a joint hockey boat on one occasion and I rowed in three successive Mays and I have to confess that I never got past the railings. The College activities and the traditions attached to the rowing and rugby were such that in 1945 the

College won the rugby Cuppers and in 1946 the hockey Cuppers and, never to be forgotten, was Head of the River. I think those typify the sort of spirit and cooperation, because for a small college, and the numbers were much lower than they are now, to have produced teams of such quality and ability was an achievement in itself.

I remember when Launcelot Fleming became Bishop of Norwich… meeting the then Master, Sir Ivor Jennings, at a time when sport was at a very low ebb. One or two of us were rather disappointed and I braved the stern look on his face to inquire about the lack of sporting prowess at the Hall at the time. He took the view that the academic side was more important and I had to gently point out to him that six members of the Head of the River crew took first class degrees.

James Sunnucks (1946)

After three years naval service as an Able Seaman (meteorologist) I arrived at the Hall in September 1946. I was urged by Launcelot [Fleming] to take up rowing because the Cambridge climate demanded physical recreation and, if I had no other sport in mind, rowing was the best choice. I accordingly rowed in the fourth boat in which we got our oars in the Bumps and on one occasion were sliced in half pulling in or pulling out during the Bumps. The Secretary of the Boat Club was Ron Scruby who had lost a leg in the war but kept a spare 'rowing leg' at the Boathouse. The spare leg – stockinged and shod – in the changing room could sometimes give one rather a shock on entry. The Master and Launcelot took great interest in the lower boats. I believe it was their interest in the lower boats which led to so many rowing triumphs at this time.

Peter Usher (1951)

In 1953 the Boat Club were having a rather lean year in the May races. Trinity Hall Rugger Club had won the Cuppers a few months earlier and were on a high, but we always felt that in the Master's eyes we came a poor second to the Boat Club. Now the Trinity Hall Rugger Boat was on the verge of winning its oars. I was stroke and

we had made all our previous bumps in the Plough Reach but already we had passed the Plough. As we approached the Railway Bridge it was our last chance. Mike Shearman, the cox, called for one more 'ten' and suddenly we were within a few feet. We made the bump just before the Railway Bridge. As we made that last effort my enduring memory is of Professor Dean cycling along the towpath, scattering all before him and shouting his head off for us. That day we felt the Rugger Club had arrived.

Caroline Newton (1977)

Once the autumn term began, the Hall had to get used to women. I was permitted to teach graduates to row in an eight after they had been properly schooled by a male member of the Boat Club in a bank tub, and so emerged the 'Gradueight' boat of 1978–79. I also rowed in the first-ever Hall women's boats, with some success. We should have got our oars in the Lents but couldn't quite manage the final bump. I rowed at 3 in the first Trinity Hall Ladies' May Boat in 1978, which was all a bit more exciting. We rowed over the first two days, but on the third day we were rammed just as we were pulling over to the bank, having bumped New Hall 3. I was literally 'rowed over' by the attackers and ended up in hospital and the papers.

John Naylor (1988)

In our third race in the Mays of 1989, we were heading into a bend in the river when our cox failed to make a sharp enough turn. I was bow and could see out of the corner of my eye that we were coming close to the bank of the outer shore. I did as I and everyone else in the boat had been instructed (which was rare) and kept my eye on the stroke and kept going. That worked fine until I and everyone on the bow side of the boat had to raise their oars because we were so close that they were gliding over the shore. I distinctly remember seeing the spectators on the bank running to get out of the way and one of my team-mates' oars slamming into a coolbox which exploded, spraying ice and drinks everywhere. We were bumped shortly after that. Fortunately, if I recall correctly, the Hall's first boat went head.

Martin Fordham, Boatman. Martin joined the THBC in 1974 after a brief apprenticeship in the College Boathouse at Eton. His reputation as a craftsman and especially as a coach has led other clubs to attempt unsuccessfully to lure him away. He and his predecessor, Percy Masters, who served for almost forty years, have been powerful influencers of the Boat Club's destiny, running the Boathouse between them for over seventy years.

Row Hall!
Tom Robins (2001)

As we charge towards one hundred and eighty years at the top of college rowing and we once again prepare the coaching bike of time for the tow path of destiny, you'll be pleased to know the club is in fine health. It is still my pleasure to find the cycle racks full, the changing rooms packed high with kit and the boat racks empty. We remain the largest club in College, with eighty members competing in the Lents and an estimated twelve black and white crews hitting the river for the Mays.

Our success in numbers is a direct reflection of the great time members have as novices. More than ever, the vast majority of members have never rowed before they arrive at Cambridge. However, with the right coaching and careful development we continue to embarrass those with much more experience. We are also lucky to receive a constant trickle of schoolboy oarsmen. It is the integration of these experienced rowers, often blues or internationals, with our own College oarsmen, that annually keeps our first eight in contention for both headships.

The first men's positions of second in the Mays and fourth in the Lents should produce some outstanding and exciting racing this year. The women are also on the up. Following a difficult few years, with the absence of any schoolgirl rowers, the squad has matured and is confidently fighting its way into contention.

As Captain, it is my job to ensure the smooth running of the club. It is a never-ending job, characterised by the highs of shiny pots and the lows of another call to our insurance company. The nightmare of last-minute injuries vanishes upon receiving the golden alumni phone call, 'is there anything you need coaching?'

Rowing continues to be an expensive sport and the manner with which the Boat Club is funded remains complicated. It would also appear to keep us eternally short of money. Nobody told Gillott when he did the calculations that one day women might want to row and it has been a long time since we've had an alumni whip-round. Thankfully our reputation is our greatest asset and

this year, for the first time, the Club will be sponsored. An approximately five-figure deal with the Scottish independent investors Baillie Gifford will allow us to continue to provide the very best rowing experience, not to mention hot water for the best showers in Cambridge.

It is the atmosphere of the Club that provides us with strength. I was flattered when a friend of mine described the noise coming from a recent Boat Club dinner as 'truly frightening'. I'm pleased to report that we are still being asked to leave from all the best colleges and 'stop riding that horse!' Martin the Boatman's ability to make boats and tea is only matched by his ability to reminisce and so it was a great privilege to hear him describe the club as 'doing good'. As the sound of 'Row Hall!' continues to reverberate across Midsummer Common, the Hall is going head, again.

Tom Robins, Captain of THBC 2003–04.

Nick Eastwell in action for THAFC, 1977.

Trinity Hall Association Football Club
John Collier

Sport in Trinity Hall has been for long so closely identified with the College Boat Club that it may surprise many alumni to be told that other games have been played here. Indeed, many of its members in the mid-1970s may not have realised that the College had an association football team until 1975, when its eleven began to progress towards the Cuppers final. This coincided with the careers of Steve Smith, who captained the University Club, and John Wilkes, who, over several periods of residence, collected five blues. He is thought to be the first person at this University to do so for any one sport and very few have done this since.

In 1976 the Cuppers final was reached but lost by an own goal to one to St Catharine's, then the heartiest college in Cambridge, with about nine blues. The losing score was again 0–1 the following year and in 1978 the Hall lost to Fitzwilliam in the final. There were other notable College matches: once we were playing Fitzwilliam at Wychfield and losing 0–4 with twenty minutes to go when a rainstorm hit Fitz in their faces and a bombardment of five Hall goals hit the back of their net. Memorable players included Nick Eastwell, Morris (Bob) Charlton, Chris McFadzean and Rick Bacon. Dr Jonathan Steinberg, a keen soccer follower (though an American, he supported Cambridge United), became Club President. On his vacating office in 1982 John Collier was appointed Jonathan's successor by the then captain, Jonathan Klein, to forestall a move by JC to the vacant manager's post at Aston Villa (JC was a shameless pluralist who was also at the same time Senior Treasurer of the Crescent Club and then added President of the Rugby Club and Senior Treasurer of the Amalgamated Club to his unpaid College jobs).

The glory days were the late 1970s and early 1980s, during which we won the Colleges' Championship in 1980 and the Cuppers in 1984, each for the only time – since 1966, at any rate. This may not seem a great record but is better than many clubs, Birmingham City, for example, have ever done. On looking at the 1980 team photograph, one is struck by how far our boys were

from being typical football hooligans; indeed, what an intellectual lot they were. The side contained several PhDs, one of whom, Ian Postlethwaite, a Research Fellow, was signed on a free transfer from St Catharine's, where he had been a research student with three blues under his belt. A number of the lads, including skipper Ian McMaster, got Firsts in the Tripos and two of them are now QCs. A blue and a star player was Steve Evans, a displaced scouse and Everton supporter, whose silken skills are legendary.

The Admissions Committee, which from 1974 to 1985 consisted of Ernest Frankl and the two Club Presidents, had been working for years to a football Cuppers win. They paved the way by letting in Mark Eardley (called Tardelli since he was half Italian), another man whose skills, as they say, were awesome. He had been on the books of Stoke City until they realised he could play football, whereupon they transferred him to the Hall. He captained the blues in 1982 and was followed by Julian Ironside, who was, atypically, a Kiwi who led the University in the centenary Varsity match in 1983. His team contained three other Hall boys: David Hudson, who was a hereditary supporter of Aston Villa; Angus Whyte, a very effective player from Wolverhampton Grammar School; and Graham Walsh, an England schoolboy international striker from Barrow. These four were the backbone of the Cuppers team which beat the Cambridge Tech, as it then was, by three goals (two by Walshie), to one (a first-half penalty). Graham went on to captain the blues in 1984, the third Hall man in a row to do so.

By a strange coincidence, 1983–84, in which the Hall won the Cuppers, was the year in which the Hall topped the colleges' Tripos Table for the first time anyone could remember.

We have had several blues since, including Will Wesson and Adrian Spurling, a public schools racquets champion who was also a golf and racquets blue. Others include Rob Mather, Paul Harris and Andy Fraser. In 1997 once again we had a blues Captain, Iain White, a Geordie central defender with a physique like a St James's Park goalpost but who could fire a football like a cannon.

But football's main contribution, like all the other sports, including women's football and men's and women's rugby, to College life has been the friendship and fun afforded to so many of our magic boys and girls who have played for the Hall.

John Collier has been tutor, mentor, guide redeemer and friend to many Hall law students and footballers from 1966–2001. He was Vice-Master 1986–90. He supports Aston Villa in tandem with THAFC.

THE 'NEARLY BOYS'
JAMES THOMAS (2002)

Football, or soccer as it is now irritatingly referred to, is the nation's game. It is said to break down barriers of language – all nationalities and tongues can communicate with a football. There are stories (true or not, they are still stories) of troops dropping arms and playing impromptu games during wars. A former England manager is reported to have said (if we believe the T-shirts): 'Football is not a matter of life and death – it's more than that.'

Based on that evidence one would expect Trinity Hall AFC to be bursting at the seams. In some senses, yes, in others, no. We are a respectable enough outfit (well, at least we have had two new kits in two seasons) and have an e-mail membership list of over 80. Nevertheless, spectators for any game other than against neighbours Trinity, are few and far between. We are one of the few colleges to boast three full teams and an MCR team (not to mention two women's teams as well). We are even a sponsored club – the first XI by Hall alumni entrepreneurs Gal•peck and the newly formed third XI by local quality food outlet Gardi's. At least we look and feel the part, even if we don't necessarily always play it.

At the alumni open day this year I had the pleasure of sitting next to a gentleman (whose name sadly escapes me) who played for the Hall many moons ago (1950s I believe). His main complaints were not that we didn't play with guts, for that we surely did, but that we so rarely had luck on our side: essentially we were 'nearly boys' too much of the time. Well, most of that which he remarked is probably still true today. We do not cause other teams to quake in their boots when we are drawn against them in the Cuppers draw, but they do need to think twice about the game. Of all the school teams and clubs I have played for (count them on one hand, folks), I've never known a team to have so much unrealised potential. I, however, can feel it in my Puma Kings that this could be the year….

We are a club that enjoys our sport. A respectable first XI who are eyeing a chance at promotion this season, a second XI who are streets above their rivals this year and a third team who smile more during 90 minutes than I have ever seen before in a team.

It can only be a coincidence that the ball most confiscated by the likes of Alan and the other porters from being illegally banded around Latham Lawn last summer was a round one. Maybe it is the College's game after all….

James Thomas, THAFC Captain 2003–04.

ROGER ALDRIDGE (1987)

In May 1988 the first ever inter-collegiate American Football competition was held. This was a knock-out competition over several weeks. The final was held on 1 May 1988 between the Trinity Hall Truants and the Jesus Cardinals. Despite the Cardinals fielding one or two ringers, Trinity Hall won the game 31–20. The Hall team was mostly graduates, with one undergraduate, and mostly Canadians and Americans. One of our stars was George Oti, whose cousin Chris played for the England Rugby team.

Hostile reception: defender and ball arriving at the same time

Playing Truants is Jesus' downfall

American Football

Trinity Hall Olympians
Bridget Wheeler (1977)

When Tom James won his place in the Great Britain eight for the 2004 Olympic Games in Athens, he joined an impressive group of Trinity Hall Olympians reaching back (at least) to the 1900 Olympics.

Trinity Hall punches way above its weight in terms of Olympic honours, bettered by only two other Oxbridge colleges, Trinity, Cambridge, and Magdalen, Oxford. At least nineteen Hall men and women (and probably more as data is still becoming available) are Olympians, the majority of them, as the table shows, medallists.

The scarcity of data which surrounds both the early Olympic Games, and indeed Trinity Hall's own students, means that the list of Olympians at present remains open, in particular in respect of non-British competitors. Nonetheless, a number of remarkable ex-Trinity Hall men and a woman have emerged with outstanding Olympic (and often other) honours. Any omissions are accidental and any additions would be gratefully received.

Hall Olympians include that most romantic of Olympic heroes William ('Billy') Fiske. Fiske's short life was packed with action. Born in 1911 in New York of a wealthy family, Fiske was educated in Europe. Aged 16 he captained the US bobsleigh team to win gold at St Moritz in 1928, making him (still) the USA's youngest gold medallist. He repeated the victory at the Lake Placid Olympics in 1932 where he carried the flag, and declined a third opportunity in 1936. He attended Trinity Hall in 1928 reading economics and history, and married the Countess of Warwick in 1938, joining (by a subterfuge) the RAF a year later at the start of World War II as its first American pilot. He died of injuries sustained in battle in 1940, the first American to die in the war. He is buried in Boxgrove churchyard, Sussex, and is shortly to be the subject of a film staring Tom Cruise. There is a tablet to his memory in St Paul's Cathedral. Of him it was famously said that Britain 'thank[ed] America for sending us the perfect sportsman. Many of us would have given our lives for Billy'.

Thirty years earlier, the Doherty Brothers dominated world tennis. Reginald Frank and Hugh Lawrence Doherty were both educated at Westminster and Trinity Hall. Born in 1872 and 1875 respectively, as well as winning the Wimbledon doubles a record eight times and being unbeaten in the Davis Cup, they took six Olympic medals between them, five of them gold at the 1900 and 1908 Olympics. Sadly neither enjoyed good health and both died young.

The 1908 Olympics also saw gold for Gordon Lindsay Thomson in the coxless pairs. Thomson had attended University College School in Hampstead before going up to Cambridge in 1909, winning his blue in 1910 to add to his gold medal. He also won silver in the coxless fours in 1908 as part of a Leander crew, behind the gold-medal Great Britain four. Thomson went on to distinguished wartime service.

The Hall was well represented on the water in 1908 with three further Hall men, Richard Frederick Boyle, Harold Edward Kitching and Douglas Cecil Rees Stuart winning bronze in the Great Britain second eight (the first eight won gold) made up entirely of Cambridge students. Yet another Hall man, Lord John Wodehouse (later the Earl of Kimberley, CBE, MC), born 1893, educated at Eton then Trinity Hall, participated in the 1908 games. Lord John had captained the winning Cambridge Polo team in 1904 and 1905, whereafter he became the Liberal MP for Mid-Norfolk. As a member of the Hurlingham team he won silver in

CHURCHMAN'S CIGARETTES

W. L. FISKE

Hall Olympic Medal Winners.

Gold		
1900	Hugh Lawrence Doherty	Tennis: Men's doubles
	Hugh Lawrence Doherty	Tennis: Men's singles
	Reginald Frank Doherty	Tennis: Men's doubles
	Reginald Frank Doherty	Tennis: Mixed doubles
	Reginald Frank Doherty	Tennis: Men's doubles
1908	Gordon Lindsey Thomson	Coxless pairs
1912	Sidney Ernest Swann	Men's 8s
1920	William Faulder Smith	Hockey
	Lord John Wodehouse	Polo
1928	Billy Fiske (USA)	Bobsleigh
1932	Billy Fiske (USA)	Bobsleigh
Silver		
1908	Lord John Wodehouse	Polo
	Gordon Lindsay Thomson	Coxless 4s
1920	Sidney Ernest Swann	8s
1948	David John Charlton Meyrick	8s
Bronze		
1908	Reginald Frank Doherty	Tennis: Men's singles
	Douglas Cecil Rees Stuart	8s
	Richard Frederick Robert Pochin Boyle	8s
	Harold Edward Kitching	8s
1952	John Ashley Cockett	Hockey
	John Taylor	Hockey

Donald Legget, rowing coach to THBC for forty years.

1908, before serving with great valour with the 16th Harriers in the First World War. Thereafter, at the relatively advanced age of 36, he became a member of the gold-medal-winning Great Britain Polo team at the 1920 Olympics. He died in an air raid in 1941.

There was (probably) only one Hall representative in the 1912 Olympics, Sidney Ernest Swann, a member of the gold-medal-winning eight and the only Cambridge man in an otherwise all Oxford crew. Indeed, of the eighteen men in that Olympic final, all bar Swann were from Oxford. He had previously partnered Thomson prior to going up to Trinity Hall in 1910, from Rugby. He won four blues, and captained the blue boat. His brother Arthur also attended Trinity Hall and was a fine oarsman. Swann further won silver in the 1920 Olympics.

In 1920 the first of Trinity Hall's hockey Olympians, William Faulder Smith, won gold. Faulder Smith had gone up from Marlborough to Trinity Hall winning his first blue in 1909 playing outside right. He won 26 international caps.

Archibald David Edmonstone Craig went up to Trinity Hall in 1904, although there is no record of him obtaining a degree. He became a star of the fencing world where he was known as Captain David Craig, having learned to fence under the Mangiarotti family in Milan. He represented Great Britain at two Olympic Games, in 1924 (when he was 37) and again in 1948 when he became the oldest fencer to take part in the Games at the age of 61. He was a lively and outspoken member of the fencing community as well as a talented artist and gave fashionable parties with his wife in Chelsea.

Trinity Hall provided more oarsmen at the 1936 and 1948 Olympics. In 1936 Hugh Walter Mason was a member of the Great Britain eight, having gone up to Trinity Hall in 1933 to read engineering, and, in 1948, David John Charlton Meyrick won silver on the water in the eights.

In 1952, however, two Hall men, John Ashley Cockett and John Taylor, won bronze for Great Britain in hockey. Both recently attended a Trinity Hall reunion. Cockett's sporting career extended not only to a further Olympic Games in Melbourne, where they were narrowly out of the medals, but to several years of high-level cricket representing Buckinghamshire and the Minor Counties (he was a blue in both hockey and cricket). He has speculated as to whether, had the draw been different, the 1952 bronze might have been silver.

The medal trail ceases with that 1952 bronze. Thereafter others have made the team, but medals have not come their way. In 1956 Kenneth Alfred Massey represented Great Britain in the eights, and in 1964 and 1968 Dr David Wilman FRSA made the hockey squad. In 1988 one of the 1977 first intake of female undergraduates, Kate Grose, rowed in the fours.

But the list of those who made it is matched by stories of tremendous achievement and the dedication of those who, for various reasons, did not. Athletics is not well represented in terms of Olympic honours even though the early British teams were made up of many Oxbridge athletes. This was by no means because Hall men lacked talent. Again, like much of the early Olympic

history, the real story has often been lost. What of A.E. Hind (1897 from Uppingham, also a cricket blue and international rugby player) who in 1900 held the University record for 100 yards at 9.8 seconds (allegedly downhill…) which should have assured him Olympic honours ? Or Forbes Horan who, in the 1933, paced Jack Lovelock to his mile world record? Most tantalising of all, Ralph Kilner Brown was tipped by his gold-medallist brother as a certainty for the gold medal in the 400m hurdles at the 1936 Games, but was dogged by a hamstring injury. His brother and sister won a gold medal and two silvers at those Games and it is most likely that Ralph would have shared in their success if fit. His fine record both in wartime and as a senior judge is perhaps some compensation.

Finally let us not forget those who, if they did not themselves participate, enabled others to. Donald Legget was from 1964–99 a rowing coach to Trinity Hall and coached several Olympic medallists at the Munich and Montreal Olympics.

Bridget Wheeler was amongst the first women undergraduates at Trinity Hall in 1977, where she read law. She was the first female member of the Hall to win a full blue and a former treasurer of the Crescent Club, she captained the Cambridge Ladies' Athletics team in 1979/80 and represented the UAU in 1980. She qualified as a barrister in 1981 and latterly as a solicitor, until recently heading up the litigation department of Coudert Brothers, where she is now a consultant.

The Hall has a strong tradition of success in rugby. In 1953 the first XV attempted to intimidate their Cuppers opponents by performing a Maori Haka (below left). In 1954 the Hall's first XV went on tour to Barcelona. Malcolm Chaplin races in to score having received a pass from Ken Rimmer (above), and Charles Stacey attempts to retrieve a memento (above left).

Alumni Association

17

Staying in Touch

BARRY LEWIS (1959)

The Trinity Hall Association (THA) was conceived in 1903 by Sir Robert Romer who assembled a few fellow members of Trinity Hall to discuss raising money to fund a memorial to the late Master Henry Latham. They did this and met again in 1904 when they decided to raise money to build a boathouse, fund a Memorial Cup and found an Association. A sub-committee established some objects (see opposite) and 50 members of the new Association held an inaugural dinner at the Trocadero in London on the 25 March 1904, the eve of the Boat Race. The first Annual General Meeting was held in London on the 5 July 1905. Membership was open to all past members of the College and was extended in 1931 to third-year undergraduates so that they were 'initiated' well before they left the Hall and ran the risk of losing contact with their friends. As early as 1922 an undergraduate was invited to be on the Committee.

The THA's main objects were to keep Hall alumni in touch with each other, promote the welfare of the College and bring alumni together by social events or otherwise. These objectives were essentially achieved in the first place by having an annual gathering including an AGM and an annual dinner. Both of these events were originally held in London although the AGM seems to have moved to Cambridge in 1927, whilst the dinner did not come to Cambridge until well after 1945. At the first Committee meeting it was resolved to 'frame a leaflet for circulation', to 'prepare as exhaustive a list as possible of all Hall men to be circularised', to 'organise a Dinner and a Committee meeting' and finally to devise

'a scheme for attracting as many Hall men to the Association on graduating or leaving College.' A list was prepared of all Hall men which was revised every five or six years at increasing cost. This became prohibitively expensive and is now done by the College on computer.

In July 1923 it was resolved that 'the Cambridge Secretaries be authorised to prepare a Newsletter to be circulated to all members of the Association'. The first *Newsletter* appeared in 1924 and in 1937 it was for the first time distributed to all Hall undergraduates. The *Newsletter* was specifically to inform members of the Association each year of what was happening in the College and relate the Minutes of the last AGM. The College, having contributed to the production of the *Newsletter*, took over the whole cost and it is now produced by the Alumni Office as a celebration of the year's events, incorporating a variety of articles. The THA used its funds to finance various presentations to the College and retiring Masters and staff. The THA raised appeals for funds ranging from £400 in 1924 for a portrait of the Master by Gerald Kelly RA to a target of £100,000 in 1947 for general use, and subsequently the Henry Dean Memorial Fund Appeal in 1961 to finance the development at Wychfield.

In 1924 a Mr Lewis suggested that the THA set up branches in 'Australia, New Zealand and elsewhere' – the suggestion was noted! Today the Association has members all over the world and the idea of local branches is as valid today as it was foresighted then. Now all those who have studied at Trinity Hall for a year or more are eligible to be members of the THA.

The Association has always sought to find more ways of bringing Hall alumni together. Years ago when the idea of the College being open to ladies was still a novelty, a fork supper was arranged for Hall men and spouses at Trinity House, which was the first mixed event of the THA. In recent years, a London event has been added to the calendar at a venue of special interest such as the Geffrye Museum and Royal Society of Arts.

Some years ago an annual careers workshop (originally in partnership with the Nick Nicholson Trust) was instituted and careers counselling is available thanks to the co-operation of countless members prepared to give their time. The THA will give modest subsidies to members of College, who cannot get funding elsewhere, to pursue some worthy goal such as international lacrosse or photography, to quote two actual examples. Contributions have for some years been made to the choir and June event.

The THA is being expanded through the Year Reps scheme and works closely with the College and the Alumni Officer. In June 2004 at its centenary AGM, new rules of the THA were overwhelmingly approved by the membership, which will enable the Association to evolve in partnership with the College and continue to foster the close alumni relations which have been built up over the years, thanks to its existence as one of Cambridge's oldest and strongest college associations.

Barry Lewis went up to Trinity Hall in 1959 to read modern languages and law. He retired from full-time practice as a solicitor in December 2001 and now works part-time as a consultant to two firms of solicitors. He has been on the Committee of the Trinity Hall Association since 1973 and London Secretary since 1975.

Errant alumni

18

IDEALISM AND TREACHERY

TRINITY HALL TRAITORS
GRAHAM HOWES

Both Donald Maclean (1931) and Alan Nunn May (1930) represent the Hall at its most 'hidden'. Indeed, neither of these notorious anti-heroes of the Cold War receives as much as a mention in Charles Crawley's otherwise generously inclusive history of the College. Nor, as undergraduates, did their strongly Communist opinions especially attract the attention of the College authorities, for, as Maclean's German supervisor recalled, 'nobody minded because it was felt that he, like most of his friends, would grow out of them.' It was also because both men (although a year apart and from very different social backgrounds) were, like so many of their peers, profoundly aware of the threat of Fascism, omnipresent poverty and mass unemployment and the cynical temporising of much domestic politics. In such a climate, Maclean and Nunn May, if never close friends, shared similar political beliefs. They were, of course, eventually to mask and act upon those in widely contrasting ways.

Alan Nunn May was born in Birmingham in 1911, the son of a brass-founder. Clever and hard-working, he won scholarships to King Edward's School and then to the Hall, where he gained Firsts in maths and physics. His supervision reports – still in the College archives – speak for themselves: 'Has done well this term' (Blackett), 'Works very hard and knows a lot' (Bullard) and, as his tutor, Wansbrough-Jones, commented,' We have every hope that he will get a First and stay on and do research.' May did both, and in June 1936 was awarded his PhD, for which Rutherford himself had

been one examiner. Finally, on 20 August of that year, May could write to Wansbrough-Jones from his lodgings at 199 Chesterton Road – on Union Society notepaper – saying that 'My post at King's College [London] has now definitely been fixed up…. I shall probably not see you before I go, so I will take this opportunity of thanking you (and the college) for your help'.

His flat tone is perhaps typical of the rather withdrawn, unmemorable young scientist, described by one contemporary as 'colourless' and by another as managing 'to convey the distant impression of always being spiritually in his laboratory', and with none of the dash or pretension of his smarter Left Wing peers. Yet the latter's high-profile Communism and anti-Fascism – coupled, perhaps, with his own painful memories of the Depression years in

Left: *Alan Nunn May, from his matriculation photograph, 1930.*

Opposite: *Donald Maclean (centre) from his matriculation photograph, 1931.*

Sir Owen Wansbrough-Jones in Australia in 1948. Elected a Staff Fellow in 1932, at the outbreak of war he was initially engaged in chemical warfare research but became a soldier and rapidly rose to become a brigadier. On demobilisation, he resigned his Fellowship to become scientific adviser to the Army Council and later chief scientist in the Ministry of Supply. He became an Honorary Fellow in 1957. As Assistant Tutor, it was he who wrote the glowing reference to the Foreign Office, commending Donald Maclean for employment.

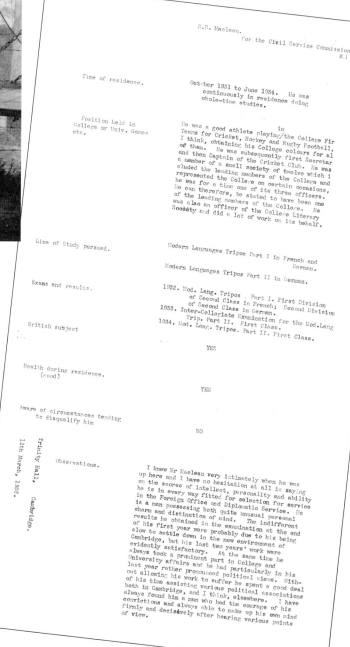

his native West Midlands – clearly radicalised May. Like Maclean, he joined the University branch of the Communist Party, and in May 1932, voted for the successful Union motion that 'This House has more hope in Moscow than in Detroit' – although predictably (and unlike Maclean) he did not speak. Less predictably, and probably through his graduate links with the charismatic physicist/crystallographer, and Marxist, J.D. Bernal, he made his own pilgrimage to Russia in 1936. One Hall contemporary described May as 'principled and an idealist.' Both were qualities, which eventually led him, in 1943–44, to pass on vital atomic bomb secrets to the Soviet Union. He did so with some personal angst. 'The whole affair,' he told the High Court in May 1946, 'was extremely painful to me and I only embarked on it because I thought this was a contribution I could make to the safety of mankind. I certainly did not do it for gain.' The presiding Judge was unimpressed and sentenced him to ten years. Granted early release in 1952, Nunn May returned to Cambridge, married and, after seventeen years at the University of Ghana, spent the last twenty-five years of his life living unobtrusively off the Milton Road. He is not known to have revisited his old College during this period.

As an undergraduate Donald Maclean's political views were far more overt and pronounced than Nunn May's. Indeed they were already largely formed by the time he entered the Hall in October 1931. They also ran parallel to other more conventional orthodoxies. Nearly six foot four, fair-haired and very good-looking, with an Exhibition in modern languages, Maclean not only worked hard, securing Firsts in his second and final years, but played hard too. He captained the College cricket XI and was also awarded 'crescents' for rugby and hockey. He was an active member of the Hesperides (hosting several meetings in his large rooms then underneath the Old Library) and closely involved in the College magazine, the *Silver Crescent*. Unsurprising, therefore that his tutor, Wansbrough-Jones (also from Greshams!) should describe him as 'one of the leading members of the College.'

Yet it is also evident from College archival sources that Maclean was already consciously conducting a double life. We know already from other published sources that Maclean was a member, from his first year, of a small, Trinity-based Communist study-group containing, among others, Burgess, Blunt and Philby as its Treasurer. We also know from Maclean's Caius contemporary, fellow-diplomat and subsequent biographer, Robert Cecil that – notwithstanding Lionel Elvin's acid comment on him, that 'such people from a comparatively affluent background… knew very little about the working classes that featured so loudly in their talk' – Maclean was, in fact, arrested in 1932 (albeit briefly – his mother obtained his release within hours) for his part in an unemployment rally in Hyde Park. He also took part, in early 1934 in a post-Jarrow 'Hunger March' which was passing through Royston. On that occasion, Cecil recalls, 'I looked ahead and saw the tall figure of Donald striding purposefully along, arm in arm with some genuine proletarian. His face wore a look of dedication I could not hope to emulate.'

Such 'dedication' was also evident to the College, too. Many Hall men would have attended or read the account in *Granta*, of the 'Moscow/Detroit' debate at the Union in May 1932, where the freshman Maclean told a packed chamber that, 'The only ultimate solution is the victory of the property-less classes'. More still would have recognized the humorous reference in the December 1933 *Silver Crescent* to 'Donald Maclenin, with a Tomb of Red bakelite in Market Square'. Maclean's own contributions to the magazine were, however, deadly serious. The December 1934 issue carries his bitter verse response to the so-called Armistice Day Riot, when the Student Anti-War Council, en route to an Armistice Day demonstration at the War Memorial, was waylaid by assorted hearties on Parker's Piece. Running battles ensued, in which Maclean – and Burgess – took part, until the police intervened. The poem is worth reprinting in full:

Dare Doggerel. Nov. 11

Rugger toughs and boat club guys
In little brown coats and old school ties
Tempers be up and fore-arms bared
Down in the gutter with those who've dared.
Dared to think war-causes out,
Dared to know what they're shouting about,
Dared to leave a herd they hate,
Dared to question the church and state;
Dared to ask what poppies are for,
Dared to say we'll fight no more,
Unless it be for a cause we know
And not for the sake of status quo.
Not for the sake of Armstrong Vickers,
Not for the sake of khaki knickers,
But for the sake of the class which bled,
But for the sake of daily bread.
Rugger toughs and boat club guys
Panic-herd with frightened eyes,
Sodden straws on a rising tide,
They know they've chosen the losing side.
D. M.

The next issue, for March 1934 was edited by Maclean himself. His editorial lays great stress on the decline in world trade precisely when traffic in arms and massive rearmament are increasing, attacks the League of Nations for 'instructing its members not to discourage territorial recruiting' and deplores 'the current politico-journalistic drive to war-mindedness.' The same issue also carries a highly polemical diatribe, signed D.M. and entitled 'Read This'. When one does, the tone and content go well beyond routine consciousness-raising. Instead it calls upon his fellow Hall students 'to identify with the working class' and for 'everyone of military age to start thinking seriously about politics'. For 'the students and workers will suffer most: it is they who will be gassed, it is they who will be shot down.' This will be 'the real position of the student during the present stage of capitalist decline.' For good measure, he also contends that 'the university is economically a capitalist institution, and for that reason the teaching and ideology are bound to be capitalist.' On such evidence (and there is much more in the same vein) it is clear that in 1933–34, his final year, and following the death of his politically conservative father the previous June, Maclean decided to give public expression – albeit through the Hall's modest College magazine – to his own political convictions. By then he had already built up a largish personal library of Marxist and Soviet books and pamphlets. One item, the newly translated *Brief History of Russia*, by M.N. Pokrovsky, with a preface by Lenin himself, had accompanied him to a small Christmas house party at Hawarden, the Gladstone family home. Page 145 has a quotation, which Maclean heavily underlined, and initialled and dated. It reads; 'Like the bourgeoisie, the intelligentsia lived on the surplus product that was extracted by force from the peasant and the workman. A communist revolution would mean that it would have to give up its advantages, renounce all its privileges and join the ranks of manual labour. And this prospect could be accepted only by a small number of the most sincere and devoted revolutionaries of the intelligentsia.'

Donald Maclean clearly identified closely with the latter, while also obediently giving up his formal membership of the Communist Party on instructions from his new Russian contacts in London, and opting for the Foreign Office rather than, as previously envisaged, graduate work or a teaching post in Russia. As for his Communist sympathies: 'I've rather given up on all that lately,' he lied to his very relieved mother. One suspects that he took a not-dissimilar line with his tutor, Wansbrough-Jones, whose own letter to Maclean (a copy is still in the archives), dated 29 August 1934, speaks for itself: 'I have very little doubt that your decision is a wise one. It may seem a little dull at first sight, but from what I have seen of people who went into the Foreign Office I gather that they have a very interesting time, and I am not sure that you will not find you have considerable talents in that direction.' The same file also contains Jones's formal reference to the Civil Service Commission concerning his former pupil, dated 11 March 1935 – when Maclean was already in contact with the NKVD. Maclean entered the Foreign Office successfully later that autumn, and the rest is, of course, history.

Jack Humphrey (1931)

I came up with Donald Maclean in 1931 and must be one of the very few surviving friends of his. I knew him very well and was co-opted by him and Harry Collier into dealing with and augmenting the material for the termly *Silver Crescent* in hilarious sessions. He was an altogether engaging person, universally liked and a good sportsman, who took the bludgeonings of forward play for the rugger team with gusto. He got a First and was regarded as a prize acquisition by the Foreign Office. Having discussed the matter with another mutual friend from the Hall, T. Mervyn Jones, neither of us caught even the faintest glimpse of anything beyond the leftist idealism common at the time among young people. Any suggestion that he would act dishonestly would have been absolutely laughable. Nor did either of us ever note the faintest hint of homosexuality, which in those days was a blackmailable peculiarity, making the subject vulnerable, nor of alcoholism or any other addiction put forward later among suggested factors in the transformation of the generous, open, friendly undergraduate into the spy.

AMERICAN PATRIOT, BRITISH TRAITOR?
JAMES A. PASSAMANO (1998)

Arthur Middleton was born in South Carolina on 26 June 1743, son of a prominent planter and land owner. His father's wealth allowed Arthur to be educated in England. He attended the Hackney School, and later the Westminster School near London. In 1762, Arthur matriculated at Trinity Hall. His biographer Charles Goodrich noted that at Cambridge Arthur was 'powerfully tempted to enter into… youthful follies' but 'left the university with the reputation of an accomplished scholar, and a moral man.' As political discontent increased in the American colonies, Arthur actively promoted rebellion and served on official committees to organize a military force and establish defenses in South Carolina. He helped draft South Carolina's first constitution in 1776. Later that year as a delegate to the Continental Congress in Philadelphia, he signed the Declaration of Independence. Middleton fought in the defense of Charleston, which fell to the British in May 1780. He was captured and exiled to Florida with other prisoners of war until 1781. After release, he returned to Congress, but was unable to rejoin his family in South Carolina until after the British defeat at Yorktown in October 1782. He died in Charleston on 1 January 1787.

Arthur Middleton, Trinity Hall graduate, who signed the American Declaration of Independence, with his family.

New freedoms, new pressures

19

James Runcie with his father, Robert Runcie.

JAMES RUNCIE (1978)

I was christened in the College chapel in 1959. The priest taking the service began with the following words:

'Man that is born of a woman hath but a short time to live, and is full of misery. He cometh up, and is cut down like a flower; he falleth as it were a shadow, and never continueth in one stay…'

'Noel,' my father hissed. 'That's the funeral service. This is a baptism.'

'Sorry, Bob,' replied the befuddled minister, switching to the correct, but equally miserable, introduction; *'Dearly beloved, forasmuch as all men are conceived and born in sin…'*

The holy water was poured over me and remains, I think, to this day, part of the Proustian, Wordsworthian, and Freudian memories I associate with the College. I can still smell the first spring cutting of grass on the lawns and picture the way in which the light falls on the honey-coloured stone of Front Court. I can taste the warm IPA of nights spent drinking after the plays had finished, and hear the optimism of the chapel bell when waking on Sunday mornings. I can still see Ginty's encouraging eyes as he gave me a sherry at ten in the morning, and I think of him every time I drink it alongside the Boat Club member who once spat:

'Sherry! What are you doing? Only vicars and women drink sherry.'

When I went up in 1978 people often referred to Trinity Hall as the warmest, friendliest college in the University; 'I deal,' Graham Howes once told me, 'in everything from broken windows to broken engagements.' 'Cripes!' I thought, 'Engagements! I've only just got here, what kind of a place is this?' Well, I suppose it was, and still is, a glorified finishing school where you can do almost anything; direct a play, row a boat, jump off roofs, learn the libel laws, *anything*. But this very freedom means that when I look back on my time as an undergraduate the prominent feeling is one of deepest embarrassment. Oh God, what on earth was I doing? I can't go to reunions because I would spend my whole time saying sorry: Sorry for the foolishness and stupidity, for the drunkenness and the misplaced wit and the hopeless flirtations and for ever thinking that I would be any good as a theatre director. Ah, theatre, the Preston Society and Peter Holland's all-forgiving eye! What mistakes he witnessed – sub-Beckettian plays about nightmares in the day; the impersonation of a chicken in the College revue; a breathless production of *Romeo and Juliet* for May Week; and Ann Jellicoe's

Far left: *'Survivors' of the 1995 May Ball.*

Left: *A boat burning to celebrate going Head of the River, 1992.*

glorious 1960s comedy about picking up girls, *The Knack*. I remember peeling 'Smile, Jesus loves you' stickers off bicycle saddles all over Cambridge and replacing them with 'Have you got the knack?'

The plays I directed were all about burgeoning sexuality, their choice influenced by the presence of so many fabulous women in the College. Debbie Wolsey! Isla Rowley! Sue Swift! Louise Croker! Amanda Galsworthy! Olivia Fane! It was impossible to concentrate, and drama was the perfect excuse to meet them. One could be sensitive and authoritative simultaneously – it would only be a matter of time before one of them cracked, just as the Christian society had been at school ('I've been having doubts, Alison…').

But no drama could disguise my great, and utterly unrequited, University love for Anne Louise, who was, and is still, beautiful, who cooked duck *à l'orange*, and who didn't mind when I ate the skin as well as the fruit of an avocado; who took pity and let me take her to the May Ball where we danced, bizarrely, to Eddie and the Hot Rods singing *Do anything you wanna do*.

That might well be the motto for the College – *Operor quisquam vos volo efficio* – except I couldn't with Anne Louise, for such a love was impossible.

'Look,' I said at last. 'The fact is you find me physically repulsive.'

'I wouldn't quite put it as strongly as that.'

So little hope in that 'quite'! And yet I persisted, for such is the confidence a college can inspire; a sense of home and belonging where no one will say stop, and that you will almost always be forgiven. I remember being almost in tears at graduation, seeing Peter Holland clapping us all, saying goodbye and God speed, a second father, wishing his students on their way into the world.

And so, whenever I return, there is the feeling of coming home. I wonder if perhaps I could live it all over again, that my life has been a marathon in which the organisers have only just discovered that there has been a false start and we can all begin again and do it properly, realising what we have been given; the privilege and glory of youth.

I still use the University Library, and I often walk through the College. At first there is jealousy, seeing students looking so carelessly young, studying in the Jerwood Library or putting up posters for plays or chatting on the bridge at the bottom of Garret Hostel Lane, their bicycles resting, their scarves blown back, and their heads tilted with the possibility that something new and wonderful might just be beginning. I am envious of their youth and security, of the hope that lies before them, until I realise that we have all been given this; a love, if that's not too strong a word, a supportive, tolerant, familial love from a college that will always be there, that forgives mistakes and allows you to become either what you had always wanted to be or what you never expected or intended. In memory, people will always be rehearsing *Romeo and Juliet*, fencing on the Latham lawn, singing revue songs in the lecture theatre or roaring into the bar after the pubs have closed; and just as, at the end of childhood, a boy and a bear will always be playing, so Anne Louise will be walking towards me, her silver jewellery tinkling over her layered clothes, smiling her eternal smile.

James Runcie read English at Trinity Hall from 1978–81 before going to Bristol Old Vic to train as a theatre director. He now works as a writer and independent film-maker. His novels include The Discovery of Chocolate *and* The Colour of Heaven. *His father, Lord Runcie, the former Archbishop of Canterbury, was Dean of the College from 1956–60.*

Trinity Hall May Ball

OLIVIA FANE (1979)

I went up to Cambridge for my interview and fell in love not only with the place but with everyone who lay in my path. I remember someone mentioning the word 'paradigm' and swooning with delight; in the world that I came from the sexiest word was 'tennis'. Jonathan Steinberg asked me supposedly searching questions about my character: as I'd been thinking of little else over the previous few years I was more than happy to answer him. If he'd asked me the date of the battle of Waterloo I wouldn't be writing this now.

I must have been the most ignorant fresher ever. I'd never been to an art gallery or a museum; I'd never been to a concert, classical or pop. Before I'd gone up, I'd bought about thirty posters from the bargain basket at Athena, some of them costing no more than 10p, and I happily blu-tacked them all up in the narrow suite of rooms at the top of D staircase. My favourite was of a melted clock by Dali, which even in 1979 had sunk to cliché. It was the first time I'd ever seen it. My one cassette was Holst's *Planets*. But more embarrassing still was my taste in poetry. One evening we were all sitting round talking about which poets we liked. For once I was off my guard. 'I just love Alfred Lord Tennyson,' I enthused. Everyone looked aghast. 'You really like that sort of stuff?' they said. Traitor, traitor that I am. After that I said Larkin like everyone else, and I even learnt a few of his poems off by heart to prove it.

I was very fortunate, or so it seemed in the beginning, to have great hordes of visitors. It never even crossed my mind they were all men, nor that they should ever want anything more from me than a cup of coffee and a chat. But I knew exactly what I wanted from them: knowledge. I wanted to break down the huge megalith of my ignorance, and I would sit them down, one after another, in my brown furry beanbag and interrogate them about their subjects. I'd ask mathematicians about imaginary numbers and parabolas, natural scientists about quantum mechanics, and historians about truth. But by the end of the first term those poor boys stopped talking and started looking miserable, so miserable, in fact, that I

couldn't just send them away. I didn't understand what they were doing there. In the end I went to see my tutor about it. 'Olivia,' said Jonathan. 'Don't you understand anything? These men fancy you. If you're not interested, just tell them to go.'

So that's exactly what I did; and over that year I got ever more brusque. I remember making a bargain with one poor chap in the summer term, 'If I take my clothes off, will you leave me in peace?' I said to him. And I did.

I got a First in my prelims, and was awarded a scholarship, which I suppose should have delighted me, but it didn't at all. I felt enormous gratitude to the College, and wanted to justify their faith in me, but for the first time in my life I felt under pressure to perform. I spent my second year lying low in a basement in Clarendon Street, listening to the World Service and pretending I didn't exist. I only emerged in my third year, when I finally entered into University life proper.

I remember feeling extraordinarily heightened. I think we all did. No one ever talked about careers or even life beyond June, and we were all conscious of having to squeeze so much in before we set off on our way in the big wide world. For myself, I wished to learn everything I possibly could, seeing as that was what the place was about, and through Greek philosophy I discovered modern philosophy, which I couldn't get enough of. I went to lectures on time, logic, happiness, beauty. I had a rather wonderful supervision with Richard Sorabji. I remember him coming into my room and looking rather awkward, and making him sit down on a chair while I sat on the sofa near him. Then I asked him – what in the world got into me? 'Would you mind terribly if I lay down? I think so much more clearly when I'm horizontal.' We didn't look at each other for the whole hour, but just chatted away quite happily about Zeno's paradoxes. He shook my hand afterwards and smiled. Over the years it has dawned on me what an extraordinary privilege that encounter was.

I became interested in trying to engineer the perfect romantic moment. For me, eroticism could be located precisely between initial eye contact and the first kiss: to this end the Reading Room of the University Library proved itself a rather exciting place to sit. To this day it gives me huge pleasure to see that occasionally I have kissed all the reporters on a single page in a national newspaper, as though there were a tiny part of me in all those far-flung places they write from.

During the week of my finals I was woken up and told I had an exam: it was a paper I'd completely forgotten about. My supervisor had fallen ill at the beginning of the year, but I'd ignored her advice to change modules and insisted I would do the work on my own. I hadn't even got as far as reading the syllabus. So I entered into the stuff of nightmares: an exam paper in which I couldn't answer a single question. Yet I felt strangely light. I looked around and thought what a magnificent room it was, how beautiful the windows were. After about twenty minutes I put my hand up. The adjudicator had pre-Raphaelite red hair and I asked if I could have a word with her. She took me into a back room and said, 'Yes?' I didn't tell her the real reason I hadn't begun to write – that was far too banal. I said, 'Will there ever be a moment in my life when I am as free as this? When I can choose to pass my finals or to fail them?' We must have spoken in this vein for half an hour. She was brilliant. She said, 'If life is a game, why don't you play it, just this once?'

In the end I got a 2ii, but my education had been perfect. Even my CD collection is based on the music I heard through the walls of the various rooms I lived in. My taste in art, architecture, literature, philosophy: those years were utterly formative. I know that I'm the product of a time and a place, but what a time and what a place.

Olivia Fane read classics between 1979 and 1982. After Cambridge she trained as a probation officer in Leicester and went on to work as a psychiatric social worker with young offenders. She published her first novel Landing on Clouds *in 1994, and her second book* The Glorious Flight of Perdita Tree *will be published in 2005.*

TERRY WAITE (1992)

I have no clear recollection of my first days at Trinity Hall. As I search the recesses of memory a host of events crowd together in my mind. I see the warm smile of the Master, John Lyons, as he welcomes me to the Fellowship. 'There is a flat available at Wychfield if you would like that,' he said. It was a kindly offer but not one I could accept. After spending years in solitary confinement all I needed was a simple room and access to other people. A small room was found that looked out across to the Old Schools. It seemed ideal. Several months later a visitor pointed out that the window of my room was barred. I hadn't noticed.

I see my room as it was; a bed, an old armchair, a desk and a wardrobe. What more did I need? After spending years chained to a wall and sleeping on the floor this was luxury. An even greater luxury was the large blank writing pad placed on the desk by the window. For five years I had been forbidden to write. Now I could write all day and throughout the night if I so desired. Protected by the four walls of my room and hidden within the heart of the College I was free to take some hesitant steps back into the 'real world'. Although I hardly realised it, I was struggling to come to terms with the world that had changed so much since my incarceration. I was also attempting to understand myself. I needed time: Time to think, to write, to converse; time to try to understand what had happened to me during the long dark days of imprisonment in Beirut.

I see the faces of the Fellows as they welcome me as a Fellow Commoner: Frank, Roy, John, Graham, Allison, Tom. Today some have departed this life, some have moved away from Cambridge but all live on in memory. Tuesday night, the evening of the Fellows' dinner, becomes one of the most important nights of the week. I sit long into the early hours questioning, theorising, listening and in the process gradually returning to life. These kindly compassionate friends can hardly know how important they have become to me. They don't patronise. They tell me frankly when I am being ridiculous and we eat, drink and laugh together.

Terry Waite, Fellow Commoner 1992–93, was an adviser and special envoy for the Archbishop of Canterbury.

I remember closing the door of my room and moving towards the desk. I don't have or require a computer or a typewriter. All I want is pen, ink and paper. I need to record my experiences before they are lost for ever. During my captivity I wrote in my head. Now, here in Trinity Hall, I want to put down on paper that which I had mentally written. I want as little as possible to come between my memory and the written word and so I choose to write every word in longhand. Once or twice a week I telephone my editor using the pay phone outside my room. How fortunate I am to have an editor who knows how to encourage. He never tells me what to write but his gentle suggestions enable me to move forward through episodes that are painful to remember and record.

I wander through the streets of Cambridge but, as I am always recognized and stopped, my journeys are few and far between. For the moment I am quite content with the companionship found in College and the security of my home in London at the weekends. Winter gives way to spring and I make my first visit to the countryside. After being deprived of colour for so long I marvel at the developing hue of the trees and the plants that are coming to life. I begin to feel that I am in tune with nature and that we are both coming alive together. I gaze at the distant spires of Cambridge and can hardly believe my good fortune.

The year moves on and my writing will soon be completed. Before me sit endless pages of handwritten manuscript. I have done my best to be honest. I am naturally apprehensive as to the book's reception, but I have written what I wanted to write and that is that. All too quickly my time as a Fellow Commoner is drawing to an end.

A farewell dinner has been arranged in the Fellows' dining room that has been the setting for so many good evenings with my friends. I want to leave behind a memento of my time spent in Trinity Hall and have purchased a small silver cup to be known as 'The Fellow Commoner's Cup'. However, the College has meant so much to me that I need to leave behind something that is truly personal.

Right: *The blindfold and magnifying glass used by Terry Waite during his captivity in Beirut, now in the College archive.*

Below: *The Fellow Commoner's Cup, which Terry Waite presented to the College in 1993.*

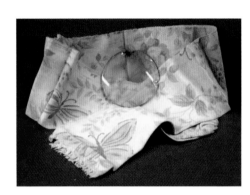

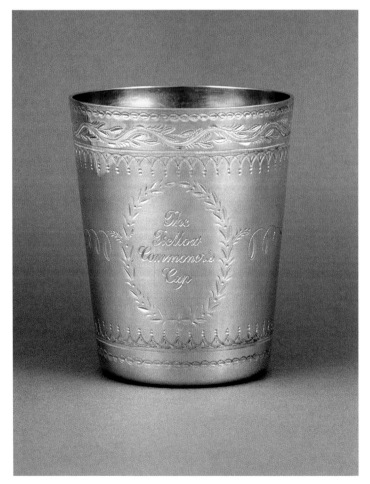

I remember that in the drawer of my desk there is an envelope. Inside is a scrap of curtain material and a chipped magnifying glass. These are the blindfold that I had to wear whenever anyone came into my cell in Beirut and the glass that I read with when after three or more years I finally received books. At the dinner I hand over both the cup and the envelope.

The book is written. The past is a memory. Master, Fellows, graduates, undergraduates and staff have come and gone. Trinity Hall remains. A milestone, an anchor and a beacon for the thousands who one day will also have memories and who, like me, eventually will look back with deep gratitude for a unique institution.

Terry Waite CBE was an adviser to the Archbishop of Canterbury when he was captured in Beirut and spent almost five years in captivity. He was a Fellow Commoner at Trinity Hall for a year from April 1992, during which time he wrote an account of his experiences in captivity entitled Taken on Trust.

ADAM BARNES (1994)

In the mid-1990s the College still extolled its 'small and friendly' reputation. Our days echoed to *Johnny Lyon's Black and White Army*, the sound of Joseph clucking concernedly about trays in the dining hall, and noisy Scottish porters charming all-comers in the Porters' Lodge. The setting was, as ever, seriously beautiful. Henry James's appreciation of the unparalleled delights of the gardens held true on a summer's day; you just had to ignore the aberration of Garret Hostel Bridge and the chatter of the punt guides.

Undergraduate rooms were still cleaned by bedders, and all meals were available in hall. 'If you come here you will have to walk less than fifty yards in order to graduate,' crowed the *Alternative Prospectus*, and it wasn't far wrong. You could drift from one courtyard to another, enjoying intellectual fuelling stops in lecture halls and science labs, and earthier refuellings in the bar. The Wodehousian days of jolly japes and larks aplenty might have passed before our arrival, but this was definitely not the real world.

There was an edge, however. Beneath the fustiness of a seat of great learning and the veneer of college scarves and bicycles was an insistent pressure. Yes, we punted, caroused, danced and tackled. Yet the most strident note, the theme that surged relentlessly through our Cambridge days, connecting Monday morning to Thursday evening to Sunday afternoon, was the intensity of the study.

The tone was set in an early class where a Director of Studies told us to split the day into three chunks: four hours in the morning, four in the afternoon and four in the evening. If we worked for two of the three chunks, five days a week, he said, those 40 hours would see us through our degrees. My hopes for three years of high living shrivelled.

Shoehorning vast courses into Cambridge's eight-week terms meant the scope for in-depth study could be limited. In my third year, the Cambridge University Students' Union campaigned to introduce a reading week into the middle of the summer term to reduce stress levels, but was laughed out of court by authorities concerned about academics' research time. Students, we learnt, were peripheral.

Of course, work was not our everything and the College had a reputation for its Saturday night bops. 'Global!' was the best known and on three Saturdays per term, queues would stretch from a side entrance in Garret Hostel Lane up to Trinity Lane. Students from other colleges salivated at the prospect of Trinity Hall's Ents, and we turned them away in their hundreds. Complaints from various sources saw these occasions scaled back, but at their best they were *the* stellar attraction of the University's entertainment scene.

Politically, the College was as apathetic as most of the others, with the time-honoured exception of King's. If student radicalism found its hotbed there, Trinity Hall was its sunbed. In my third year we marched through the streets to complain at Tory underfunding of higher education; and the words 'rent' and 'strike' shared a sentence in a couple of JCR Committee meetings. But when the Labour Party took power for the first time in eighteen years shortly before summer exams, we just buried our heads further in our books.

Any angst which did exist was frequently alcohol-exacerbated. My father was at Cambridge 35 years earlier and told me that alcohol simply did not matter, beyond the occasional sherry party. Fast forward to the mid-1990s and it dominated. The College's drinking societies were going strong, appalling some, enthralling others (law firms loved employing Presidents of the Crescents), and the bar – the apotheosis of all that was small and friendly about the College – buzzed most nights. The Sunday after finals, Suicide Sunday, was the seedy crowning glory of the University's preoccupation with the bibulous, but hey, it was fun at the time. Just about everyone got drunk at some point, or at many points, like everyone else of our age across the country. Except that our version often involved blazers. That's what I mean: playing at being grown-up.

So, the 1990s… playing hard, but working harder; scrabbling for working space in the library and worrying about careers. The pressure started early, with final-year job applications depending heavily on second-year exam results, and even second-year summer placements highlighting first-year efforts. Anyone less sure of the five-fold way to job enlightenment and less inspired by the travelators of professional careers was often just caught in the maelstrom. We were still vaguely renowned for our lawyers, and the Boat Club toyed with the Headship of the River. We raised more money for RAG than virtually all the other colleges put together, got a mention in *The Sun* after the JCR passed a motion forbidding public displays of affection between two lovers, and spent a lot of time explaining to people that we weren't at Trinity. Happy days indeed, but hedonistic? No.

Adam Barnes read English from 1994 to 1997. Whilst at the Hall he was JCR secretary and played for the rugby, football, cricket and hockey teams. Since leaving Cambridge, he has worked in management consultancy, sports journalism and guidebook publishing.

All undergraduates are now accommodated on the central site in their first year.

BEN RAWLINGS (2001)

Small, friendly and by the river: That was what both the official Trinity Hall paraphernalia and the alternative student publications said, and it pretty much summed up the impression I got when I came for interview. After walking past the pomposity of King's frontage and the austere formality of Senate House, the unassuming entrance to the Hall opened into the pretty and unintimidating vista of Front Court. I remember thinking at the time that it looked like a homely and welcoming place, and I don't think I've ever been so prescient. Whenever I walk into Front Court it feels somehow right, the place I'm meant to be: for good or ill, with all the positive and negative aspects of living here.

One of my first impressions (and I suppose prejudices) was that a Cambridge college – particularly one as small and self-contained as Trinity Hall – would be a bubble of unreality, a haven sheltered from the real world. In some ways it is: Bedders, DoSs, gowns, formals and such-like are not really of this earth. So many things here are unreal, even ridiculous: but as a third year, even the Harry Potter-like halls of the older colleges just seem normal. Cambridge is a totality, an all-consuming atmosphere, and it's only when I get home to Scunthorpe that the differences between the two worlds come into focus.

But this bubble cannot shelter us from the financial burdens and hardship that characterise student life today, nor from any number of other worldly pressures. In fact, life here can in some ways be more difficult: this is no haven of tranquillity; there is no time to be dreaming amidst the spires. The pressure to perform academically is intense, as is the workload. This continues despite the fact that for many students their tripos is no longer the main reason for being here. A degree is increasingly a prerequisite: it does not get you a job. Extra-curricular activities, 'transferable skills', experience – these are the things that count. And, depending on one's career interests, being in plays or working on *Varsity* are equally, if not more, important than doing the best you can academically.

In the face of the pressures exerted by the demands for academic excellence, the endless form-filling of the career game and those all-important extra-curricular commitments, the College is in many ways losing its centrality in Cambridge life. As the academic structures of most courses become increasingly faculty-based, the modern Haller may have little physical need of the College beyond board and lodging. College-based societies often can't compete with the plethora of opportunities offered at a University level or beyond, and heavier involvement in College life is now an option on a par with alternatives outside the College. JCR Open Meetings are usually poorly attended, too many elections are uncontested and turnout is quite low. Some College societies, such

Left: *North Court.*

Below: *Flyer for 2004 June Event.*

as THEFT (film society) and the Mountaineering Society, run only intermittently, when one or two enthusiastic individuals take them on and there is enough interest in the wider student population. The Preston Society (drama and theatre) rarely performs, functioning more as a means to distribute funding to students who want to produce or direct a play. Attendance at formal halls has also fluctuated, as even the communal dinner is sacrificed to the ever-increasing individuality of life. On the other hand, the College is well-represented in every field, from theatre to student politics, sports to academic excellence, by individual members. In Cambridge, college scarves still abound, but a student is as much if not more defined today by their main pursuits, rather than their collegiate affiliation.

In some ways, however, Tit Hall is bucking the trend. Despite, or maybe even because of, the increasing diversity of student activity and the decreasing practical importance of the College in individual student life, the sense of community is stronger than ever. The need for the College as a haven from work and other commitments, a safe and comforting anchor from which to explore all the opportunities Cambridge offers, has grown. There is a sense here that we are all in this together: surviving this madness is our aim and at times we will need each other. That need can be financial or practical, but very often it is mental or emotional. Bops (Viva!s) may no longer be the University-wide phenomena they once were, although Open Bops still sell out and our June Event remains the best in town. Instead, bops and Superhalls provide regular occasions when we can all get together, take a break from the incessant work and let our hair down without worrying about work, the future or our image. Cheese still reigns supreme, although Ents are starting to branch out into unexplored territory and new genres. But the fun-loving element seems unlikely to leave. The almost perverse inclination to fancy dress is as strong as ever, and the Tom Peck's propensity for shirt-loss at Viva! is becoming a worryingly widespread phenomenon despite the fact that he has graduated.

Life as a Tit Haller in the 'Naughties' is frenetic. The pressure comes from all angles, all of the time, and via every media conceivable bar sky-writing. Free and fast access to the internet seemed originally to be a huge advantage,

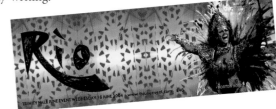

but its dark side soon became clear: with email, we can be set, reminded and chased for work instantly, constantly and at any time. There really is nowhere to hide here.

Caught up in this maelstrom of academic rigour, career-planning, CV-enhancing activities, financial tightrope-walking and the demands and complexities of simply living, it is difficult to step back and look at what our lives are like. If the hedonistic, care-free, non-stop party lifestyle of the stereotypical student can be found anywhere, though, it isn't here. We have our moments, and blazers, punts, drinking societies and garden parties all have their place. They haven't died out, and they won't because we need them. Time is so precious here that we often simply cannot wind down and relax: our leisure activities need to be as intense as every other aspect of our lives.

Perhaps these are just the ramblings of an increasingly eccentric third year, besieged by essays, application forms, job fairs, the not-so-distant spectre of finals and the even closer spectre of the bank manager. I don't know how we'll feel when we look back in one, ten, fifty years on this Cambridge chapter of our lives. But if I may borrow a phrase that has been popular in my time here, then I can say one thing with certainty: it's been emotional.

Ben Rawlings studied social and political sciences from 2001–4, during which time he was JCR Access Officer (2002–03), JCR President (2003–04), was involved in RAG and played on the Ultimate Frisbee team and volleyball team.

'I remember in 1993, at one of David and Ellen Flemings' celebrated parties in the Fellows' Garden, I was talking to the Bursar – Joanna Womack – who asked me if I felt there was room for a new building in Latham Court. I imagined that she could only mean along the mediaeval wall dividing it from the Fellows' Garden and said that I doubted it. However, she then pointed to the small, flat-roofed garden store overlooking the river and asked – 'What can you do with that?' Those simple words were the conception of the Jerwood Library and a wonderful commission for me.'

–Tristan Rees Roberts.

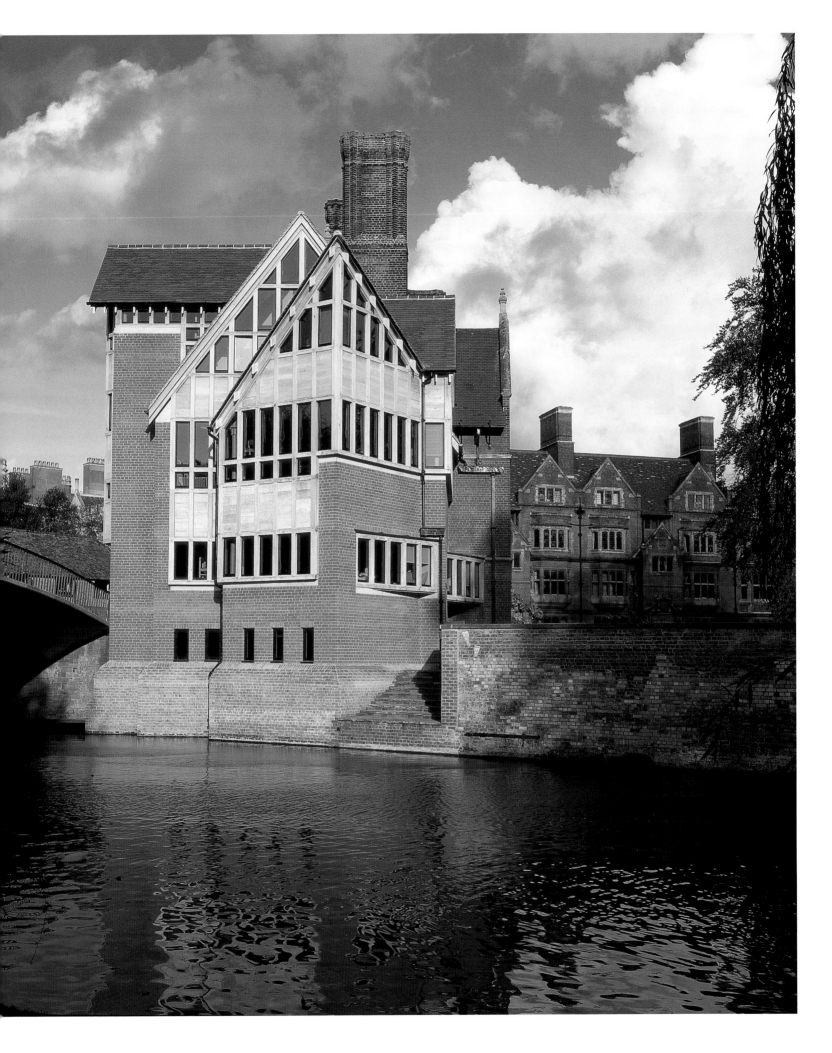

A diverse community

20

GRADUATE PERSPECTIVES

CHRISTOPHER PADFIELD, GRADUATE TUTOR

In a University that has been slow to treat graduate students as the equals of the undergraduates, Trinity Hall has been a shining example among the traditional colleges. Trinity Hall has approximately the same proportion of the University's graduates as it has undergraduates. Given the existence of specialist graduate colleges, this gives the College a slightly higher proportion of grads than most of the older colleges, and offers the enormous advantage of creating a population of critical mass – the Trinity Hall MCR is, by reputation, the most successful in town. Trinity Hall is also at the top of the list of the traditional colleges in the admissions league table, measured by the number of our students who put the College as their first choice on the application form. This translates into really excellent students. Only the specialist grad colleges, and the big name colleges with especially generous scholarships on offer, rank higher.

Trinity Hall has made enormous strides in regard to grads in the last two decades, building upon a very happy legacy of small graduate populations before that. We increased our intake of grads in 1990 in response to a crisis in the University, caused by an insufficiency of college places. Since then, we have maintained our numbers approximately constant, overshooting on admissions for a couple of years in the late 1990s when admissions statistics threw out our careful forecasts, and in recent years dipping temporarily, in response to a crisis of accommodation in College, while we build new accommodation at Wychfield.

In admitting graduate students, we endeavour to select people who will play some part in College life, and create the widest possible community. On this basis the grad community is quite different from the (predominantly British) undergraduates. We admit roughly equal numbers of men and women, and beyond that we try to admit something of everything – race, creed, subject specialisation, type of course, orientation and eventual career ambition. There are some students with experience of business, studying the MBA, and professional lawyers (LLM) and teachers (Med, PGCE), typically younger clinical medical and veterinary students, and recent graduates from all parts of the world, pursuing MPhils and PhDs in the widest diversity of subjects.

Grads are, of course, older than undergraduates, and have normally chosen graduate study because of a well-developed interest in the subject, and an ambition to pursue it afterwards. They are committed, can often be passionate, and they intend to work hard. But they are also at the peak of their intellectual and social powers, often multi-talented, mature and sophisticated, and determined also to have a hectic social life. By offering a largish community of between 150 and 230 individuals (depending upon the time of year and how many grads choose to establish their social life around the clinical school, or the management school rather than round College), Trinity Hall becomes an extremely exciting place to hang out.

With this quality of intellectual and social horsepower available, the most important thing College has to do (rather like good government) is to provide the environment and the infrastructure for the community to grow and to flower. Every year, new grads arrive looking uncertain, and at the end of every year, grads leave having

Graduating students,
June 2003.

enjoyed a blazing whirl of social life, a pot-pourri of intellectual stimulation, the nurturing of enduring new friendships, and, very often, the achievement of a distinction in their study. Of course, with this raw power available, the Graduate Tutor needs to maintain a watchful eye on things, sometimes applying a little moderation.

Graduate students, as a population, probably experience a great deal more financial stress than undergraduates. With the passing years, fewer and fewer are able to win full scholarships, as governments throughout the world trim their sails, and spread the funding out more thinly. The College is fortunate to have certain funds devoted to the support of grads, but it covers the costs of less than 2 per cent of our students. The awards come in different forms: full-cost studentships, or part-funding alongside other funding bodies; smaller top-up bursaries; funding for 'research-related' expenditure; and hardship funding.

The availability of full-cost studentships is a vital feature in attracting first-choice students. We do extremely well in comparison to many other colleges, but the traditional colleges who beat us in this measure are all able to offer more generous support. We have to remember that we are in competition for the best students in the

world, and leading North American universities' ability to offer full-cost studentships puts us at a serious disadvantage.

Research-related expenditure takes many forms, ranging from enabling grads to present their research at academic conferences (an essential feature of academic education) through to part-funding of fieldwork, whether in jungles and deserts, or in libraries and archives. Our hardship funding protects students from deprivation in the face of unexpectedly disastrous changes in their circumstances, and makes a contribution to the unfounded costs of those who over-run with their PhD.

Grads need less of the Fellowship's attention, but they do need some. One very promising initiative we have taken this last year, is to appoint a new cadre of Graduate Mentors from among the Fellowship. This has attracted an extremely interesting range of Fellows, who have started to develop a closer relationship with students within their general subject area than was possible for the Graduate Tutor alone. Their role is to provide academic stimulation and strategic advice that complements and does not conflict with the students' supervisors and other teachers in the University. We all hope that this helps to enhance the College as an academic, as well as a social community. The style differs from that which applies to the undergraduates, who are taught and have Directors of Studies in College. It is more in keeping with the grads' relative maturity and sense of professional purpose. It reflects the College's complementary role to that of the University, providing the nurturing but stimulating environment within which grads may develop social and generic skills.

We have made other changes that are small enough in themselves, but which are symbolically important. This year, grads who obtained a First or a distinction in their final assessment were admitted, formally in chapel, as Scholars of the College, and invited to the Eden Feast. In all the history of the College, the only students who have been inscribed as members of the Foundation have, until now, been high-performing undergraduates. Now grads are recognised, in this and in other important ways, as equal but different junior members of the College, alongside the undergraduates.

The sense of membership grads feel for College is considerable, but if it needs any underlining, one only has to remark that two of the College's most munificent benefactors in recent years were never undergraduates – they remembered their experience of Trinity Hall's MCR in this extremely important way.

In its accommodation to the realities of research and graduate study, Trinity Hall is moving rapidly with the times, while retaining the best of the values of the past, the fabulous environment we inhabit, and the powerful sense of community. Perhaps the next stage will be to make a move towards integrating our share of the disenfranchised post-docs into collegiate Cambridge.

Christopher Padfield graduated in engineering from Fitzwilliam College, taking his PhD at Darwin College. He worked for 14 years in international engineering and rural development consultancy, before returning in 1988 as Director of the Cambridge Programme for Industry. At that point, he came to Trinity Hall as an Engineering Fellow, and has been co-Director of Studies in Engineering all this time, and since 1991, Graduate Tutor.

J.P. Gonzalez Blanco (1957)

In 1957 I joined Trinity Hall as a research student. My goal was to obtain a PhD, working as hard as possible in order to do so. My research outreached the usual requirements. Thus, before long my sleepless nights and poor diet caused my health to deteriorate.

My tutor, Trevor C. Thomas, called me in order to discuss, at great length, my life's hopes, and ambitions. After listening to me, he told me I was going entirely the wrong way about it. He told me that if I wanted to become a politician, I should look beyond books, and concerning my education, he put a greater emphasis on getting to know people, political parties, cultures, towns, foods and women; suggesting all that England and Europe had to offer would hold me in greater stead for the future, than being a round-the-clock bookworm.

'Go out. Make friends. See how we live and what we are like. Find out what you could do in your country, as well as what you should not allow to happen if it is ever in your hands to prevent it. Forget about the PhD because you are not going to be a scholar and it would not make you a better politician.'

I changed. I took full advantage of the opportunity given to me together with Mr Thomas's advice, which led me to become a much better politician. Since then I have been Director of Federal Public Investment, Vice-Governor of Mexico City, Mayor of one of its counties, Dean of the Anahuac University Law School, Member Elect of the Federal House of Representatives, Senator Elect of the Republic, Governor Elect of the State of Chiapas and Minister of the Interior. This is why I have always said that I owe so much to Cambridge and to Trinity Hall, but especially to the life-changing advice of Mr Trevor Thomas. To me he is a shining example of such teachers who become 'unsung heroes'.

Dennis Stanton Avery (1980)

On a windy September evening in late September 1980, I towed my suitcase through Parker's Piece, having disembarked the train in Cambridge after a flight from California. The Hidden Hall was

Dennis Avery, graduate student 1980–81.

found and I, as an endangered species (a mature American student), settled in, not before exercising the egregious error of walking on the grass in Front Court. Correction was swift and not again repeated, until, of course, graduation day the following year.

What a year it was! In fact, it is a year which has never ended and for one reason: people. If any facets of Hall life endure – beyond fond buildings, that is – acquaintances nurtured to friendship over time do. And what staying power members of the Hall have. Now with THA in its centenary year more than six thousand living members survive globally, all indelibly and in highly personal ways, touched by each other amid their enduring experiences.

My experience was immediately coloured by being drafted into the graduate boat and, as a rated pilot, discovering, inevitably, the museum at Duxford. As a lawyer, it was coloured by meeting John Collier, the ubiquitous Fellow and advisor in law. 'What are you going to do?' he queried, and barely did I know, until the Easter Term. It seemed I would write as part of my degree a paper on international law, perhaps international law of the sub-terrain. Lo, I discovered there was no sub-terrestrial law delimiting the whole of our planet, and took on the task of so doing. This, and publishing it, has carried me years beyond that important non-ending degree day at the Senate House.

Surely other members find themselves, decades beyond coming up, reflecting on it all.

Dennis Stanton Avery took his LLB at Trinity Hall in 1981. He is married to lawyer and educator Sally Tsui Wong-Avery and was President of the THA in its centenary year.

Arkady Ostrovsky (1991)

I first came to Cambridge in 1990. I came as a visitor from a country which was still called the Soviet Union and which was about to collapse. I studied theatre history in Moscow and came to Cambridge on the invitation of Peter Holland, a professor of English at Trinity Hall.

Trinity Hall was my first port of call. The contrast between Moscow and Cambridge could not have been greater.

Quiet medieval lanes, tidy green lawns, libraries full of rare manuscripts, unhurried atmosphere – these could impress any foreign visitor. But coming from Russia which was in a state of turmoil and flux, the world of Cambridge academia seemed almost unreal. Back in Moscow, you could come out of the library and see tanks roll down the streets. In Cambridge you came out of the library and saw a don cross a lawn in his gown.

It was hardly surprising that I was totally seduced by the place, and particularly by a small college called Trinity Hall. But the prospects of coming to study in Cambridge at the time were as distant as flying to the moon. More distant, in fact.

One could fly to the moon, but one could not enter the world of a fairy-tale or a fantasy, which is what Cambridge seemed to me then. It was a place frozen in time, separated from the rest of the world by centuries – not miles – populated, I thought, by the happiest, freest people. On my first visit to Cambridge I stayed with an undergraduate student from Trinity Hall. I can't remember his name. I can't remember the street or the house where he lived. When I came to Cambridge two years later as a graduate student, I tried, several times, to find his place. I never did. It was as if the place vanished – like in a fairy-tale.

On the last day of my first visit in Cambridge I told Peter Holland, that I wanted to do my PhD there. He smiled back at me: 'A lot of people do'. Two years and a lot of effort later, I proudly entered Trinity Hall as a graduate student. Peter Holland, who helped me all the way through, was to be my supervisor. I was given a room at 9 Bateman Street for £25 a week. It was the smallest and nicest room I ever lived in.

The idea of a college as club or a union of people with different interests was alien to me. I grew up in Moscow trying to avoid being a member of any union. The only organisation one had to belong to in the Soviet Union was the Komsomol – the young Communist party league – and though the membership was effectively compulsory, I certainly did not want it to be part of my social life.

This is why, perhaps, I shied away from being a member of an MCR or any other group. I felt I did not fit in. Perhaps if I was a member of any other college, this feeling of awkwardness would never have gone away. But after a while, I realised that Trinity Hall was drawing me in, that it was becoming my safe haven, that I was feeling proud of it, that I belonged to it and it belonged to me – for ever. (When I invited friends from other colleges for dinner or lunch, I felt particularly proud as Trinity Hall had the best food among colleges).

I was falling in love with Trinity Hall – with its old dining hall, with its modest and dignified chapel, with grumbling porters, with the tree you could lie under in the summer months, with the herbaceous border in front of the Old Library.

The subject of my PhD was Russia's perception of England and Englishness at a time of social upheaval: the First World War and the Bolshevik Revolution. I was writing about the myth of England in Russian culture as a safe haven, a shelter from chaos and turmoil, a blessed island, a fair and fairy land. The more I worked on my thesis, the more I felt that I was succumbing to this myth and becoming part of my own story: the Soviet empire was crumbling, academic work had been made impossible by social and economic chaos and Trinity Hall was my shelter and my safe haven, my personal corner of England where I could hide. My Hidden Hall.

It was the only institution I wished to belong to. Unlike almost any other place in the world, it wanted to give me something rather than taking something from me. I was lucky, of course. Trinity Hall had generously given me a scholarship for three years to finish my PhD. For that I will always be grateful.

But it was more than money that Trinity Hall gave me. Being part of this small College, I felt part of a very large world. The diversity of nationalities and interests of its graduate students made Trinity Hall a kind of microcosm of the world. And whether you live in Moscow or Tokyo, Bangkok or Paris – you always feel part of this small big world.

Arkady Ostrovsky is now a journalist working for the Financial Times.

Postscript

PROFESSOR MARTIN DAUNTON
(MASTER 2004–)

The nine months between my election as Master in January 2004 and my admission in October were a period spent in learning about the Hall, meeting Fellows and staff, and being briefed about future strategy. I learned what any old member of Trinity Hall would have known instinctively: that the Hall is friendly and inclusive. Many wrote to welcome me to the College and to share memories of their days as students or Fellows. During these months, drinks in the Fellows' garden; a concert in the Senior Combination Room; a wonderfully stimulating Leslie Stephen lecture by Amartya Sen; and the glittering new song cycle of our music Fellow Richard Baker at the Aldeburgh festival, already made me appreciate the stimulation of the Hall's community. The essays and reminiscences in *The Hidden Hall* are confirmation of the affection in which the Hall is held.

The Hidden Hall celebrates centuries of achievement since 1350 and demonstrates that we have an impressive past: our role now is to ensure that we have an impressive future. The Master and Fellows must look ahead to the next century, in order to ensure that we hand on the Hall to our successors in as good a shape as we found it. Peter Clarke provided a foundation on which we can build, and I am particularly delighted to be following in his footsteps. We were colleagues for a brief period at University College London, that Godless institution in Gower Street, and we have worked together, as colleagues in the Faculty of History, since my arrival in Cambridge in 1997. At the same time that I arrived as Master, the tower cranes rose at Wychfield to build student accommodation – an essential part of our future plans. Our new organ will soon be installed. We have recruited outstanding young Fellows; and we can look forward to

some expansion of the Fellowship. We have appointed an excellent new Bursar who will work alongside our first-rate Senior Tutor, Admissions Tutor and Graduate Tutor. We have experienced a period of renewal, without sacrificing the best of the past. We are fortunate that the Hall has a strong team to provide us with a base from which to face immense challenges – both in terms of student and University finances and of the competing pressures of faculty and college – confronting all Cambridge colleges and the University.

I arrived in Cambridge without prior experience of a collegiate system from my own education and previous career. My experience in Cambridge since 1997 means that I now have the fervour of a convert to a collegiate university. How else could we meet undergraduate and graduate students from so many intellectual and cultural backgrounds? Where else would it be possible to discuss academic work with colleagues from such diverse disciplines in relaxed sociability? The colleges in general, and the Hall in particular, are an antidote to the over-specialism of the modern academic world, a place to think in new ways and to make friends. The Hall has thrived since 1350 – we must now work together to ensure it continues for another seven hundred years.

Index of Names

List of Subscribers

Trinity Hall MCR
The Jerwood Foundation
Helen Abbott
William Abraham 1994
Colonel M.B. Adams 1936
Dr Robin Adams 1954
Chris Adams 1975
Alexandra Adams 2003
Ben Adcock 2002
Marcus Agius 1965
Jo Allan 1998
Dr Bernhard Altehenger and
   Dr Sherida Altehenger-Smith
Jennifer E. Altehenger 2001
Peter Alter
Victor Alvarez- de la Torre 1975
Ian Andrew
Dr Christopher H. Anderson 1962
Robin Anderson 1970
David Anderson 2001
Rebecca E. Anderson 1999
Chris Angus 1967
Professor M.R. Anseau 1970
Kate Arkless Gray 1998
Jackson W. Armstrong 2001
I.M. Arnott 1962
Dr Jens Aschenbeck 1994
J.G. Ash 1937
Nicholas Ashby 1976
V. Athanassoulia 1986
Mike Atkins 1977
Rosie Atkins 1993
Alastair B. Atkinson 2001
Sakura Atsumi 1994
Marc Attwood-Wood 1959
Dennis Stanton Avery 1980
R.B. Backhouse 1958
Ronald W. Bailey CMG 1936
Anthony Charles Bailey 1954

Philip R. Baines 1943
Russell Baker 1973
Estella Baker 1987
Kevin Ball 1970
Professor William Ballantyne 1940
Revd Professor Paul H. Ballard 1953
Dr Nick Bampos 1999
Simon Barclay 2002
Rodney M. Barker 1952
Jayne Barlow
David Barlow 1987
David Barnes 1973
D.M. Barnett 1964
Max Barnish 2003
Jessie Barrett 2001
Roy Barter 1948
Mrs Joan Barton (née Durrant)
Dr D.J. Basnett 1993
Dr John L. Batten 1958
Micha Battsek 1944
Jim Baxendale 1948
R.A. Bayford 1968
Hugh R. Beadle 1964
David Bean QC 1972
Ms Rosie Beaufoy 1978
Katya Belichenko 1999
Peter Bell 1943
David Bell 1965
James Bell 1996
Andrew Bellars 1959
A.F. Bennett 1942
Marcus Bennett 1953
Derek H. Benson 1955
Annabelle Berenzweig (née Sidhu) 1991
C.J. Beresford-Jones 1959
Nicholas Beresford-Jones 1962
Olivier F.L. Bertin 1992
Kirstie Bewers 2003
David W.S. Beynon 1954

Rajat Bhatnagar 1997
Dr David Bickley 1959
Michael Biddle 1958
Tim Bilham 1967
Katerina Biliouri 2000
Dr David Billett FRSC 1968
Charles Bird 1972
Andrew Bird 1983
Neil Birkett 1999
Paul Black 1974
Chris Blackhurst 1979
Andrew Blankfield 1981
Richard Blomfield 1951
David Blunt QC 1963
Caroline Boggust 1998
C.S. Bolton 1942
Alan Bolton 1974
Sarah Bolton 2001
Judy Szemere Boughey 1992
Michael Boulton-Jones 1960
Sir Jeffery Bowman 1955
A.D. Bowyer 1959
Thirza P. Boychuk M.Phil 1999
Sarah Brace 1998
Dr J.L. Bracegirdle 1966
Anthony W. Bradley 1960
Dr Robert Bradley 1973
Dr R.H. Bradshaw 1986
Geoffrey Braithwaite 1950
Professor C.P. Brand 1941
J. Martin Brand 1958
James H. Brandi
R.J. Brandon 1964
Michael Brear 2002
Tom Breeze 1994
P.M. Brennan 2000
Ian Brentnall 1942
Charles Brewin 1957
Professor A.D.P. Briggs 1958

Mr J. Brinsmead-Stockham 2000
Dominic Brooks 1954
Kenneth F.C. Brown 1935
Dr J.M. Brown 1952
George H. Brown 1957
Dr Richard Brown 1961
Ann Brown (née Cheesman) 1980
Graham Browne 1963
Alan and Avril Bruce
Matthew Bruce 1996
Tanja Bruns 1997
Oliver Mark Brupbacher 2003
Dr Charles Bryan 1974
Deborah Bryce 1998
Stephen Buckley 1995
Amy Buckley (née Reneker) 1999
Dr Maurice H. Bull MD 1951
Tim Bullimore 1986
Michael I. Bultitude 1955
Nicola Bunn 1990
David D. Burgess 1954
Richard Burnett-Hall 1956
Andrew Burr 1977
Professor Donald Burrows 1964
Mr J.D. Bush 1943
S.C. Bushell 1943
Nick Butcher 1964
R M. Butterworth 1944
R.M. Cadman 1948
Jeremy Callman 1987
Adam Calvert 1975
Angela Campbell
Sophie Candfield 2002
Peter Cannon-Brookes 1957
Ralph Cantor 1958
Edd Capewell 2002
Derek Capon 1964
Brian Cappell 1974
M.V. Carey 1945

Name	Year	Name	Year	Name	Year	Name	Year
Dennis C.P. Carey	1949	Napier Collyns	1948	Esha Dasgupta	1998	Andrew Dyke	1964
Guy Carless	1951	Ian E. Colston	1954	Penny Davenport	1989	Kerry Eady	
Dr Michael Carlile	1951	S.D. Colton	1994	Rosemary Davidson		Richard Earlam FRCS	1952
Malcolm J.C.G. Carlisle	1965	Alan J. Colvill	1975	Laura A. Davidson	1998	Phyllida Earle (née Gerrard)	1977
E.J. Carr	2003	Duncan Colville	1950	C.B. Davies MA, PH.D	1935	Nick Eastwell	1975
S.H. Carriere	1996	C.R. Cone	1973	Derek Davies	1952	Linda and Barry Ebbutt	
J.A. Carruthers	1956	Frank Conley	1964	Greg B. Davies	1997	J.R.R. Ebsworth	1960
Ian Carson	1957	Shruti Contractor	1993	Alice M. Davies	1999	Robert E. Eckton	1941
Margaret Emma Carson	2001	Anthony M. Conway	1957	Gary M. Davies	2003	D. Edwards	1948
David Cassidy	1995	H.Basil S. Cooke	1933	Peter A. Davis	1983	Professor Steven Edwards	1966
Christopher Causer	1972	Terry Coombes	1968	James Dawnay	1968	Gwendolyn A. Edwards	2001
Charles Cavanagh	1970	Paul corben	1975	Roland A. Dawson	1960	Tamerlane Edwards	2003
Mrs Kathleen Cavill		R.L.B. Cormack	1956	Edward R. Day	1952	Thomas A. Ehrensberger	1999
Esther M.R. Challis	1996	Dr Fiona Cornish (née Cameron)	1978	James Trelawny Day	1955	Stephen Elkington	1950
Douglas M. Chalmers	1990	D.N Cornock-Taylor	1937	Ed Day	1989	John Ellard	1971
G.Jeannette Chamberlain		Jonathan Cornwell	1992	Mr Ivor Daymond	1959	Alan Elliot	1951
Anthony Chamier	1956	Fiona Cousins	1986	John de Figueiredo	1962	D.E. Elliot	1965
Dr Nigel Chancellor DL	1990	Ian Coward	1958	Sophie de Laguiche	1993	Steven Elliott	1973
Dr Theodore K. Chaplin	1943	M.L. Cowper	1949	His Hon. Alan de Piro QC	1938	Enass Salah Elmaghraby	1991
Alastair Chapman	1994	Barry W.M. Cowper	1953	C.D. De Puy	1976	Daniel Elton	2001
Bob Charlton	1975	Tony Cowsley	1969	Filip De Schouwer	1998	Professor Lionel Elvin	1924
Revd Alan Charters	1956	Nick and Cathy Cox	1982	Professor Jose de Souza Martins	1993	Robert Ely	1950
Krishna Chatterjee	2003	A.A. Crassweller	1941	Julian de Zulueta	1945	Professor John Erskine	1960
Professor Philip Chatwin	1960	P.J. Crawford-Taylor	1965	Meryll Dean	1978	A.B. Evans	1948
Revd Eric Cheetham	1954	John Crawley		John E. Denison	1960	Anna Burch	1977
Claire Chelton (née Turnbull)	1985	Tom Crawley		John Denton	1958	Philipp Fahr	2002
Mary Cherical	1998	Breen Creighton	1969	Berjis Desai	1980	Olivia Fane	1979
K. Chiappe	1982	Mrs P. Cremona		Chaz Dheer	1992	Barry Farnham	1947
Dr Anthony Childs	1953	James D. Crerar	1953	John Dick	1967	Dr Chris Farrer	1950
Revd Alan M. Chilver	1955	Dr Bob Crichton	1967	Cameron R. Dick	1996	Peter Faulkner	1953
Vassiliki Chondrogianni	2002	Bob Critchlow	1969	Nicholas B. Dill JP	1951	Dr Birte Feix	1999
Chun Yip Chow	1999	John L. Crockatt	1938	Carl Dinnen	1990	C. Richard Ferens	1957
Sarah Clapson	2000	Piers Crocker	1971	Gareth Dobson	2003	Dr Arthur Ferguson	1941
Colin Clark	1955	Alex Crockford	2003	Brian Donaldson	1957	Andrew Ferguson	1973
Simon Clark	1975	Sophie Crossfield and		Luke Donnan	2003	David G. Ferguson	2002
Nicholas Clark	1991	Nicholas McKay	1996	C. Douglas-Jones	1936	Roberto Fernandez-Medina	2001
Dr L.W. Clarke	1940	James Cruise	2001	Andrew Dowden	1983	Georg Feulner	1997
Dr P.John Clarkson	1981	Dr John Cule	1938	Stuart Downhill	1957	Dr M. Field	1983
John D. Clifford	1998	Jonathan Cullis	1979	Paul Dowthwaite	1965	D. and G. Field	1989/1990
David Cluer	1966	Robert Cumming	1962	M.G. Draper	1978	Kim Field	2002
Dr Rosamunde Codling	1978	J.H. Cunningham	1955	Iain N. Drayton	1991	Philip Fine	1989
Alan Cohen	1950	David Cunningham	1959	Bruce Drew	1963	His Honour Judge Stuart Fish	1957
Bill Coldrey	1952	James Curtis	1973	J.W. Drummond	1954	David G. Fison	1970
Canon Alan Cole		J.O. Cutler	1953	Guy Du Bose	1980	David Fleming	1965
Dr B.I. Coleman	1966	Dr John Dalby	1944	Michael Dubois	1987	Tim Flew	1958
Kirsty Colman	1992	Keith Daley	1973	P.J. Dudley	2000	Mark Ford	1989
Dr Lucy Coles	1991	Neil L. Dallas	1944	Nigel Duncan	1944	Vic Forrington	1955
Deirdre Collings	1993	Christopher Daniels	1992	Rafal E. Dunin-Borkowski	1987	J.P. Foster OBE	1937
Douglas L. Collins		D.C. d'Arcy Orders	1956	Aquilino Duque	1954	Karen and Duncan Fowler-Watt	1981

Dr Cyril Fox	1950	Geoffrey Gornall	1962	Sir Michael Harrison	1959	Michael Holter	1984
Mark Fox-Andrews	1970	A.J. Gorton	1955	Laura Harrison	2001	Tahl Holtzman	2000
Elizabeth A. Franey-Kottke	1984	Tony Gosse	1962	David Hart	2000	Michael Hood	1957
Gerry Frank	1945	Andrew Gowans	1990	David Harte	1963	(Eric) Stanley Hooper	1964
Revd Cortland Fransella	1967	Kevin Grafton	1971	Giles Harvey	1952	David Horne	1957
John R. Freed	1999	Tamsin Llwyd Graves	1982	Eric Hawkins	1933	Stephen Horne	2001
James Freeland	1957	Peter J. Gray	1974	J.J. Haydn-Williams	1976	Arthur Horrocks	1939
Peter Freeman	1959	V. Greany		Hilary R. Haydon	1951	Peter Horrocks	1973
Howard Freeman	1973	Edward Greenfield	1949	Josephine Hayes		William (Bill) R. Horsfall	1938
Denzil K. Freeth MBE	1943	David Greenwood	2003	Colin Hayes	1962	William A. Horsley	1943
Paul Frost-Smith	1986	A.L. Greer	1973	Bruce Hayllar	1946	Sharon Horwitz	1988
Chris Fry	1972	M.D.A. Gregson	1955	Douglas S.E. Hayward	1947	Brian Hoskins	1963
Isaac Chun Hai Fung	2000	Sukhjit Singh Grewal	1996	Liz Hayward	1997	Frances Houghton (née Carr)	1978
John Gale	1976	Alan Grieve CBE	1945	Dr Louise M. Haywood	2000	Richard G.G Howard	1952
Nigel Gallop	1949	John Griffith-Jones	1972	Dirk Hazell	1974	Paul Howcroft	1976
Dr Christoph Gallus	1991	Paul Griffiths	1976	Nicolas Heath	1973	Charles Howe	1954
John S. Gammon	1956	Trevor Grigg	1955	Mr Richard Heginbotham	1966	Michael R. Howe-Smith	1953
Geoff Gardiner	1972	Chris Grigg and Fionna Stirling	1978	J.Warwick Hele	1948	Dr Frank-Erich Hufnagel	1991
Paul Gardiner	1980	Mr Michael Grime	1960	Kevin Hemmings	1980	H. Gray Hughes	1943
Edmund P. Gardner	1957	Harry Guest	1951	Michael Hender	1958	A.V.M. David H. Hull RAF (RETD)	
Robert C. Gardner	1959	Simon D. Guest	1994	Dr Anne Henry	1995	John E. Humphrey	1931
Laura Gardner	2003	Sir John Guinness	1956	J.R. Herklots	1950	R.E.L. Hunt	1944
Stephen Gare	1970	Frank Gutteridge	1939	A.C. Herring	1983	Robert Hunt-Grubbe	1959
Matthew Gaskarth	1988	Sam Gutteridge	1996	Barbara Hewson	1979	Henry P. Huntington	1988
Daniel and Mary Gaskarth	1991/1994	Revd J.A. Guttridge	1948	Matthew J.K. Hickman	1983	John Huskins	1957
Dr Y. Gaspar	1996	Jonathan Hadley	1990	Dr Tom Hill	1956	Dr C.R. Hutchison	1964
Nicola Gaukroger	2001	Knut Haenelt	1980	Rachel Hill	1981	Verity Rose Ibbotson	2002
Lord Gavron		Tristram Hager	2002	Weston Miles Hill	2003	Jennifer E. Ifft	2002
Mr C.R. Gee	2003	David Halfpenny	1968	Andrew J.W. Hilson	1961	Irving Igra	1967
Jeremy Gibb	1981	Colin Hall	1961	Dr Yasmine Hilton		Dr Annette Imhausen	2002
Revd Dr Robert P.P. Gibbons	1999	John W.L. Hall	1990	David L. Hinds	1969	Jeremy Inglis	1950
Dr R.G. Gibbs	1941	Revd Canon P.H Hallam MBE	1953	Richard Hine	1965	Duncan Ingram	1950
W.S. Gibbs	1958	A.G.W. Hallgarth	1991	Rachel Hinton	1991	Colonel C.J. Isaac	1944
John Gibbs	1962	Dr Peter R Handford	1968	Chris Hipwell	1955	Dr A.G. Ives	1964
C.T.Barney Gibbs	1991	Professor Emeritus G.C. Harcourt	1955	C.H. Hirst	1966	S.W. Jackman	
Sheriff W.E. Gibson	1955	Robin Hardie	1958	Stephen Hodges	1972	Dr Clare Jackson	2000
Robert Gilchrist	1951	Rupert Harding	1976	John Hodgkinson	1948	Ian and Julia (née Betnell) Jackson	1981
A.O. Gilchrist	1955	J. Harding-Edgar	2001	Christine Hodgkinson		Ian and Julia Jackson	1981
Amanpreet Gill	2000	Dr C. Hardwick MA, MD, FRCP	1929	(née Watson)	1985	Maharaj Jai Singh	1951
Charlotte Gill	2000	Benedict Hardy	1999	T.C. Hodgson	1983	Rajan S. Jain	1997
Victoria Gillard	1987	Neil Harman	1979	Thomas Christian Hörber	1999	Matthew James	1950
Derek Gilyard	1951	Dr Philip Harmer	1987	Roderick Hole	1958	Dr Eleanor James	1996
Magnus R.E. Gittins	2002	Jackie Harmon	2003	Professor Clive Holes	1966	Nick Jamieson	1990
Samantha Godden (Williams)	1988	P.H. Harper	1968	Matt Holgate	1995	The Hon. Daniel Janner QC	1976
Charles Goldie	1955	Sue Bilton	1979	Peter Holland	1969	Dr Jerome P. Jarrett	1993
Jose P. Gonzalez Blanco	1957	Claire C.M. Harrington		Donald Holliday	1964	Richard Jarvis OBE	1960
G.E. Goodall	1969	(née Long)	1993	M.G. Holloway	1962	Simon Jeffreys	1976
Abigail Goodwin	2003	Graham Harrison	1957	Rupert Holmes	1992	Peter J.L. Jenkins	1957
Henry Gordon-Clark	1954	Richard Harrison	1957	Dr Bodil Holst	1994	Richard Jenkins	1962

M Jenner	1948	Michael Laurens	1952	Dr Iain C. McMillan	1979
Catharine and Paul Jessop	1980	Alfred Laux		Magnus Arni Magnusson	1999
Victor Joffee QC	1970	Dan Lawrence	1957	Alison Maguire	1990
Vegard Johnsen	1998	Casper Lawson	1981	James D. Malcolm	1956
Arwen Johnson (née Handley)	1989	Henry Lawson	1983	Jonathan Malcolm	1957
Mr Angus C. Johnston	1999	Mark Le Brocq	1978	Colin Mallet	1962
Professor John Philip Jones	1950	Richard Lea	1960	Robert Mallows	1994
Simon J. Jones	1969	John D.A. Leaver	1948	J.L. Mangan	1951
Roderick B. Jones	1993	W.A.J. Leaver	1950	Peter Mansfield	1968
Mr Lindsay Jones	1995	Dr N.G.M. Legg	1957	Anne Marden	
Geraint Jones	1999	B.A. Lennon	1998	David Marples	1932
David Alma Jordan	1953	Richard H. Levy	1951	J.C. Marriott	1991
Dr Michael Jordan	1968	Barry Lewis	1959	D. marshall Evans	1956
Martin Josten	1968	Daivd Morgan Lewis	1962	Graham Martin	1957
The Very Revd Peter Judd	1968	Laura Ley		Gerard Martin	1974
Tobias Jung	1997	Dr Alison Liebling	1981	Sophie Martin	2003
Dr Amalia-Emma Karamitrou	1994	Yee Wei Lim	1999	Jeremy Mason	1968
Gillian Karran	1982	C.M. Lind Holmes	1956	Rob Mather	1988
Azim H.A. Kazzam	1993	Robin Lindsay	1947	Ben Maude	2002
Lila Kazemian	2002	F.J.M. Lindsay	1952	Anthony P. May	1955
Sarah Keen	2003	Frances K. Linehan	2003	John McCaig	1953
Canon D.P. Keene	1953	Colonel Ian S. Lister FRCS	1946	Dr Lucy McCorkell	1977
Katherine Kell (née Pearse)	1991	John Lloyd	1946	Sir Charles McCullough	
D.F. Kelly	1957	Charles Lloyd	1980	Fiona C.B. McDermott	1999
Ralph J. Kemp	2002	Hugh Lloyd-Jukes	2001	Sinéad McDonald	1994
N.J. Kenealy	1960	Carina M.C. Lobley	2001	Alexander McDougall	1987
C.G. Kershaw	1944	Amanda Lomas	1996	John McEwan	1947
Mohammed Awais Khan	1997	Glen Long	1990	Des McEwan	1998
Hanah Kilduff	2003	Mr Chris Lord	1973	Chris McFadzean	1976
J.H. King	1948	David Loring	1987	B.T. McGeough	1954
D. D. King	1953	Rupert Lowe	1982	Dr I.R & Mrs J.M. McLauchlin,	
James King	1958	Anthony Lucas	1954	in memory of Elizabeth	1993
William King	1967	Marian Luff	1999	Ian McNeil	1964
Dr W.H. Kirkaldy-Willis	1933	H.C. Lumsden	1929	B.H. McPherson CBE	1957
R.W.F. Kitchin MBE	1950	R.W. Lunnon	1970	Steve McTiernan	1969
John Kitching	1955	Revd S.B. and Dr C. Lynas	1977	Lesley McWilliam	1992
Revd Dr Peter Knight	1973	Edward Lyndon-Stanford	1956	Andrew Medlicott	1961
Gillian Koh Tan	1997	Dr Arthur Lyons	1961	Elizabeth S.M. Mellen	1977
Dr Katerina Krikos-Davis	1986	Sir John and Lady Lyons	1984	Paul Melshen	1990
Thomas Kvan	1975	Sir John Macdermott	1945	Aamir Maerchant	1989
Professor J.C. Laidlaw	1956	Revd R.W.K. MacDermott	1952	Dr Paul Meredith	1974
Robert Lamb	1947	His Honour Angus Macdonald	1951	Dr B.D.G. Mickley	1948
Stephen Lane	1975	Hon Donald S. Macdonald	1956	Dr L.P. Middleton	1998
Peter D. Lane	1986	David J. Mack	1977	Richard Miles	1954
Kevin John Lane	1999	P. Mackie	1958	Robert Glendinning Miller	1937
Dominic Lang	1975	Keith Mackiggan	1990	Dr Kenneth Miller CBE FREng	1943
Mr S.L. Larcombe	1949	David MacLean Watt	1959	J.I. Miller	1952
M.J. Larkin	1951	Patrick H. Macleod MBE	1935	Tony Miller	1956
Dr B.A. Latham	1951	Martin MacLeod	2001	Douglas Miller	1958

Nargis Miller	1996
Anthony Mills	1960
Stephanie Mills	1993
Alan C. Milne	1943
Michael Milne	1978
Melissa Jane Milner	2002
Dr Peter Milton MA, MD, FRCOG	
Natasha Minchella (née Kennedy)	1990
R.J. Mitchell M.Chir, FRCS	
Sir John Mitting	1966
R. James Miura	1973
Edmwnd Moelwyn-Hughes	1958
Carolin Moje	2000
P.B Monahan	1957
C.J.E. Moody	1975
John Moore	1948
Dr D.F. Moore	1984
Dr Simon Moore	1991
J.R. More-Molyneux	1939
P.W.L. Morgan	1956
Frank E. Morgan II	1974
John K.S. Morgan	1974
Charlotte Morgan (née Balaam)	1986
Iain R.M.R. Morley	2000
Group Captain Roy Morris	1942
D.J. Morris	1947
R.J. Morris	1948
Richard G. Morris	1966
Dr Peter Morton	1946
R.J.P Morton	1972
Carolyn Moule	2002
Jan Mouton	2001
Mark Mulrooney	1986
Dr Keith Mundy	1971
Professor B.O. Murdoch	1989
Liz Murphy	1981
Caryn Myers	1996
Professor Tony Narula	1973
John Naylon	1991
Revd J.W. Naylor	1949
John and Emilia Naylor	1988
Professor B.G. Neal	1947
John Neame	1944
Peter G. Needham	1958
Tracy L. Nelson	2002
Ambassador Matthew E.R. Newhaus	1985
David Newby	1951
George Newlands	1982

221

Roger Newman	1954	Nigel Parker	1976
Alan Newman QC	1964	Amy Parker	1995
D.A. Newton	1942	Dr Ann Parker-Smith	
Hedley J. Newton	1954	Sarah and Brandon Parkes	1989
John Nicholls	1982	Mrs S. Parks, widow of P.C. Parks	1949
Lord Nicholls of Birkenhead	1956	Jeremy Parr	1980
Dr A.E. Nicholson	1942	Christopher Parr	2002
G.B. Nicholson	1968	Giles Parsons	1974
Jane Nicholson	1977	James A. Passamano	1998
Dr Timothy Nicholson	1981	Benjamin G. Paster	1970
Adrian Nickson	1999	Ms Sabine Patarin	2003
Mladen Ninkov	1984	John Paton Walsh	1960
Tony Nixon	1973	David Patrick	1991
Dr Chileshe Nkonde	1997	Susan Pattison-Wait	1989
John Nolan	1957	Dr Andrew Pauza	1989
Michael Norman	1967	Roger Payne	1957
Mr and Mrs Arthur Dalton		Jonathan Pearce	1985
S.R. and S.V.A. Norman		Dr Alan E. G. Pearson	1944
Ian Nutt	1972	Tristan E.C. Pedelty	2002
R. K. Nuttall	1930	Martin Peers	1964
Jonathan Oakley	1980	D.G. and J.E. Penfold	
Mary Ellen O'Connell	1981	Chris Penn	1958
Ambassador E.A. Odeke	1961	Liz Pentlow	
Dr Ian Michael O'Donnell	1988	Jane Pepperall	1984
Patrick (Tony) O'Donovan	1972	David C. Peters	1970
T.W.B Ogilvie	1950	M.T. Petsalis-Diomidis	1990
W.S Oglethorpe	1948	P.C.F. Pettit	1956
Sarah O'Hara	1979	Harald Pfeiffer	1998
W.P. Oliver	1942	The Revd Canon	
Katherine Olsson Carter	1999	Dr Anthony Phillips	1969
Douglas Oram		Simon Pilcher	1984
Sebastian Oram	2002	Norman Pinch	1942
Tim Orchard	1991	Philippe Pinguet	1977
J.C. Orr	1957	David Platt	1983
David Orrick	1968	John Polkinghorne	1949
Charles Ortner	1953	Dr John Pollard	1963
Sir John Osbourn	1941	Hugo Pooley	1972
Alan Oswald	1963	Winston Poon	1972
Emma Owens	1989	Katrina Porteous	1979
Martin Pacey	1978	D. M. Potash	1990
Nicholas Padfield	1969	Jocelyn Poulton	
Michael Page	1935	Richard and Helen	
G.T. Pagone QC	1982	(née White)Powell	1988
Count Stephen Pálffy	1957	A.C. Powers	1949
Neil Palmer	1991	Mr M.A.G.R. Prabhu	1998
Dr Edward Pank	1963	Jisa Prasannan	2003
Professor W.E. Parish	1956	Tim Pratt	1961
Hugh Parker	1937	Patrick R. Prenter CBE	1959
Adrian Parker	1974	Petré Prins	1971

Revd R.H Procter	1951	Charles Rome	2002
Simon Pudsey	1986	Martin Roper	1982
Dr Graham Pullan	1993	Canon Paul Rose	1953
Philip E. Purcell	1947	Edward Roskill	1987
Mr and Mrs Purchase		Graham Ross Russell	1953
Asha Puttaiah	1999	Dr Rob Ross Russell	1976
Richard Quesnel	1995	David E. Rothera	1957
Paul Quinton	1963	Hazel Rothera	1990
Matthew Rachleff	1994	Tanya Roussopoulos	1985
John Raison	1944	David Rowlands	1952
David W. Raistrick	1957	A.P. Rowlands	2003
V.K. Rajah	1985	Clive Rumbelow	1953
Aroul Selvam Ramadass	2000	Philip Rumney	1953
David A.J. Rand	1961	Michael Rusbridge	1951
Mark Ransom	1955	Alex Rushmer	2002
Ben Rawlings	2001	J.C. Russell	1953
Prue Rayner	1997	Steve Russell	1964
Dr N.G. Reading	1973	Hilary Russell	1994
Peter Readman	1966	Wendy Russell Barter	1992
Dr Roger E. Reavill	1958	Mrs Fiona M. Rutter	1989
Dr Auberon Redfearn	1952	Fiona Sandeman Hall	
Douglas Redfern	1952	(née Steward Sandeman)	1988
Michael Redmayne	1954	Mike Sandland	1957
David Morgan Rees	1949	C. Bevis Sanford	1936
Tristan Rees Roberts	1967	Dominic Sargent	1981
Aidan Reilly	2002	Pierre and Carolyn Sarrau	1996
P.W. Ricardo MBE	1931	Dr Nicola Perkins	1993
Denis Richards	1928	Malcolm Savage	1961
Wyn Richards	1966	Adrian Mark Savage	1990
Right Revd John Richardson	1958	Paul and Georgina	
Nigel Richardson	1967	(née Bates) Scholl	1976/1978
Mark Richardson	1974	Dr Alex Schroeder	1995
Nina E. Richardson	1998	Kerry Scott	1964
Natalie Ridgard	2003	David Scott-Jones	1972
Arne Riedlinger	1998	Philip L. Scrowcroft	1953
Ken Rimmer	1953	Professor C.B. Scruby	1964
Guiseppe Risino		Jon Seddon	1986
Mr R. Roberts		Mark Sellers	1941
S.C. Roberts	1963	Rob Severn	2003
Selwyn Roberts	1976	Morley Sewell	1951
Christopher Roberts	1981	Thomas Sharpe	1971
Quentin Roberts	1989	E.N. Shaw	1954
Suzanne Roberts	1998	Richard Shayler	1992
Caroline H. Roberts	2002	Peter Shellswell	1988
Nicholas John Rock	1988	Fiona Shelmerdine	1986
James R. Rogers	2001	Rt Revd Lord Sheppard	
Jonathan Rohrer	1993	of Liverpool	1949
Charles Rolland	1939	Rebekah Sherwin	2002
Mike Romanos	1973	Michael Shipley	1956

David C. Shipley	1963
Graham Shorter	1973
Dr E.P.H. Shortt	1941
Anna and Daniel Shrimpton	1990
Rory Silkin	1976
Brian A. Simpson	1967
Rachel E. Simpson	2003
Boyd Sims-Williams	1959
Nicholas Sims-Williams	1968
Rosalind D.A. Sipos	2001
Neil Slater	1977
Amelia Sleat	2003
Roger J.W. Sleigh	1960
Dr D.J. Slotboom	
Maurice Smelt	1943
Revd Alan Carlton Smith	1938
Ian P.D. Smith	1960
Gerald C. Smith	1961
Dr Andrew L.H. Smith	1976
Simon Smith	1986
Natalie R. Smith	1992
Donna Smith	1998
W.D.F. Smyly	1948
Francisco Solorzano Santos	2003
Bryce Somerville	1976
Gavin Southern	1993
Sir Robert Spencer-Nairn Bt, DL	1957
Roger Spurling	1952
C.A. Stacey	1953
J.B Stainton	1951
James Statham	1992
Cathy Staveley (neé Kendall)	1983
Christopher Steele	1968
G Stelmaszczyk	
A.M.M. Stephen	1948
Peter Stephens	1998
Tim Stevenson	1970
W.J. Stewart	1952
Catherine Stewart	1977
Bobby Stewart	1984
Geoff Stewart-Smith	1976
Andrew Stilton	1975
Richard Stone QC	1948
Joanna D. Stott	2001
Dr Peter Strangeways	1957
Phil Stratford	1992
E.P. Stuart-Williams	1928
J.H.G. Sunnucks	1946
Stephen J. Surgeoner	1988

Alexander E. Sutton	1945
David Swann	1939
Jack Sweeney	1949
Michael R. Sweet	1961
Jonathan C. Sweet	1994
Peter H.B. Sykes	1974
Brian Symes	1955
Chris Symonds	1963
Dr Arch Tait	1961
John Talbot	1955
Geoffrey A. Taylor	1945
James C. Taylor	1960
Hugh R Taylor	1962
Richard Taylor	1975
Stephen C. Taylor	1977
Paul Malcolm Taylor	1986
Alison Taylor (née Newton)	1999
Sir Donald Tebbit GCMG	
Anoush F. Terjanian	1995
Alison Tesh	2003
Jacuqes A. Thiemard	1967
Nigel Thomas	1955
Michael Thomas	1961
Dr Noel B.W. Thompson	1953
Clive D. Thorne	1971
Christopher J. Thornton	1963
Jane Thorpe (née Hillier)	1982
I.C. Tickler	1962
Neil Tidmarsh	1978
Gordon Tilsley	1936
Robert Todd	1934
Dr Julian Toms	1964
Dr Peter Tomson	1944
Beth Townsend (née Nolan)	1992
Anthony Trenton	1987
Peter Trier	1938
Dick Tripp	1952
Mike Tucker	1956
Iain Tuddenham	1993
Mark Tully	1956
David Tunbridge	1977
Natasha S.J. Turner	
Peter J. Turner	1964
Neil Twiddy	1968
John N. Tyake	1959
David Tyler	1971
Roger Unite	1974
H.J. van den Berg	1950
J.N. Van Leuven QC	1966

Charles J.P. Van Maele	
Mark Venn	1987
Louis G.S. Verdi	2002
Petra E. Vertes	2002
A.S. Veys	1983
Professor Nigel Vincent	1966
Dr Detlef Wächter	1991
Dr John Waddington	1960
A.J. Wade	1945
D.W.M. Wade	1960
Aaron Walder	2000
Lyndsay Walker	1983
Richard Walker-Arnott	1957
Jon Wallis	1967
B.D.J. Walsh TD	1941
Andrew Walsh	1975
Dr Michael J.K. Walsh	1993
Kate Ware	2001
Derek H. Waters	1942
W.Watkins	1999
Laura Watkinson	1999
Shirley Jennings Watson, daughter of Sir Ivor Jennings	
David G. Watston	1945
Michale G. Watson	1972
Amy Watson	1999
Amy Watt	2003
Ron Watts	1962
Dr Ray Weatherby	1969
Michael Webb	1992
Nick Weber-Brown	1956
Colin T. Weeden	1975
Bjoern Weidner	1999
Jeremy Weinstein	1982
Kevin Welch	1969
A.L. Wells	1943
John Wells	1983
Peter J. Wentzel	1975
Dr Donald Wesling	1960
Ed Wesson	1984
David West	1954
Maurice West	1969
Samantha Isabelle West	2000
Tony Westlake	1979
John Weston	1955
Sue Whalley	1984
M.C. Whear	1941
Mark Wheeler	1970
Miss Bridget Wheeler	1977

His Hon. Judge Guy Whitburn QC	1963
Dr Colin Whitby-Strevens	1965
Phil White	1968
Martin and Lucy White	1982
Gillian White	2003
Christopher Wilcock	1957
Edward Wilde	1961
Dr Ian Wilkinson	2001
Peter Willers	1969
Sir David Innes Williams	1937
Edward T. Williams	1948
R.K. Williams	1952
Paul W Willams	1965
Martin Williams	1966
M.D. Williams	1970
Mark Williams	1971
Jonathan Williams	1973
Paul H. Williams	1978
Gareth Williams	1979
Dr David A. Williams	1981
Sarah Willicombe	2001
Revd Dorothy Wilman	
Dr David Wilman	1964
Leslie Wilson	1937
Richard H. Wilson	1967
Jonathan Wilson	1981
Strahan L.A. Wilson	1994
Tim Winchcomb	1996
G. Windsor-Lewis	1956
Tony Wingate	1951
Paul A. Wolter	1974
M.T. Womack	1966
Michael C. Wood	1965
A.J.P. Wood	1997
Ben R. Wood	2001
Philip Woodcock	1958
John R. Woodman	1975
Clive E. Wouters	1970
Andrew Wowk	1999
Captain A.C. Wray RN	1946
William Wright	1972
Christian Wuthrich	1999
David Wyatt	2003
Malcolm Wylie	1967
Michael Young	1949
Dr Joanne Young	
Daniel Seidan	2002
Hong Zhang	1998
Lawrence Ziman	1956